# THE HISTORY OF THE EUROPEAN MIGRATION REGIME

After the Second World War, the international migration regime in Europe took a course different from the global migration regime and the migration regimes in other regions of the world. The free movement of people within the European Union, European citizenship, and the Schengen agreements in their internal and external dimensions are unique at the global level for the openness they create within Europe and for the closure they produce towards migrants from outside Europe. On the basis of relevant national and international archives, this book explains how German geopolitical and geo-economic strategies during the Cold War shaped the openness of that original regime. *The History of the European Migration Regime* explains how the regime was instrumental for Germany to create a stable international order in Western Europe after the war, conducive to German reunification, the rollback of Russian influence from Central Europe, and German economic expansion. The book embraces a large time frame, mostly between 1947 and 1992, and deals with all types of migration between and towards European countries: the movements of unskilled labourers, skilled professionals, and self-employed workers, along with the migrants' family members, examining both their access to economic activity and their social and political rights.

**Emmanuel Comte** is Lecturer in European History at the University of California, Berkeley.

ROUTLEDGE STUDIES IN MODERN
EUROPEAN HISTORY

www.routledge.com/history/series/SE0246

40 RESISTANCE HEROISM AND THE END OF EMPIRE
The Life and Times of Madeleine Riffaud
*Keren Chiaroni*

41 THE SUMMER CAPITALS OF EUROPE, 1814–1919
*Marina Soroka*

42 GERMAN REUNIFICATION
Unfinished Business
*Joyce E. Bromley*

43 OIL EXPLORATION, DIPLOMACY, AND SECURITY
IN THE EARLY COLD WAR
The Enemy Underground
*Roberto Cantoni*

44 DIVIDED VILLAGE
The Cold War in the German Borderlands
*Jason B. Johnson*

45 PROPAGANDA, PERSUASION AND THE GREAT WAR
Heredity in the Modern Sale of Products and Political Ideas
*Pier Paolo Pedrini*

46 THE AGE OF ANNIVERSARIES
The Cult of Commemoration, 1895–1925
*Edited by T. G. Otte*

47 THE HISTORY OF THE EUROPEAN MIGRATION REGIME
Germany's Strategic Hegemony
*Emmanuel Comte*

# The HISTORY of the EUROPEAN MIGRATION REGIME

## Germany's Strategic Hegemony

*Emmanuel Comte*

LONDON AND NEW YORK

First published 2018
by Routledge

2 Park Square, Milton Park, Abingdon, Oxfordshire OX14 4RN
52 Vanderbilt Avenue, New York, NY 10017

*Routledge is an imprint of the Taylor & Francis Group, an informa business*

First issued in paperback 2019

Copyright © 2018 Emmanuel Comte

The right of Emmanuel Comte to be identified as author of this work has been asserted by him in accordance with sections 77 and 78 of the Copyright, Designs and Patents Act 1988.

All rights reserved. No part of this book may be reprinted or reproduced or utilised in any form or by any electronic, mechanical, or other means, now known or hereafter invented, including photocopying and recording, or in any information storage or retrieval system, without permission in writing from the publishers.

Notice:
Product or corporate names may be trademarks or registered trademarks, and are used only for identification and explanation without intent to infringe.

*British Library Cataloguing-in-Publication Data*
A catalogue record for this book is available from the British Library

*Library of Congress Cataloging-in-Publication Data*
A catalog record for this book has been requested

ISBN: 978-1-138-06052-4 (hbk)
ISBN: 978-0-367-34872-4 (pbk)

Typeset in Perpetua
by Apex CoVantage, LLC

 Printed in the United Kingdom by Henry Ling Limited

*To my family, Eugenia, and my old friends*

# CONTENTS

| | | |
|---|---|---|
| | *Illustrations* | viii |
| | *Abbreviations* | ix |
| | Introduction | 1 |
| 1 | An unstable regime, 1947–1954 | 10 |
| 2 | A new regime taking shape, 1955–1964 | 42 |
| 3 | A shrinking dynamic, 1965–1973 | 76 |
| 4 | A protectionist status quo, 1973–1984 | 110 |
| 5 | A selective and regionalist regime, 1984–1992 | 143 |
| | Conclusion | 177 |
| | *Acknowledgements* | 184 |
| | *Notes* | 185 |
| | *Sources* | 212 |
| | *Bibliography* | 226 |
| | *Index* | 233 |

# ILLUSTRATIONS

| | | |
|---|---|---|
| 1.1 | The rise of unemployment in West Germany, June 1948–March 1950 | 22 |
| 1.2 | The dual migration regime in Western Europe in the early 1950s | 29 |
| 2.1 | The high electoral results of the Italian Communist Party: elections for the Chamber of Deputies (1946–1963) | 46 |
| 2.2 | The geostrategic vulnerability of West Germany in Europe in May 1955 | 47 |
| 3.1 | West Germany absorbing most of Italian emigration in the Community, 1963–1970 | 81 |
| 3.2 | West Germany dominating family benefits transfers in the Community in 1965 | 89 |
| 4.1 | Convergence of extra-Community immigration with intra-Community migration after 1973 | 111 |
| 4.2 | Foreign residents from Mediterranean Europe in Germany, France, and Benelux in 1980 | 112 |
| 5.1 | The rise in the number of Erasmus students, 1987–1993 | 159 |
| 5.2 | Russian losses, risk of armed conflicts in Europe in 1990 | 166 |

# ABBREVIATIONS

| | |
|---|---|
| AAMS | Associated African and Malagasy States |
| AAPA | Auswärtiges Amt, Politisches Archiv, Berlin |
| ACCUE | Archives centrales du Conseil de l'Union européenne, Brussels |
| ACE | Archives centrales du Conseil de l'Europe, Strasbourg |
| ACP | African, Caribbean, and Pacific States |
| AHCE | Archives historiques de la Commission européenne, Brussels |
| AHUE | Archives historiques de l'Union européenne, Florence |
| AN | Archives nationales, Paris |
| AOECD | OECD Archives, Paris |
| CAP | Common Agricultural Policy |
| CEEC | Committee for European Economic Cooperation |
| CFDT | *Confédération française démocratique du travail* |
| CFSP | Common Foreign and Security Policy |
| CGT | *Confédération générale du travail* |
| COREPER | Committee of Permanent Representatives |
| CSCE | Conference on Security and Cooperation in Europe |
| DGB | *Deutscher Gewerkschaftsbund* |
| DOM | *Département d'outre-mer* |
| ECA | Economic Cooperation Administration |
| ECSC | European Coal and Steel Community |
| ECU | European Currency Unit |
| EEC | European Economic Community |
| EFTA | European Free Trade Association |
| EPC | European Political Community |
| ESC | Economic and Social Committee |
| EU | European Union |
| FRG | Federal Republic of Germany |
| GEQ | Council Group on Economic Questions |
| GDR | German Democratic Republic |
| GSQ | Council Group on Social Questions |

## ABBREVIATIONS

| | |
|---|---|
| ICEM | Intergovernmental Committee for European Migration |
| ICM | Intergovernmental Committee for Migration |
| ILO | International Labour Organisation |
| INSEE | *Institut national de la statistique et des études économiques* |
| IOM | International Organisation for Migration |
| JORF | *Journal officiel de la République française* |
| MSA | Mutual Security Agency |
| NATO | North Atlantic Treaty Organization |
| OCT | Overseas Countries and Territories |
| OECD | Organisation for Economic Co-operation and Development |
| OEEC | Organisation for European Economic Cooperation |
| OJEC | Official Journal of the European Communities |
| OJEU | Official Journal of the European Union |
| SNCB | *Société nationale des chemins de fer belges* |
| TOM | *Territoires d'outre-mer*, French overseas territories |
| UNICE | Union of Industrial and Employer Confederations of Europe |

# INTRODUCTION

In the beginning of the twenty-first century, the European migration regime had emerged as the distinctive feature of European Integration. The European migration regime refers to the set of rules, formal or informal, at the European level governing international migration movements.[1] Until this book was written, this regime was unique in the world through the free movement of people within the European Union, European citizenship, and the Schengen agreements in their internal and external dimensions. In comparison to migration regimes in other regions of the world, those instruments created a higher degree of openness for migrants within Europe, with the absence of border controls, a general right of residence, the access to employment, the right of establishment, the recognition of qualifications, the export of social security benefits, and certain electoral rights. Elsewhere, for instance in North America, Southeast Asia, or the Middle East, migration movements were more constrained. The rules of the migration regime in Europe were also unique insofar as they had created a deeper closure for migrants from outside Europe than was the case for any other region in the world. Europe's external borders became the bloodiest globally, with 9,000 migrant deaths in 2015 and 2016 in the Mediterranean alone, accounting for over 60 percent of all deaths worldwide.[2]

Its uniqueness at the global level is not the only reason why the European migration regime deserves attention. It was also an engaging regime in its internal dimension, insofar as it entailed the management of international inequalities associated with international migration in a way that minimised coercive restrictions against migrants. Migration may open up new opportunities, allowing people to make a better use of their talents and fulfil their aspirations. Those born in poorer countries may improve their condition by accessing the opportunities existing in richer countries. The primary focus of this book is therefore to explore the formation of the open migration regime within Europe and, in doing so, investigate an instance in which an open international migration regime was able to occur. The presence of both great openness and closure in this regional migration regime makes its existence even more intriguing.

In addition, this open migration regime deeply shaped European economies and societies. A closed migration regime within Europe until the 1950s had resulted in emigration overseas outstripping emigration to Europe.[3] As late as 1954, 57 percent of Italian emigrants still moved to non-European destinations.[4] With more open migration arrangements in Europe, by the mid-1960s nearly 80 percent of Italian emigrants moved to continental countries of North-West Europe.[5] The same happened with Greece, which benefited from more open migration arrangements in Europe as early as the beginning of the 1960s. Whereas two-thirds of Greek emigrants went overseas in the 1950s, 70 percent migrated to West Germany by 1964. In parallel to that change, annual Greek emigration increased fivefold, from 20,000 to 100,000.[6]

The more open migration regime contributed to the convergence of living standards with the rest of Western Europe for Italy, and later on for Greece, Spain, and Portugal. Italian gross domestic product (GDP) per capita was still 15 percent lower than the average in Western Europe in 1960: twenty years later it was equivalent.[7] With the enlargements of the European Union in Central Europe in 2004 and 2007, the populations of European Union citizens living in another country than their own more than doubled, from 5.9 million in 1999 to 13.6 million in 2012. Between 2000 and 2012, the number of Romanians residing in Western Europe multiplied tenfold and reached 2.4 million. Britain integrated a large number of Eastern European migrants in the decade following the 2004 enlargement: whereas there were only 1 million European immigrants in Britain in 2001, the number increased to 2.3 million by 2012.[8] Such flows had a profound influence on British society.

In 2015 and 2016, the regime entered a period of uncertainty for its future, as did European Integration in general. Voters' concerns about immigration in Western Europe triggered the outcome of the June 2016 referendum on British membership of the European Union. Anti-immigration had been a major theme for British politicians opposing the European Union well before the referendum.[9] During the referendum campaign, immigration was the key concern for 'Leave' voters.[10] This theme included the impact of European and non-European immigration on the labour market, the payment of benefits to European immigrants, and the control over non-European immigration. Meanwhile, migratory crises in the Mediterranean highlighted the restrictive side of the European migration regime, in the face of increasing migration inflows. For instance, in August 2015 – just one month – almost 200,000 migrants entered the European Union.[11] Between November 2015 and March 2016 the heads of state and governments of the European Union met three times with their Turkish counterparts. The European Union granted €3 billion to aid the Turkish government in stabilising refugees from Syria. The Europeans also promised to make progress regarding the liberalisation of visas for Turkish citizens in the European Union and for the talks related to the Turkish accession to the Union. Those considerable concessions were all driven by the importance of securing Turkey's participation in stemming the flow of migrants to Europe.[12]

To highlight this situation, both within Europe and at its borders, it is necessary to know how and why the regime that prevailed until 2016 was formed. Such development started around 1947 with the first European negotiations intending to define lasting rules for migration movements in Europe. This was the time when the first European international organisation, the Organisation for European Economic Cooperation, was created in the wake of the Marshall Plan. The year 1992 marked an attainment in the formation of the regime. The Treaty of Maastricht, creating the European Union, and coinciding with the end of the Cold War, introduced the final elements of the regime that prevailed for the following twenty-five years, by establishing Union citizenship and a common policy on extra-European migrants. After 1992, already negotiated agreements, such as the Schengen Convention, entered into force and the regime, initially centred on Western Europe, gradually expanded to encompass almost all the continent.

## Argument

In this book, I will show that the internal opening of the European migration regime had, despite widespread conviction,[13] little to do with the negotiation tactics of the governments of emigration countries. The largest countries of emigration in Europe never had the privilege of introducing migration questions in international negotiations. Often, European states debated about migration in international frameworks that excluded them. In many cases, raising the question of migration was a counterproductive move for the governments of emigration countries. Above all, there was no trade-off between trade liberalisation and migration liberalisation.[14] Even though these governments sometimes tried to threaten to block trade liberalisation if no progress was achieved in migration liberalisation, they were never credible and always ended up as the main supporters of trade liberalisation, which was vital for their exports.

More generally, I will show in this book, contrary to widespread conviction, that domestic demands in secondary states implying concessions from foreign governments do not explain European Integration.[15] The weakness of certain states to fulfil the economic needs of their populations never played any major role in achieving that process. It is exact that European Integration was decisive in helping a number of governments in their efforts to eliminate important domestic social and political tensions.[16] But those states that thus benefited from this process were not driving change. Above all, European Integration did not happen as a way for other European states to control Germany.[17] European Integration had nothing to do with a quest for preventing German resurgence. Quite the opposite: most other governments became heavily dependent on German support and were desperately looking for German help.

In this book, I will show that West Germany emerged as the most important actor in the European migration system in the post-war decades and led other immigration states into an open migration regime in Europe that favoured German geopolitical and economic interests over the long-term. I will show that the German economy was the main stabiliser of the open migration regime in Europe. German companies provided the jobs that the vast majority of migrants occupied, and German institutions paid the overwhelming majority of social transfers associated with migration flows between European countries. Without the German support, social tensions in destination countries would have rapidly led to the suppression of open migration arrangements, so that such arrangements probably would never have been implemented at all.

I will explain that West Germany accepted extensive concessions to other countries in order to define an international order in Western Europe favouring German interests over the long run. After the Second World War, the West German government had to cope with a geopolitical predicament that had considerably reduced German territory, divided it in two parts, and led to foreign occupation. It was of major importance to stabilise Western Europe and prevent any development that could lead to further German isolation in the long run. Additionally, it mattered to create a liberal international order in Western Europe that would help to absorb immigrants from Eastern Europe and act as a magnet for people of that region. This would not only contain Soviet influence, but also undermine it. By the end of the Cold War, the open migration regime in Western Europe was a powerful force, prompting support in Eastern Europe for membership to the European Union. An important contribution of this book will therefore be to emphasise that the formation of the European migration regime was a major political enterprise by West Germany in the unfolding of the Cold War in Europe.[18]

I will also highlight how West Germany integrated in the migration arrangements in Europe a number of provisions that were likely to promote German economic and social interests. Those arrangements facilitated the movement of German companies' staff. They facilitated the establishment of German independent professionals, such as lawyers, architects, and doctors, who could play an important role in the subsequent installation of German companies. I will demonstrate that the rules governing the transfer of social security benefits, even though expensive for Germany, aimed at reducing tensions in the German housing market and public infrastructure by promoting circular migration movements. Families of migrant workers could stay in the origin countries and still receive all the benefits to which they were entitled. These benefits included first and foremost family allowances, but also health care. In this way, workers too would return more easily in their countries of origin or move to another country as they could receive abroad their unemployment benefits and their pensions.

I will highlight that the open migration regime in Europe rested as well on some kind of support by secondary immigration states. These were chiefly France and Britain. But even though France played a role at the beginning of this story and Britain an important role at the end, I will show that none of these players was deeply enthusiastic about the open migration regime in Europe, and accepted it in many instances as long as Germany supported the most important part of migration flows and benefit transfers. I will present evidence about how their support was based on German concessions to them in other fields of European Integration, such as the Common Agricultural Policy, the Single Market, and the Economic and Monetary Union.

As a result, it will be the argument of this book that the open migration regime in Europe emerged in the Cold War under German hegemony. *Hegemony* refers to the superior position of a state in the hierarchy of power of an international system, and the use of that position to promote the interests of that state.[19] This power derives from the control by the hegemon of the scarce resources in the system, making other actors vulnerable to its decisions. In the European migration system, the scarce resources were the means of production that provided the jobs that migrants sought. With the largest economy and the greatest number of job vacancies, West Germany was in position to define the rules within the Western European migration system. This does not mean that the rules of the European migration regime were tyrannical;[20] it only means that they developed under German guidance and matched German preferences over the long run. The objective of long-term stability precisely invited to some balanced distribution of costs and gains in the European migration system.[21]

As I will show, the restrictive side of the regime derived from this same reason. There were geographical limits within which an open migration regime could actually foster German interests. Protectionist concerns both in Germany and other immigration countries should find compensation to greater openness within Europe by greater closure towards the rest of the world. More generally, I will depict European Integration as the result of extensive German concessions to create in Western Europe an international order conducive to German reunification and the rollback of Russian influence from Eastern Europe.

# Sources

For this research, I have used the archives of all the international organisations at the European level involved in the formation of the European migration regime.[22] These were the European Coal and Steel Community (ECSC) and the European Economic Community (EEC), whose records are held by the Archives of the

European Union. They also included the Organisation for European Economic Cooperation (OEEC) and the Council of Europe. In the archives of those various organisations, I have exploited exhaustively the documents of intergovernmental institutions: the Council of Ministers of the ECSC, then of the EEC, including the Committee of Permanent Representatives (COREPER) and the various Council working groups; the Council and the Executive Committee of the OEEC; and the Committee of Ministers of the Council of Europe.[23] In those documents, I could directly observe governments debating. The minutes of meetings reveal not only the positions taken by different governments, but also the underlying reasons for those positions. Government representatives explained their motives to their partners as often as they could in order to strengthen their positions.

In the archives of the European Union, I have also used the documents of non-intergovernmental institutions, which provide information on intra-national interests. The documents of the Economic and Social Committee show debates among trade unionists and employers. The documents of the European Parliament allow observing local interests. The Commission documents are useful to monitor the application of agreements made by governments and to go beyond an official approach to the functioning of the regime, even though, most of the time, governments respected these agreements, which were incorporated into national law. The documents of cases before the Court of Justice of the Community, available in the Commission documents, provide a similar clarification. They sometimes allow observing domestic political tensions and violations of European agreements.

International archives offer rich material on most questions, and I have used national archives only selectively. International archives are underdeveloped for the period from 1947 to the mid-1950s. To fill this gap, I focused on the archives of German diplomacy, the Auswärtiges Amt, as Germany was about to become the most important immigration country in Europe in the following years. I also used the documents of the French Ministry of the Interior on immigration in French Eastern borderlands for the period until the mid-1950s, to observe considerations against German immigration that were unlikely to be expressed in an international organisation. I also used national archives for the late 1980s, when Western European states negotiated outside the European Community questions related to Schengen cooperation. French archives are the most important, because France was the most concerned about the migratory consequences of the abolition of border controls and wielded important power to decide whether to abolish these controls. The presidential archives of François Mitterrand hold the most useful documents on the subject. I was able to access international and national documents despite the thirty-year rule governing such access. My information has been equally complete for the entire period covered by this book.

INTRODUCTION

# Outline

This book is divided into five chronological chapters that reflect the evolution of the European migration regime from the beginning of change in the wake of the Second World War until the full-blown configuration that the new regime assumed after 1992. In the period from 1947 to 1954 (Chapter 1), the prevailing migration regime in Western Europe was still a legacy of the Depression of the 1930s and the Second World War. Immigration states controlled bureaucratically every aspect of migration. The defeat of Germany had led to a regime unfavourable to German interests. The excess workforce in certain countries could often not find even temporary migration opportunities in neighbouring countries. That regime was a regular source of international tensions in Western Europe. France initially attempted to transform it, but could not absorb alone the increased migration flows that a more open migration regime with Italy would create. The U.S. government intervened and developed a large Western organisation allowing migrants to move towards other Western countries overseas. Meanwhile, the migration regime started becoming more open between the countries of North-Western Europe (i.e. between the Nordic countries, the Benelux countries, Britain, Ireland, France, and Switzerland). West Germany, Austria, and the Mediterranean countries in Europe (Italy, Spain, Portugal, Greece, and Turkey) remained outside this more open migration regime. During that period, the West German government started promoting a new migration regime in Western Europe, based on the principle of the free movement of persons. The economic difficulties in West Germany in the years following the Second World War meant that these attempts were overall unsuccessful.

From 1955 to 1964 (Chapter 2), owing to economic growth in the country, the West German government gained a greater influence on the European migration regime. Cold War constraints determined the German strategy. Providing permanent migration opportunities for Italian workers, and later on for Greek and Turkish workers, would firmly fasten those countries to the German camp. Securing strong alliances in Western Europe would in turn reduce German vulnerability towards the USSR and lead to German reunification. A more open migration regime started in a geographical setting matching German preferences. Centred on the six countries of the European Coal and Steel Community and then the European Economic Community, it was manageable and excluded the populations from the colonies. In accordance with French and Belgian preferences, opportunities were subject to labour demand increases in immigration countries in order to avoid downward pressure on local workers' wages. To discourage family flows, West Germany started exporting allowances for the families of Community migrant workers. France followed the German positions, not without linking this to German support for the Common Agricultural Policy, which was to enormously benefit French farmers.

From 1965 to 1973 (Chapter 3), West Germany managed to make further progress towards a new migration regime in Western Europe, but growing disagreements with France and increasing tensions within Western European labour markets slowed down this movement. France became less and less eager to accept unfettered migration flows of workers and arranged to tailor immigration in accordance with the interests of local workers. The French arranged various barriers in the Western European migration regime in order to prevent immigration from threatening French workers' status and wages. As immigration was increasing in West Germany, the government was eager to prevent huge family migration flows; it exported even more generously social benefits and arranged for other countries to do the same, with France obtaining a temporary exception. During that period the regime also touched independent professions. In that sector, flows were in the majority directed towards France, with farmers, shopkeepers, and self-employed professionals (e.g., architects) opposed to foreign competition there. This prevented significant opening, with several barriers subsisting such as public monopolies or the lack of recognition of qualifications. Regarding immigration from outside the Community, West Germany, France, and Britain, which joined the Community in 1973, favoured opening up towards different regions. Yet, none of them, including West Germany, had the capacity to support an open migration regime with any of those regions characterised by rapid population growth and expanding emigration. The distinction between migrants from inside the Community and outside the Community started being consolidated during that period.

From 1973 to 1984 (Chapter 4), the evolution towards a more open migration regime in Western Europe came to a standstill. In West Germany, a decline in the demand for goods and services led to a decline in the demand for labour. The government consequently stopped immigration from outside the Community. This policy provided an additional incentive for Greece, Spain, and Portugal to join the Community. The demographic growth of these countries was weak and the GDP per capita was comparable with those in the Community; this helped accession talks to succeed. In the case of Turkey, with a lower GDP per capita and higher demographic growth, the Community did not respect the already signed migration agreement. For Community migrants, migration opportunities stagnated because of higher minimum wages in immigration countries and the absence of progress on the recognition of qualifications and on the movement of self-employed professionals. In addition, infractions of Community rules increased as governments strove to protect their national workers. While Western European governments developed employment policies to foster the employment opportunities of their national workers, they could not agree on specific programmes to help migrant workers. Eager to limit its financial commitments, the West German government even called into question the amounts of family allowances to be exported, after increases in German family allowances to stem population decline. A stalemate in

INTRODUCTION

those negotiations ensued and the exception recognised to France persisted. European cooperation developed during this period only to reduce migration from Arab and African countries.

The new migration regime in Western Europe took on its final shape between 1984 and 1992 (Chapter 5). The regime, even though open, developed a selective and regionalist character. This was at the time of the negotiations of both the Single Market, of great interest for Britain, and of the Economic and Monetary Union, of great interest for France. These negotiations helped secure British and French support to German plans affecting the European migration regime. This led to the abolition of internal border controls through the Schengen agreements, with Britain opting out, and France and Germany agreeing on strong external borders for the Community. Where Britain and West Germany converged was in the willingness to move forward in the recognition of qualifications in the Community. This was a necessary precondition for the movement of managerial staff – itself essential for the expansion of their firms in Europe. The upheavals in Eastern Europe, which led to the end of the Cold War, interfered with these developments. In such an unstable environment, it mattered for the German government to reinforce diplomatic or even military integration among the states of the European Union. That signal was intended to discourage Russia to try to preserve the status quo or to use force. European citizenship became an important piece of a common foreign and security policy, as it was a way to create the civic base necessary to make this common foreign policy credible. Citizenship rights included the right for European migrants to reside in any country of the Union, and the right to vote and stand in local and European elections. Finally, as immigration flows were increasing in the early 1990s, the member states of the European Union agreed on greater closure towards trans-Mediterranean migration flows.

After 1992, continuing along those lines, the European Union implemented previous decisions, integrated Central Europe, and kept developing its policies to stop immigration in the Mediterranean. By then, the migration regime in Europe was quite different from what it was in 1947.

# 1

# AN UNSTABLE REGIME, 1947–1954

After the massive population displacements at the end of the Second World War, international relations over migration questions in Western Europe returned to normal around 1947. The migration regime then prevailing in Western Europe was largely a legacy of the interwar period and remained, overall, in place until 1954. In this chapter, I shall examine how this regime was subject to a series of tensions. I will show how the Allies in Europe tried to transform it but failed, before going on to discuss how, in the context of the Cold War, the United States intervened to resolve the most serious migratory tensions in Western Europe. In the first half of the 1950s, the Western European migration regime was then dual, with a movement for a more open regime concerning only certain countries. I will end the chapter with an account of the first steps taken by the Federal Republic of Germany (FRG) to champion an open migration regime in Western Europe.

## Disturbing tensions

Around 1947, disturbing tensions wracked Western Europe's migration regime. A bureaucratic management of migratory movements created costs and pressures, even for countries of immigration. In addition, this regime, which the victorious powers in Western Europe had tried to mould to their own ends, clashed with German and Italian revisionism.

### A bureaucratic migration regime

Migration flows within Europe had regularly increased over the previous century. The number of Italians in France had increased from 63,000 in 1851 to 419,000 in 1911.[1] In the decade leading up to the First World War, between 300,000 and 600,000 Polish seasonal workers were travelling each year to Germany and France for work.[2] The number of Dutch workers in Prussia reached a peak of 118,390 in 1912.[3]

After the First World War, immigration states developed a bureaucratic framework to manage international migration, in order to protect wage and employment levels for national workers. In Germany in the 1920s, firms had to register their workforce needs with local labour offices, and the Reich administration centralised such information. Foreign workers had to apply for new work permits each time they changed jobs, and employers had to apply for new permits to employ them. The labour administration granted permits according to the situation of the labour market. Residence permits could be valid for all or just a part of German territory and, in the latter case, had to be renewed for all changes of residence. These measures remained in force after the war.[4] In France, Articles 6 and 7 of the ruling of 2 November 1945 on the entry and residence of foreigners stipulated the need for a residency permit after three months, and a work permit issued by the Ministry of Labour to exercise any professional activity.[5] In the sectors that the ministry classified as having labour surplus, authorities had to check that an unemployed French worker could not be assigned to the company that had applied for the permit, before issuing a permit to a foreigner.[6]

After the Second World War, states also organised workforce recruitment during peacetime. In France, the ruling of 2 November 1945 set up the National Office of Immigration:

> The operations to recruit [labour] for France and the introduction in France of workers from overseas territories and foreigners . . . are the exclusive competence of the National Office of Immigration set up by the Ministry of Labour. No individual or group other than this office can engage in such operations.[7]

Yet, such a monopoly led to recruitment centres being overloaded and unable to respond to the labour needs of companies.[8]

Other bureaucratic procedures limited migration flows. After the Second World War, France drew up a list of countries whose nationals were entitled to take out a licence to run a coffee bar (*débit de boissons*). The list excluded former enemy countries or countries that had 'collaborated in the policies of the Axis [powers] voluntarily or otherwise': in other words, Germany, Austria, and Italy, but also Romania, Bulgaria, and Hungary.[9] Belgium insisted on a compulsory 'moral standards certificate [as well as a] medical certificate certifying [that the foreigner] does not suffer from any contagious or transmittable illness.'[10] Belgium also deferred immigration of the worker's family. A wife was not eligible for a work permit if her husband had a job and if the couple only had a small number of dependent children.[11] As regards remittances sent by workers to their families in the country of origin, in France all remittance operations were handled by the Exchange Office, which dealt with them according to the balance of payments and the availability of foreign currency.[12]

Rare bilateral agreements with emigration states mitigated arbitrary decisions by immigration states. The Franco-Italian Treaty of 15 April 1904 had recognised rights to Italian migrants in France. Through this concession, France had tried to get Italy to impose greater social security obligations on its employers, and in this way to limit Italian competition for French industry.[13] Between 1919 and 1932 France had also signed bilateral agreements to facilitate migration with the new countries of Central Europe. In offering migratory opportunities to the workforce of such countries, France had tried to stabilise them socially and politically, as a way to achieve greater stability for Europe and greater safety for France. France signed agreements with Poland in 1919, 1920, and 1925; with Czechoslovakia in 1920 and 1928; and after the crisis of 1929 with Austria, Romania, Hungary, and Yugoslavia.[14] With the Cold War, Central European countries became separated from the European migration regime, and only the agreements between Western European countries remained active.

Immigration states' bureaucratic regulation of migration movements was thus the characteristic feature of the migration regime prevailing in Western Europe around 1947. Immigration states' actions were leading to recurring tensions with emigration states.

## German concerns

After the war the winners were able to draw on the pool of German labour with no concern for the needs of economic recovery in Germany. During the Moscow Conference in April 1947, French Minister of Foreign Affairs Georges Bidault declared himself in favour of German emigration. Under the agreements with the U.S. government, on 29 September 1947, and the British government, on 25 October 1947, France obtained the right to recruit 25,000 German workers in the American and British occupied zones.[15] Germany no longer had a central state, but the administrative authorities in the *Länder* were still standing and were alarmed by French recruitment of German labour, while German recovery required a large workforce. The number of jobs in the American and British occupied zones went from fewer than 9 million in mid-1946 to more than 11.5 million in the first three months of 1949. The unemployment rate was stable. German authorities therefore opposed the emigration of their productive forces.[16] The representatives of the eight *Länder* in the American and British occupied zones created, from their first congress in March 1947, a permanent secretariat for emigration issues, charged with combating 'the emigration fever.'[17] During its congress of 8–9 September 1947 in Lübeck, the committee representing the government of the eight *Länder* in the American and British occupied zones regarded French recruitment harmful for the German economy.[18] In Austria, too, local authorities were hostile to French recruitment.[19]

German *Länder* favoured the emigration only of the non-working population. And yet occupation powers restricted precisely this sort of emigration. Indeed, these powers had a monopoly on issuing exit visas and only granted them rarely when this emigration was not part of regulated recruitment. In February 1948, the congress of the *Länder* in the American occupied zone requested that the U.S. government extend potential exit visas to the non-working population. *Länder* authorities also requested that German immigrants from the East (*Volksdeutsche*), who were not yet well integrated into the German economy, be a priority when filling immigration quotas for Germans to the United States. The Truman administration, keen to help West German recovery, accepted these demands. These U.S. concessions had no equivalent in the policies of France and Britain. Contrary to German concerns, the British and French governments asked U.S. authorities to extend exit rights in the American zone to German men joining their families in Britain or France.[20] The British government wanted the emigration of German workers to be liberalised.[21]

When forced to accept the emigration of people of working age, the West German authorities preferred newcomers, not yet well integrated into the West German economy. French policy was the exact opposite. In early 1948, in the context of the Cold War and after the French strikes of November-December 1947, French Minister of the Interior Jules Moch considered it vital to prevent the immigration of Communist agents to France from the Soviet occupied zone of Germany. In March 1948, the Ministry of the Interior ordered the Security Force for the control of the foreign workforce recruited in Germany and Austria to block the entry of all Germans without long-term domicile in one of the three Western zones.[22] This went directly against the interests of the West German *Länder*. The level and composition of German emigration were thus a source of tension between France and Britain on the one hand and West German authorities on the other.

Last but not least, the status that immigration states granted to German nationals once in their territories alarmed the West German authorities. After a certain number of years of residence, most immigrants were usually free to live anywhere in the host country. Yet Germany's neighbours prevented the settlement of Germans in the provinces bordering on Germany and which the latter had formerly occupied. During the Congress of Europe in The Hague on 8 May 1948, the Danish delegate to the economic commission, shipping magnate Arnold Peter Møller, objected to the wording of the congress' final resolution, which planned to 'promote labour mobility as much as possible,' fearing German immigration in Northern Schleswig.[23] Furthermore, in France, an order of the Minister of the Interior on 18 March 1946 made the settlement of foreigners in the *départements* of Alsace (Haut-Rhin and Bas-Rhin) and Moselle subject to prior authorisation by the Prefect, as a way to prevent German immigration.[24] In vain, the Department for Mines within the French Ministry of Industrial Production tried to oppose these measures by stressing in August 1947 the risk of a labour shortage in the Lorraine coalfields.[25] For the German authorities, this discrimination prevented the settlement of German nationals in the nearest zones, from where they would have been likely to return to Germany to fill the job vacancies to be expected in the near future or to repopulate Eastern territories after an equally expected German reunification.

Given the nature of the German emigration that the international regime in Europe favoured and the discrimination against Germans in neighbouring Western countries, the West German authorities favoured a deep revision of this regime.

## Italian revisionism

The Italian government also favoured revising the regime. Italy had experienced a demographic explosion in the previous century and a half, and the Italian population had shot up from 18 million in the early nineteenth century to over 47 million after the Second World War. The share of the population living in poverty had been exacerbated by the forced drop in emigration under Fascism,[26] and then by the postwar return of Italian settlers from former colonies. Moreover, labour demand in Italy had dropped due to the destruction caused by warfare and economic disruption in the wake of the war. The number of unemployed, which had already reached 1.32 million in 1946, rose to over 1.74 million in 1948.[27] The Italian government worked to broaden emigration opportunities in Europe, and a department dealing exclusively with emigration was set up under the aegis of the Italian Ministry of Foreign Affairs. In March 1949, the workforce surplus in Italy was estimated at 4 million.[28]

As the historian Federico Romero emphasised, there was a consensus among Italian party leaders on the need for emigration:

> Within the Constituent Assembly, the opinion of the political majority, not only of centre parties, industrialists and a large body of economists, but also of several representatives of the left, was that it would not be possible to reabsorb unemployment without constant emigration.[29]

In May 1948 the Liberal Party deputy in the Italian Constituent Assembly, Quinto Quintieri, explained to the economic commission of the Congress of Europe in The Hague why Italy had constituted a factor of instability in Europe in the previous half century. The main cause had been 'a lack of primary materials, natural resources and capital on the one hand, and continual population growth, on the other.'[30] After this reference to Italy's irredentist and colonial policies, he stressed that only emigration would absorb Italy's workforce surplus. As regards Italy's dominant party of government, the Christian Democracy, Christian Democrat deputy and party leader in the Veneto, Mariano Rumor, declared during the party congress in 1949 that emigration was a 'vital necessity.'[31]

Immigration states did little to help Italy. Recruitment agreements of Italian workers with Switzerland, France, and Belgium were asymmetrical. They limited total immigration to an annual quota, which was not always filled as immigrant workers had to meet the needs of employers in the destination country. Work permits were temporary and often limited to a particular place and job. The Swiss government favoured the replacement of immigrants by others after a few months, so as to avoid long-term settlement.[32] French officials were involved directly in recruitment, so that this was not left entirely to Italian bodies.[33]

In France, the *département* of the Alpes-Maritimes, which bordered on Italy, was the only administrative area that the Ministry of the Interior managed in the same way as the three Eastern *départements* bordering on Germany: as of 1946 foreigners could not settle without the prior authorisation of the Prefect. With this decision, the Ministry of the Interior wanted to offset the growth of the Italian population in the Alpes-Maritimes.[34] In November 1946 the Prefect of the Alpes-Maritimes, Paul Haag, pointed out that in the 1945 census 85 percent of the 68,000 foreigners in his *département* were Italian. The presence of this Italian nucleus meant a continual flow of Italian migrants who used their contacts, kinship links, and local information to obtain housing and work. The Prefect feared the creation of a 'pure and inassimilable Italian bloc' in the Alpes-Maritimes. He raised the spectre of a possible re-emergence of pre-war irredentist and fascist leagues, such as the *Groupes d'action de la Marche sur Nice*, which had prepared Italian occupation during the war.

Behind the geopolitical reasoning, the determined action of the Prefect also responded to sustained local pressure for restricting Italian immigration on economic grounds. In Cannes in February 1947, the *Amicale des anciens de la résistance* (Association of the Resistance) plastered the city walls with 300 posters that attacked 'those boycotting French goods in Italy and about to seize our work in France.'[35] The local labour demand was too weak to absorb immigration, and in the end the Prefect ended up expelling foreigners of all nationalities.[36] Given the way the Prefect was treating Italian immigrants, the National Office of Immigration closed the reception centre in Menton in order to avoid incidents likely to damage relations with the Italian government.[37]

## Inference

The constant intervention of immigration states on migration flows in Western Europe was thus the cause of recurrent tensions. The sheer number of documents required to migrate was a bureaucratic burden. These practices aroused the hostility of the German authorities and the Italian government. Even within the French government, ministries frequently opposed each other over immigration issues. In the end, these tensions weakened the prevailing migration regime.

## France failing

France was concerned about this unstable regime and was the first to try to make it less bureaucratic and more open. Episodes that previous studies associated with calls from the Italian government were, I show here, the result of the position taken by the French government. France wielded the resources to change the regime and tried to win the support of other countries in order to do so. In what follows I will explain why the French approach failed.

### French resources

France's capacity to absorb additional migration flows generated by a more open regime was key to redefine the European migration regime. France had a vast and underpopulated territory and had been trying to boost its population for some time. Geographically it was twice the size of Britain or West Germany, but at the end of 1947 its population was only 41.6 million, in comparison to 49.6 million in Britain[38] and 47 million in West Germany.[39] In the wake of the two world wars demographic growth was the key to rebuilding French power. In a speech to the Consultative Assembly on 2 March 1945, Charles de Gaulle, president of the Provisional Government of the French Republic, stressed that France's problem was its 'population shortage,' which he described as 'the underlying cause of our misfortunes' and 'the main obstacle to our recovery.'[40]

The pressing demand for labour by French companies was also conducive to the integration of new immigrants. In 1946, the French Planning Commission (*Commissariat général du Plan*) estimated that France needed an extra 1.5 million workers over a period of five years in order to maintain economic growth.[41] In 1947, the imminent release of 500,000 German prisoners of war then working in French industry and agriculture, and the repatriation of tens of thousands of Polish workers under an agreement with the Polish government, made the need for immigrants an imperative. Immigrant workers from other Western European countries were often trained in industrial work and mechanised agriculture, making them crucial for French economic growth. Bureaucratic obstacles blocked the entry of this needed foreign manpower.

Moreover, the unresolved tensions with Germany and Italy caused by the Western European migration regime jeopardised the stability of the Western European order. A more open migration regime, with openings for migrants from poor regions or from countries hit by labour-market problems, including during economic downturn, would generate greater stability for the Western European order. On 1 May 1930 the French government had issued a memorandum for a 'Federal European Union,' drafted by Foreign Minister Aristide Briand to combat 'employment crises, [and] sources of political and social instability.' As recession hit Europe, unemployment increased in Germany and Italy, two countries whose instability had an impact on French security. The French memorandum supported a 'progressive liberation . . . of the movement . . . of people' in Europe.[42] In the following years the failure of this plan and labour crises in Germany and Italy were to play a key role in the destabilisation of the European order. For French diplomats the experience of the 1930s only confirmed the arguments already presented in the Briand Memorandum.

Yet France's capacity to absorb migrants around 1947 did not mean that it could transform the Western European migration regime single-handedly. In 1946 the immigration plan of the French Planning Commission did not rule out a future downsizing of the demand for foreign labour.[43] It was important to involve other countries of immigration in this process, so that the largest migratory flows created by an open regime would be absorbed by several counties rather than triggering extreme tension in France alone.

### The French impetus

In summer 1947 the Conference on European Economic Co-operation in Paris brought together the sixteen Western European states that had accepted Marshall Plan aid. Besides France, the other countries of immigration in this group were Switzerland, Belgium, and Britain, but their capacity to absorb immigration was limited. In the Committee for European Economic Cooperation (CEEC), created by the Paris Conference, France declared a need for 300,000 foreign workers, in contrast to 60,000 for Switzerland, 26,000 for Belgium, and only 24,500 for Britain.[44]

France called for[45] and obtained the creation of a committee of experts 'to evaluate the [labour] supply and demand of participant countries and to decide the measures to promote and coordinate the transfer of workers between them.'[46] In addition to French and Italian experts, this committee brought together representatives of the destination countries of Italian emigration: Belgium, Britain, and Switzerland. To promote the movement of labour also towards Belgium and Britain, France needed to involve the International Labour Organisation (ILO), for example in recruiting workers for Belgian and British mines.[47] In June 1947, French delegate to the International Labour Conference (ILC) and trade union leader Léon Jouhaux pressed the ILC to adopt a resolution declaring the availability of the ILO for the implementation of the Marshall Plan. Shortly afterwards, French representatives in the CEEC together with Marius Viple, vice director general of the International Labour Office and a French senator, insisted that a reference to the Jouhaux resolution be inserted in the CEEC report of 23 August 1947 on labour issues.[48]

At the Paris Conference, France was keen to benefit from U.S. financial aid, and made clear that it was ready to resume the U.S. plan for a European customs union. In the meantime, the CEEC study group on customs unions was adopting a broad definition of customs unions, including migratory issues.[49] From 13 September 1947 France and Italy decided to examine the prospect of a bilateral union of this sort.[50] In his speech to the CEEC, the French representative, Hervé Alphand, argued that the barriers to the free movement of people among European countries constituted a major obstacle to their economic recovery. France did not want a bilateral relationship with Italy but a broader multilateral agreement. According to Alphand, the condition was that the economies to be combined together constituted a viable economic unit, meaning that the migration pressure had to be balanced.[51] In his speech to the CEEC on 15 March 1948, French Foreign Minister Georges Bidault repeated France's call to 'study similar [unions] with its Northern neighbours grouped in the Benelux and with Britain' – that is, the main countries of Italian immigration apart from Switzerland, which was not a member of the study group on customs unions. At the time, France was unable to deal on its own with the changes generated by a more open migration regime with the main country of emigration of the Western camp, namely Italy. France needed the involvement of other immigration countries. Bidault's plan was to subsequently extend this more open migration regime to all of Europe:

> Let us hope that soon on a territory in which we do not set *a priori* limits, the only limits will be as a result of refusal or impossibility, men . . . will be able to move and settle wherever they are most needed for the free community with a minimum of obstacles. . . . Our wish is to extend the free movement of people as far as possible.[52]

Nevertheless, Britain's low labour demand and its hostility to French plans presented at the Paris Conference[53] led to a scaling down of the migratory objectives of the Convention of European Economic Cooperation signed on 16 April 1948, which created the Organisation for European Economic Cooperation (OEEC). On 22 March, Article 8 of the draft convention provided:

> The [High Contracting Parties] will cooperate to make the best possible use of all available labour and to that end they will take the measures necessary to promote the movement and to ensure the settlement of migrant workers in satisfactory conditions from a social and economic perspective. They will cooperate . . . to progressively remove the obstacles to the free movement of persons between them.[54]

The problems of labour supply in the countries taking part were thus considered as a focus of cooperation; a plan for the free movement and settlement of migrant workers was drafted. In the days that followed, the aim of cooperation, top of the list in the original plan, was replaced by simple consultations.[55] It was no longer a question of managing the labour supply in all the countries taking part, but of each country committing to making the best use of its own national workforce.[56] It was no longer a question of 'removing' obstacles to the free movement of people, but only of 'reducing' them.[57] Finally, a special mention in the minutes made the application of the convention conditional on national security.[58] The plan to transform the migration regime at the Western European level within the framework of the OEEC had failed.

### The attempt of coalition with Britain and the Benelux states

France then tried to push the plan forwards in a narrower framework, which could subsequently be extended. Cooperation emerged between the countries of the Brussels Treaty, signed on 17 March 1948 by France, Britain, and the three Benelux states, which created the Western Union. The five powers agreed to extend social security rights to migrant workers on their territories. On 7 November 1949 in Paris they signed two conventions on social security for migrants. The balance of flows between the contracting parties played a key role in facilitating this agreement: each government had to pay for migrants on its own territory, without having received contributions beforehand.[59] In 1950, the five states also drew up a plan for a monthly exchange of information between their Ministries of Labour to help match labour supply and demand.[60] Cooperation among allies, with similar living standards, and balanced and reduced migratory flows, helped enlarge migratory opportunities.

To transform the European migration regime, the agreements between the five powers of the Treaty of Brussels had to be extended to the rest of Western Europe, because the migratory stakes were high at that level. Referring to the Social Security Convention of 7 November 1949, a March 1950 Report by the OEEC Manpower Committee mentioned a plan to study the 'possible extension of the application of principles included in the Convention of the Brussels Treaty to other OEEC members by means of a multilateral convention.'[61] In the meantime the British economy continued to decline. From mid-1949 Britain indicated to the OEEC that its future workforce needs would be negligible.[62] Unemployment was continually rising, affecting 518,000 people in mid-1952, and outstripping the number of available jobs. Hostility against foreign labour grew among miners, and immigration remained weak.[63] From then on, Britain opposed any extension of the agreement among the five powers.

Faced with the failure to reach an agreement with Britain, France did not find the required support to resolve the issue of Italian immigration. In the Franco-Italian Treaty on a Customs Union finally signed in Paris on 26 March 1949, Article 6(2) stipulated that limits to the free movement of people should be lifted in the course of a protracted transitory period.[64] The potential costs of these subsequent adjustments did nothing to encourage treaty ratification. Given the existing opportunity for Italians to transfer remittances to Italy, France's balance of payments with Italy deteriorated and the Finance Ministry called for limiting this opportunity.[65] Without being submitted to the French Parliament for ratification, the Treaty was abandoned.[66]

France pursued the plan with Italy by trying a coalition with the Benelux countries. At the Council of Ministers meeting in France on 8 August 1947, Bidault had already declared: 'With Benelux, which has a large productive apparatus, and Italy, which has a great workforce, France could receive a big boost.' He declared that the union should not be limited to France and Italy: 'If this union is limited to France and Italy, we will lose.'[67] After the collapse of the planned Franco-Italian Customs Union in spring 1949, French Finance Minister Maurice Petsche submitted a plan to involve the Benelux countries. The U.S. State Department and the U.S. Economic Cooperation Administration (ECA) intended to earmark USD 150 million of Marshall Plan aid payments for countries taking part in the French initiative.[68] The so-called Finebel negotiations were then opened with France, Italy, the Netherlands, Belgium, and Luxembourg.

Yet the economic situation was unfavourable. Whereas Belgium received the largest share of Italian migrants in the Benelux, unemployment exploded from 5.2 percent to 12.7 percent of insured workers over the course of 1948 in that country. From 30 March 1948, the National Labour Conference criticised competition from foreign labour. The Belgian Ministry of Labour and Social Insurance decided to suspend the recruitment of foreign workers for all sectors except mines as of 1 October 1948. On 22 December 1948 the delegate of the Federation of Christian Trade Unions asked the Belgian Tripartite Commission on Foreign Labour to halt all immigration, even in the mining industry.[69] Foreign recruitment in the mining sector was brought to a halt early in 1949. In 1949, Switzerland, which did not take part in the negotiations but which absorbed many Italian migrants each year, cut the number of incoming migrant workers by around one-third, from 100,000 to 30,000 or 40,000.[70] Excess Italian labour risked ending up in the other countries of Italian emigration. The labour-market situation was therefore not conducive to a relaxation of migratory regulations for Italian labour.

In the framework of the Finebel negotiations, the Dutch Ministry for Social Affairs feared that the free circulation of labour would exacerbate domestic unemployment by causing an influx of Italian, and even German labour, if the plan was subsequently extended to West Germany.[71] Finally, the Italian government agreed not to make the liberalisation of migration a condition for accepting the Finebel Treaty, since in any case the Italian economy would benefit from the liberalisation of trade.[72]

## Inference

The French initiative in the CEEC thus failed due to the weak labour demand in other immigration countries and the decline of the British economy. There was an imbalance between French resources on the one hand, and the weight of migratory pressure, particularly in Italy, on the other. That imbalance would have persisted even if Britain or the Benelux countries had adopted the French approach: this is why France was unable to establish coalitions with them. Finally, after Algerian Muslims became French citizens in September 1947, the number of those who had immigrated to France increased tenfold between 1946 (22,000) and 1954 (212,000).[73] At the same time, the higher labour costs caused by the 1945 social security reform[74] led to a lower labour demand in subsequent years. The number of those looking for work soared from 45,000 in 1947 to 153,000 in 1950, and immigration fell, with only 26,000 entries of foreign workers in 1950, of which 16,000 were seasonal.[75] This new situation put an end to French initiatives.

## Developing overseas emigration

After the failure of French initiatives, the migratory tensions in Western Europe not only persisted, but actually increased, leading to U.S. intervention in European affairs. Earlier studies only tackled this episode from the perspective of U.S.-Italy relations.[76] In this section I will show how the migratory flows from Eastern Europe to West Germany determined U.S. intervention as of 1949.

### The influx from the East

In the immediate postwar period, 12 million emigrated from Eastern Europe. Many were Germans expelled from Central Europe. West Germany took in 9.4 million. Turkey received a further 945,000, Italy 570,000, and Austria 300,000.[77] As a consequence, the population of Western Germany increased by 20 percent in the period 1939–1949.[78] Yet immigration from the East continued. German partition, the creation of the German Democratic Republic (GDR) in October 1949, and the Communist reforms in the GDR meant a 50-percent increase in the flow of migrants between the two Germanys, from 129,000 in 1949 to 192,000 in 1950. In 1953, the year of the workers' uprising in East Berlin, 331,000 people defected from East Germany to West Germany.[79] The Federal Republic of Germany (FRG) was determined to restore German unity, and welcomed these migrants, who were German nationals under its new Basic Law (*Grundgesetz*). The aim of weakening the Communist governments in Central Europe also meant that the FRG remained open to those defecting from the Eastern bloc. The Basic Law of the FRG provided that 'victims of political persecution enjoy the right to asylum.'[80]

This migratory pressure coincided with an economic downturn. The production of manufactured goods in the United States dropped by 8.5 percent between July 1948 and May 1949, following the high rates of production of previous years. That recession affected exports from the sterling zone to the United Sates, leading to a devaluation of the pound sterling against the U.S. dollar. Britain accounted for a third of international trade in Western Europe, and this devaluation affected regional economic prospects.[81] After the 1948 monetary reform in the FRG, the West German economy was particularly affected. Unemployment increased throughout 1949, reaching 1.85 million in March 1950.

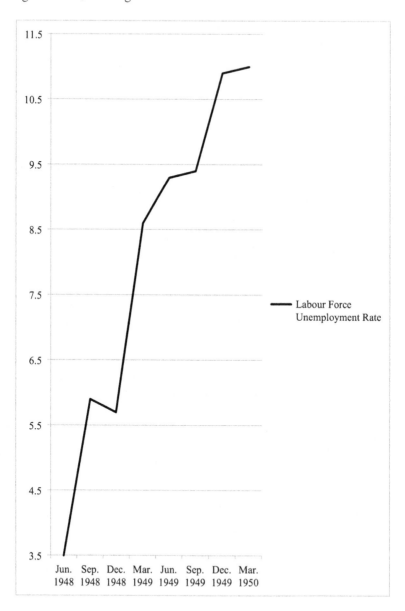

*Figure 1.1* The rise of unemployment in West Germany, June 1948–March 1950[82]

Unemployment was higher in the eastern regions, facing the arrival of migrants from Eastern Europe. From July 1948 to October 1949, the unemployment rate rose from 2.5 percent to 22 percent in Schleswig-Holstein, from about 3.5 percent to 13.5 percent in Lower Saxony and Bavaria, and from 3 percent to around 8.5 percent in Hessen, Bremen, and Hamburg.[83] The Netherlands faced similar problems, with the return of migrants from Indonesia in the wake of decolonisation, and the sharp drop of jobs in the farming sector.[84] The growing needs of these emigration countries collided with the limited migratory opportunities available in Western Europe. In 1950 emigration collapsed. Even Italy, the country the most committed to organising emigration, recorded a net emigration of only 3,500 people in 1950.[85]

In West Germany, demographic pressure and the lack of migratory opportunities created the conditions of a political crisis. Hundreds of thousands of migrants had been living in camps since 1945. An OEEC report of February 1950 highlighted the serious risk posed by a crisis in such a strategic country as West Germany:

> The fact that such an extremely high rate of unemployment . . . prevails at the border of Eastern territories under Soviet rule is a serious threat not only for West Germany, but also for the whole of Western Europe.[86]

## The failure of regional emigration

Forced to accept emigration, the West German government preferred it to be nearby and temporary, on the one hand because it considered unemployment as temporary, and on the other hand because it anticipated the return of German Eastern territories at some point. During an interministerial meeting in Bonn on 14 January 1950, Rudolf Petz, from the Ministry of Labour, declared: 'If one takes Germany as a whole, there is no surplus workforce.'[87] The outflow of migrants from the East reduced the population, making it necessary to preserve a sufficient German workforce nearby to repopulate the Eastern territories when partition would come to an end. To achieve that goal, the West German government had to promote only short-term emigration to neighbouring Western countries rather than to distant destinations. From this perspective, that government still pursued migratory opening up among OEEC member states. At the same meeting Otto Rieck, from the Ministry for Marshall Aid, pointed out that the free movement of labour was essential in any movement towards a common economic space in Western Europe. Moreover, Helmut Meinhold, of the Ministry for Economic Affairs, and Julius Scheuble, from the Ministry of Labour, backed the free movement of international payments, to ensure the maintenance of families who remained in their countries of origin thanks to the remittances of émigré workers. The upkeep of families in West Germany favoured returns and these transfers made emigration more profitable. Finally, Interior Minister Gustav Heinemann stressed that measures be proposed to eliminate discrimination suffered by Germans abroad.[88]

Following this meeting, the German delegation submitted to the OEEC Manpower Committee on 15 February 1950 a plan to promote migration among the OEEC member states, the right of the migrant to choose their job and place of work freely, and the free transfer of remittances to their families in their country of origin for short-term male emigrant workers.[89] In July 1950, during a conference at the Quai d'Orsay with American, British, and French delegates, German delegates repeated their call for European solidarity, affirming that West Germany had 450,000 workers willing and ready to emigrate.[90] In a letter of 26 January 1951 to the Secretary General of the Council of Europe, the German government forecast emigration of around 1.2 million people, including workers and their families.[91]

The emigration of farmers mattered. Many arrived from Eastern Germany, and urbanised Western Germany did not offer them many opportunities. For them, too, emigration was to be temporary, and consequently nearby. During the interministerial meeting of 14 January 1950, Türk, from the Ministry for All-German Questions, was worried by the trend towards emptying the 'Eastern German territories' of Germans. He stressed the importance of not moving farming families too far away: 'in case of return of the Soviet zone to Germany, a new agricultural reform would be needed, which would create a demand for farming families to work the land.'[92] In September 1952, twenty-two members of the Consultative Assembly of the Council of Europe, half of them German, were led by the German representative Hans von Merkatz, future Federal Minister for Expellees, and called for 'appropriate ways to integrate refugee or surplus farmers in the agricultural economy of the member states of the Council of Europe.' They called for Western European countries to settle these thousands of farmers before looking for outlets overseas. Furthermore, they argued that the freedom of movement and settlement of Europe's population, in a spirit of solidarity, was vital for the constitution of a free community in Western Europe.[93] In 1954 the West German government still forecast the emigration of at least 60,000 farming families.[94]

Youth emigration also mattered. In West Germany, the number of young people leaving school to look for apprenticeships outstripped the number of training places available. Due to the high birth rate until the early 1940s and the influx of young migrants from the East, in 1952 around 150,000 people under the age of twenty-six were unable to take up vocational training or were unemployed. The surplus was to last until around 1960. The German government wished to create a European exchange for young people looking for vocational training.[95] It called on its Western European partners to 'help deal with the professional crisis affecting young people . . . in offering to them apprenticeships in other [OEEC] member states.'[96] In their case the proximity of migratory destinations was essential, because it was meant to be temporary emigration limited to the period of training.

In spite of this call for help, in Europe, the countries of immigration did not accept German proposals. West Germany could count on the support of the United States in the OEEC. In December 1949 and January 1950, the ECA representative in the OEEC Manpower Committee declared: 'The dual purpose of the recovery programme is the viability and integration of European economies. The latter . . . unquestionably implies the free movement of labour.'[97] The delegates of the countries of immigration in Europe pointed out that a 'policy of total freedom would mean public opinion and the trade unions contesting the hiring of foreign workers much more forcefully than at the present.'[98] Two years later, when the German representative in the Manpower Committee again stressed the critical state of affairs in his country, France expressed that it was ready to accept migrants from other member states, 'subject to positive developments regarding the labour market and population surpluses of French territories overseas,' including Algeria.[99] Within the Executive Committee, apart from the French delegate, only the delegates of countries affected by high unemployment rates or immigration from Eastern Europe or former colonies also expressed an interest: West Germany, Greece, Italy, and the Netherlands. The British delegate, Hugh Ellis-Rees, stressed his government's opposition to the plan, which was then abandoned.[100]

## The actions of the United States

The Western European migration regime was unable to resolve migratory tensions, and the Europeans appealed to the United States to shift the issue to another level. Within the OEEC Manpower Committee, the United States, France, and Britain recognised the importance of encouraging emigration outside Europe.[101] In May 1953, a resolution of the Committee of Ministers of the Council of Europe on 'the social and political stability of Europe' argued the need to facilitate 'the departure of surplus European population to regions overseas.' The resolution appealed to 'extra-European governments . . . to facilitate the flows of European emigration to their countries.'[102]

The United States had a vested interest in keeping opportunities open for migrants from the East, encouraged to flee to the West by U.S. propaganda, and in order to help Western Europe attain social and economic stability.[103] A State Department memorandum of June 1951 stressed that 'continuous emigration on a much broader level since the war should be encouraged as a means to relieve the pressure' on the countries of the Atlantic Pact.[104] In a speech to Congress in March 1952, President Harry S. Truman declared that the problems linked to the density of population in some countries and to immigration from the East meant that Western Europe would have to make 'attempts to cooperate with all the countries involved' in order to reinforce the security of the North Atlantic community.[105]

Yet Congress refused to relax its quotas for European migrants and adopted the Immigration and Nationality Act to that end. Notwithstanding Truman's veto, the Act came into force on 24 December 1952. In his veto message to Congress, Truman cited the importance of guaranteeing migratory opportunities for those who had fled the Eastern bloc.[106] In the last instance, Congress granted special opportunities for migrants from the East to enter the USA. With the Refugee Relief Act of 7 August 1953, Congress agreed to issue up to 209,000 special non-quota visas in the following three years. Of this number, up to 90,000 would be for refugees in West Germany who had fled Eastern countries, most of them ethnic Germans; 45,000 for ethnic Italian refugees residing in Italy; 15,000 ethnic Italians, not necessarily refugees, residing in Italy; and up to 15,000 ethnic Dutch refugees residing in the Netherlands.[107] Potential candidates for emigration meeting the range of conditions for refugee status, ethnic origin, and residence were more often the migrants from Germany than those from other countries. This programme targeted help to the FRG, the most strategic in the context of the Cold War.

In a broader perspective, the U.S. government developed migratory cooperation on a supra-Western level to manage the problems that Europeans were unable to deal with regionally. From June 1950, it voiced its concern for demographic growth in Europe during the third session of the Economic Commission for Latin America at Montevideo. The Latin American states requested that the International Bank for Reconstruction and Development be involved in these plans so that transfers of population would be matched by investments.[108] The U.S. government then used its financial influence to guarantee the opening up of other Western countries to European emigration.

To implement these migration movements, in December 1949, the ECA's Special Representative in Europe indicated to the Secretary General of the OEEC, Robert Marjolin, that the ECA envisaged 'an arrangement under which the International Labour Office guarantees the execution of a programme under the aegis of the OEEC and designed to facilitate European migration.'[109] The Office, with its own expertise, brought together European countries of emigration and countries of immigration overseas.[110] The preparatory conference on migrant workers convened by the Office in April–May 1950 in Geneva brought together the greater part of the countries of Western Europe and the Americas, as well as Australia.[111] Even though West Germany was not a member of the Office, a German observer was invited to participate,[112] and the Conference tried to speed up its admission to membership of the International Labour Organisation (ILO); it was admitted in June 1951.[113] The United States was ready to pay out USD 988,000 in financing. The Europeans committed to USD 200,000, distributed according to the normal budgetary rates of the OEEC. Therefore, Britain accepted to take on nearly a third of the European expenses for the programme, 'given the extreme urgency and importance that this presented.'[114] These sums were earmarked for the exchange of information necessary to manage migratory movements.[115]

The sums required for transportation were expected to come to tens of millions of dollars. Congress refused to award such a large sum to a body like the ILO, which included Communist states.[116] During the Brussels conference in November 1951, the U.S. government proposed the payment of USD 10 million to a new body to cover the transportation of emigrants: the Intergovernmental Committee for European Migration (ICEM). It included the main countries of emigration in Europe, which were close to the border with Eastern Europe and welcomed migrants from there: West Germany, Austria, Italy, Greece, and the Netherlands. It also included their close neighbours, concerned about their political stability and subject to indirect immigration from the East: Switzerland, France, Belgium, Luxembourg, Sweden, and Norway. Finally, it included the overseas countries of immigration, members of the Western camp and in a position to welcome migrants: Canada, the United States, Costa Rica, Venezuela, Brazil, Paraguay, Chile, Argentina, Australia, and Israel. From 1 February 1952 to 31 July 1953, the ICEM transported around 120,000 people: half were from West Germany, 18,000 from Italy, 14,000 from Austria, and 12,000 from the Netherlands.[117]

## Inference

The U.S. intervention was not determined by the situation in Italy, which remained unchanged, but by the new migratory pressure and the rise in domestic unemployment in West Germany. The United States decided to relax its immigration quotas and created the ICEM to transport European migrants to the Americas and Australia. Guaranteeing political stability in Western European countries meant ensuring the strength of the Atlantic alliance. It also helped maintain pressure on Eastern European states by incorporating the inflows of their émigrés, thus serving the Cold War interests of the West. Following this impetus, the structures thus created could help emigration from other less strategic Western European countries, starting with Italy. One condition of U.S. aid was officially that the countries involved provide evidence of their support for the principle of the free movement of people.[118] This pressure eased the ratification of the Convention by Western European states on the status of refugees in the United Nations, signed in Geneva on 28 July 1951. Even if each state was free to grant refugee status, the contracting states undertook to extend to refugees the benefits of existing agreements between them on the social security rights of migrant workers.[119] The Convention came into force on 22 April 1954, ratified almost only by Western European states. However, this small measure and the lack of any real progress otherwise, revealed the weak capacity of the U.S. government to reshape the migration regime among the countries of Western Europe.

## A dual regime

The overall Western European migration regime had hardly changed. Bilaterally or among small groups of neighbouring countries, attempts were being made to relax migratory relationships. In this section I will present the characteristics of the regime in the early 1950s and reveal the persistent opposition between two different parts of Western Europe.

### The two parts of Western Europe

The divide in the Western European migration regime was due to the different conditions prevailing in regional labour markets. France, Switzerland, Luxembourg, Denmark, and Sweden were industrialised countries with full employment. Belgium and Britain were also industrialised countries with limited unemployment. There were pockets of underdevelopment in Ireland, the Netherlands, and Finland, but the capacity of neighbouring countries to absorb labour guaranteed regional stability. By contrast, the labour markets in central and southern Western Europe were unbalanced. In West Germany, this was due to the destruction and dismantling of industrial plants at the end of the war and to the arrival of millions of immigrants from Central Europe. Southern Italy, Spain, Portugal, Greece, and Turkey had a mix of low development and strong population growth. Migratory pressures basically originated in one of the two parts of Western Europe, and this geo-economic dualism had implications for the overall migration regime.[120]

In North-Western Europe the migration regime evolved in a more open sense. People could move between France, Monaco, Luxembourg, and Belgium without a visa or passport by simply presenting an identity card, which facilitated job searching.[121] As of April 1952, all border controls were abolished between Britain and Ireland, taking into account that their migratory policies were identical. As of July 1952, Danish, Finnish, Norwegian, and Swedish nationals could travel between their countries without a passport.[122] Visas for trips of less than two months were also abolished between Britain and Ireland, and among the Scandinavian countries.[123] The signatories of the Brussels Treaty agreed on social security conventions to guarantee the maintenance of rights acquired abroad by migrant workers and frontier workers, particularly as regards the payment of old-age pensions.[124] Work permits were abolished among the Scandinavian countries in the framework of a common labour market as of July 1954.[125] Employer demand for manpower and worker demand for job opportunities and continuity of social security rights thus led to a slight relaxation of the migration regime in that part of Western Europe.

The regime between the north-west of Western Europe and the other countries of Western Europe remained more inflexible. Short-stay visas were still mandatory for movement between West Germany, Austria, Portugal, Greece, and Turkey on the one hand and the other Western European countries on the other. Consulates were normally authorised to issue entry visas, but for France, Sweden, and Belgium, key destination countries for German emigration, consulates had to obtain the prior agreement of their diplomatic service to issue visas to Germans. Portugal and Turkey were also partly responsible for this visa regime, insofar as the fear of uncontrolled emigration led them to accept the need for a visa, which their nationals came up against when trying to travel abroad. Visa requirements remained intact between Italy on the one hand and Denmark, Norway, Iceland, and Ireland on the other.[126]

*Figure 1.2* The dual migration regime in Western Europe in the early 1950s

Other restrictions affected German migrants. In 1950 there were only 700 German frontier workers in France, compared with 53,000 Belgians, whereas the Germans were one of the main migrant groups in France.[127] This weakness of Franco-German border movements echoed opposition to German immigration in Eastern France with the decree of 18 March 1946. On 2 April 1951, French Prime Minister and Interior Minister Henri Queuille sent a letter to the Prefect of Moselle, reminding him that this decree was to prevent German immigration. In December 1951, an internal note on this measure in the Ministry of the Interior stressed that it meant being able to avoid strengthening 'certain annexationist positions.'[128] The restrictive migration regime also affected Italy: the four-year programme that the Italian government submitted to the OEEC in 1948 forecast the departure of 364,000 Italians to other parts of Western Europe, but for the period 1949–1952 this figure dropped to 180,000.[129]

## A difficult opening up

In the OEEC Italy tried, in July and December 1950, to make trade liberalisation conditional on migration liberalisation.[130] Yet since Italy would also benefit from trade liberalisation, these threats were not credible. In 1952, France and Britain suspended OEEC trade liberalisation due to a balance of payments deficit: Italian textile exports plummeted from 385 billion to 207 billion lire in 1952 while agricultural exports fell slightly from 205 billion to 197 billion lire. Trade with France and Britain had until then provided Italy with over 80 percent of its foreign currency reserves from the European Payments Union. On the other hand, Italian imports of coal and machinery from France and Britain remained stable throughout 1952, since the Italian economy depended on these. As a result, in October 1953, Italian Prime Minister Giuseppe Pella proposed that the OEEC introduce measures to deter the suspension of trade liberalisation for balance of payments problems. For emigration, Italy had no choice but to stick to the preferences of immigration countries, thus undermining the prospects for Italian manpower abroad. In 1951 the British government suspended the signed recruitment agreement for Italian workers in British coalmines following the protest of the British National Union of Mineworkers to the influx of Italian labour in Welsh mines.[131]

For the West German government, the abolition of visas was a priority in promoting labour mobility, business travel, and tourism. Immediately after the Allies had made the German authorities responsible for issuing passports, on 1 February 1951, the West German government proposed that the member states of the Council of Europe and the OEEC abolish entry visas,[132] and it renewed its demand in late 1952. However, on the request of Swedish delegate Erik von Sydow, the other governments accepted to recommend not to abolish visas, but simply to study the option for doing so.[133] The visa procedure allowed these states to expel former Nazis. In the absence of action by the other governments, the West German government decided as of 1 July 1953 to unilaterally abolish visa obligations for stays of less than three months in West Germany for citizens of all OEEC or Council of Europe states.[134] It was only during 1954 that the other Western European states recognised reciprocity to the Germans: Belgium and Luxembourg as of 1 January, France from 15 May, Sweden from 1 June, and Britain and Ireland from 1 October. West Germany was almost the last country for which short-term visas were abolished in Western Europe. Visas were only kept up between Portugal and some other countries in line with Portugal's goal of reining in emigration.[135]

Furthermore, the West German government supported a recommendation of the Committee of Ministers of the Council of Europe, in July 1952, calling for a standardised procedure for issuing passports.[136] Other governments proved willing to work on this issue, as it would help remove congestion at borders, since passport controls slowed down cross-border traffic and were costly for trade.[137] The Consultative Assembly of the Council of Europe also recommended to the Committee of Ministers to extend the existing agreements between Britain and Ireland and among the Scandinavian countries on the abolition of border checks. Due to British opposition, the Committee of Ministers rejected such recommendation. In the Committee's opinion, this type of agreement meant that 'nationals of each group of countries [could] enter, reside, and work in any other country free of restrictions,' and that these countries apply identical policies on the admission of third-state nationals.[138]

At the same time, the West German government attempted to ensure the maintenance of social security rights acquired by migrant workers abroad. Since the end of the war, many Germans had worked under different welfare systems in other Western European countries and had acquired social security rights that were important to safeguard on their return to West Germany. In early 1950, West Germany was in a marginal situation in Western Europe. It had not passed any social security agreements with other states. In a memorandum to the OEEC in January 1954, the German delegation specified: 'The steps taken to boost manpower mobility and encourage freedom of movement on European territory will only be successful if we manage to harmonise the various national social security regimes.'[139] The plan to extend the social security conventions of the Brussels Treaty to the other countries in the Council of Europe was then revived also thanks to support from Belgium, where the unfavourable demographic situation called for increased immigration.[140]

In the negotiations that followed, the French delegate defended the principle of territoriality in the conventions of the Brussels Treaty: the costs of social benefits should be borne by the country on whose territory they were paid. This principle of territoriality was unacceptable for the delegates of states of emigration – Italy, West Germany, and the Netherlands – which did not received the contributions paid by migrant workers likely to compensate the costs of social benefits provided on their territories. The West German delegate reminded other delegates 'that a large number of German workers were leaving for abroad' and that as a result 'he could not accept the conclusions of the French delegate.'[141] The British delegate supported the French position. Unable to come to a permanent multilateral convention on social security in the Council of Europe, the delegates negotiated two temporary agreements on social security, signed on 11 December 1953 by the Committee of Ministers, and an additional agreement on social and medical assistance. These agreements were based on the principle of territoriality, reflecting the preferences of immigration countries.[142]

## The failure of the U.S. initiative

Due to the difficulties faced by West Germany and Italy, both key allies of the United States, the U.S. government pushed for new negotiations among the Western Europeans. After the outbreak of the Korean War, that government indicated that mobilisation for defence should mean improving the mobility of international manpower in Western Europe. As a result, on 1 December 1950, the OEEC Council instructed its Manpower Committee to examine appropriate measures to improve international manpower mobility.[143] In the discussions that followed in August 1951, the U.S. representative in the Executive Committee, Henry Tasca, drew attention to 'the need to make full use of the vast European manpower resources.'[144] In January 1952 the Dutch delegate to the OEEC Manpower Committee highlighted the rise of unemployment in his country and called for more opportunities for intra-European emigration.[145] On 25 February 1952, the Final Communiqué of the Lisbon conference on economic cooperation between the North Atlantic Treaty Organization (NATO) and the OEEC recognised the seriousness of limitations to labour movement among its member states.[146] The Mutual Security Agency (MSA), which had replaced the ECA and coordinated military, economic, and technical aid to the United States' allies, then asked the OEEC to liberalise labour movement in Europe.[147]

In return for U.S. aid, on 28 March 1952, the OEEC Council recognised, as one of the basic conditions for the success of the planned economic expansion 'the maximum progress possible in the next five years towards the removal of restrictive regulations, procedures, and other obstacles to the free movement of workers among member states.'[148] A working group to liberalise labour flows was created, to which Italy submitted a plan to abolish work permits,[149] supported by the FRG and the MSA. In 1952 and 1953, a transition began to hint at German support for these plans. In October 1953, at the end of negotiations, the German Minister for Economic Affairs, Ludwig Erhard, declared himself in favour of 'the total liberalisation of labour movement in Europe.'[150] He then backed the relaxation of the Western European migration regime, no longer so much to provide German workers with short-term emigration opportunities in case of Eastern inflows or economic downturn as to create transitory immigration inflows to meet the manpower needs of German employers, whose interests Erhard represented.

However, the Belgian, British, and French representatives in the working group opposed the Italian plan. They cited the need to protect sectors hit by unemployment and to prevent wage reduction caused by greater immigration. In limiting labour activity to a particular sector and in setting wage levels in the average range for that sector, work permits allowed these states to avoid such problems. The British expert stressed the risk of 'the failure of any immigration plan' without 'a more effective demand for foreign labour.' Unions, he argued, would prevent immigrant workers from taking jobs. The French expert pointed out that there would be 'strikes, serious incidents, a wave of xenophobia against which all efforts of pacification would be useless.' He pointed also to France's need to first find work for the one million unemployed from North Africa.[151]

The other Mediterranean countries were not even supportive of the project. Portugal and Turkey did not want to take part in the agreement, but only communicated this at the end of negotiations in October 1953.[152] For Turkey, with an average annual income per capita of only USD 316 in the mid-1950s, migratory liberalisation with the rich countries of Western Europe could have triggered an unregulated emigration of skilled labour.[153] Political considerations also explained their positions: in Turkey, in relation to possible Greek immigration, and in Portugal, in favour of emigration to the colonies and against immigration of potential political opponents to the *Estado novo*.

Given the position of the main immigration countries in Western Europe, the decision on the employment of member-state citizens adopted by the OEEC Council on 30 October 1953[154] only proposed that member states would issue work permits to workers who were member-state citizens within a month of the notification of job vacancies by employers. In the meantime, national workers would have priority to respond to those job offers. This deadline could be extended to two months if a country applied for it. France did so, raising the problem of the integration of North African workers in the French economy.[155] In Switzerland, Britain, Belgium, and Sweden, the decision did not introduce any new element because the one-month deadline was already common practice in their employment services.[156] The decision also planned the automatic renewal of work permits after five years' employment. Sweden already applied automatic renewal after only two years, and Britain after four years. The decision did not deal with the issue of trainees, which interested West Germany.[157]

## Inference

The migration regime in Western Europe was thus split in two. On the one hand were the countries of the North-West, where the labour market situation was favourable and migratory movements were facilitated. On the other hand were the countries of central and southern Western Europe plagued by unemployment or under-employment, for which migratory opportunities in Western Europe remained limited. This distinction only blurred when it came to short-stay visas. The influence of the United States was not sufficient to win French, British, and Belgian support to transform this regime.

## Preparing change

Although unsuccessful within the OEEC and the Council of Europe, the West German government was preparing change in the migration regime in Western Europe and with rapid economic growth was already likely to obtain results. Strategically, the German government used and promoted smaller international frameworks, where the heterogeneity of member countries was lower and their interests less divergent.

### Coal and steel workers

By spring 1950, U.S. efforts to strengthen West Germany and protests in West Germany threatened the International Authority for the Ruhr, which had until then controlled German coal and steel in favour of the occupying powers and Benelux countries.[158] Unable to stop U.S. resolve to abolish the International Authority for the Ruhr, in May 1950 French Foreign Minister Robert Schuman proposed to integrate the sectors of coal and steel in France, West Germany, and other interested Western European countries.[159] The French opened the negotiations on a European Coal and Steel Community (ECSC). West Germany had key resources in these sectors, with its many coalfields and industrial plants, and this increased the ability of the West German government to promote discussions on the movement of coal and steel workers. Furthermore, labour-market conditions in these sectors were then favourable. In France, the number of foreign coal and steel workers had dropped sharply after the repatriation of prisoners of war.[160] Belgian firms were in such need of trained workers in the mining sector that the government excluded this category from its general stop to immigration in 1949.[161] West Germany suffered a labour shortage in winter 1950–1951 in the sectors of coal and steel.[162]

In autumn 1950, Julius Scheuble from the German Labour Ministry pushed for the inclusion in the ECSC treaty of the principle of the free movement of workers in the coal and steel sectors, but only for skilled labour.[163] The objective was to promote a principle, likely to be extended to other sectors, more important for German emigration. The objective was not to open up the coal and steel labour market of West Germany to immigrant workers from other participating countries. In addition to France and the Benelux countries, these also included Italy.

With the most important coal sector among those six countries, West Germany risked becoming the main country of immigration. General unemployment among unskilled German workers would worsen if unskilled migrant workers were also allowed to migrate to West Germany. To ensure that this particular negotiation would herald a more general reconfiguration of migration relations in Western Europe, Scheuble proposed a general agreement on social security for migrant workers among the participating states, to be applied to all migrant workers, and not just those in the coal and steel sectors.

The Belgian government anticipated that the ECSC had a role to play in the difficult recruitment of labour for Belgian coalmines. As a strategic country for the success of the Schuman Plan, thanks to its important coal resources, Belgium gave its general backing to German proposals.[164] The French were initially reluctant.[165] Yet in early October 1950, the French government feared that with the first U.S. calls for German rearmament after the outbreak of the Korean War, West Germany would abandon negotiation for an ECSC. U.S. calls meant that West Germany was not obliged to enter negotiations with the French to exploit German resources for the benefit of France in order to gain international respectability and integration into Western Europe. West Germany's bargaining power was high, and France had to make concessions to speed up negotiations.[166] On 11 October 1950, French delegates proposed the introduction of an article on the movement of workers. Without going as far as the principle of the 'free movement of labour' wanted by the Germans, the proposed article accepted to 'abolish, as regards the workforce of the various participating countries, all discrimination for the employment of workers of proven qualifications in the coal and steel sectors.'[167] This proposed abolition of 'all discrimination' marked a break with the limited migratory opportunities of traditional bilateral agreements.

Article 69 of the final ECSC Treaty, signed on 18 April 1951, provided that member states 'bind themselves to renounce any restriction based on nationality against the employment in the coal and steel industries of workers of proven qualifications for such industries who possess the nationality of one of the member States.'[168] To respond to Belgian concerns, they had to work out 'technical procedures to make it possible to bring together offers of and demands for employment in the Community as a whole.' Finally, as far as German requests on social security were concerned, the member states had to find 'necessary arrangements so that social security measures do not stand in the way of the movement of labour.' This outcome was a success for Germany. As an emigration country, Italy was deeply attached to the principle of the free movement of workers and the Italian government loyally backed all German proposals. Constant references to migration issues by Italian delegates also facilitated German moves.

France had managed to exclude Algerian coalfields from the scope of the ECSC, so that the resources to be shared were only those in Europe, that is, mostly in

Germany and Belgium. On the basis of this exclusion of Algeria from the ECSC territory, Italian delegates proposed to exclude Algerian workers from the benefit of the treaty. France wished to avoid having to recognise different rights for different categories of citizens. In addition, the various participating states admitted that the agreement could be the starting point for future broader migratory arrangements among them. Both France and West Germany therefore wanted to include in the scope of the agreement the populations of their respective hinterlands. The promotion of the economic interests of those populations was strategic to allow Germany to re-establish its borders and France to keep its empire. France and West Germany thus agreed to reject Italian proposal and to apply instead the ECSC agreement 'to nationals of Contracting Parties and to persons who, according to national constitutions, [were] considered as such.' Besides people with French citizenship overseas, this referred to Article 116 of the German Constitution, which considered as German 'whoever . . ., as a refugee or displaced person of German race, . . . has been accepted on the territory of the German Reich such as it was on 31 December 1937.' As they defended emigration interests, France and Germany had to make concessions to Belgium, a key immigration country in the ECSC. In case of labour market instability, the rights recognised under the agreement could be conditional on prior occupation on Community territory for a period of two years.[169] Neither Algeria nor the territories lost by Germany were part of Community territory.

During the negotiations to implement the Treaty, the German government reasserted its commitment to the principle of free movement of labour in Western Europe, while regretting that it was first applied in sectors where its workforce would have no opportunities to emigrate and where its employers did not experience a strong need of foreign manpower. German Labour Minister Anton Storch repeatedly declared that the principle of the free movement of labour was 'profoundly just.'[170] Yet from the early 1950s, the competition of oil caused the decline of the coal industry.[171] The opposition of German workers to immigration grew accordingly. German mining unions insisted on safety in the mines and demanded that foreign workers be able to speak German – a safe way to exclude most foreign workers.[172] In June 1954, the German Confederation of Unions, *Deutscher Gewerkschaftsbund* (DGB), stipulated conditions on the free movement of coal and steel workers: 'Germany must not suffer from unemployment; full-scale immigration must not occur and above all not in sectors where the standard of living is low, due to the danger of pressure on wages.'[173]

The German government was receptive to those protests. The migration opportunities created by the Treaty were restricted to skilled workers. In order to define this 'proven qualification' cited in the Treaty, German delegates, supported by French and Luxembourg delegates,[174] pushed for tough criteria. They included a minimum duration of employment in the coal and steel sectors, but also training in one of the skilled trades mentioned in a specific list of occupations.[175] These tough criteria were to reduce the number of beneficiaries and reassure German trade unions.

German Labour Minister Anton Storch indicated that German workers were opposed to free job search by migrants,[176] as this would tend to increase immigration and depress wages. Luxembourg Minister for Economic Affairs Michel Rasquin also wanted to avoid 'a downwards levelling of wages.' In France, the main trade union, the *Confédération générale du travail* (CGT), imagined an invasion of unemployed Germans reducing the wages and living standards of French workers.[177] French Labour Minister Eugène Claudius-Petit and the Belgian member of the High Authority of the ECSC, Paul Finet, pointed to the potential risks of migrant manpower unable to find work in destination countries and causing disorder or being a burden on welfare services. ECSC member states thus agreed not to recognise free job search for migrants.

So as to use the migratory agreement in the ECSC to recruit for Belgian mines, the Belgian representative proposed the creation of 'an international placement body that [would receive] job offers and requests directly from employers and workers.'[178] In this way, emigration states would not be able to limit the emigration of skilled workers, which is what Italy and the Netherlands opposed. France and Germany, which would be the main contributors to the ECSC budget, did not want to support the cost of this body. These positions prevailed in the final agreement. The national employment services remained in charge of linking up job offers and requests. The employment services of emigration countries could thus dissuade the most useful workers from leaving and the employment services of immigration countries could check whether job offers were in line with normal wages and working conditions.[179]

The representatives of the four immigration countries – West Germany, Belgium, France, and Luxembourg – also wanted to avoid the free passage of workers from one sector to another. The scenario of workers recruited for the mines moving to the steel sector was a source of concern for the Belgians, who experienced acute difficulties to recruit for their mines. The Belgian representative highlighted 'the tendency . . . [for] mineworkers to move to the steel sector.'[180] Belgian Minister of Social Insurance Léon-Eli Troclet stressed the risk of 'a reduction of levels of wages and working conditions' in the steel sector.[181] The German and Luxembourg representatives stressed that the 'proven qualification' differed between the two sectors.[182] While Italy and the Netherlands called for a single work permit, valid for both sectors, the final agreement reflected the preferences of immigration countries: it created two work permits, each valid for a single sector.[183]

The German government thus managed to promote the principle of free movement of labour thanks to the ECSC, even if internal reluctance in the coalmining sector meant taking a more restrictive position in implementation negotiations. These negotiations resulted in the decision of 8 December 1954 taken by the ECSC Special Council of Ministers and did not open up many migratory opportunities.

## The free movement of persons

Meanwhile, the general demand for labour started to rise in Western Europe. In March 1951 the French Labour Ministry called unsuccessfully on the Interior Ministry to 'relax the regulations in force' for the transfer of foreign manpower to Moselle and Alsace.[184] In May 1953, the Chamber of Agriculture in Moselle once again called, unsuccessfully, for the abolition of the decree of 18 March 1946, due to the obstacles it created for hiring much-needed agricultural labour.[185] In West Germany, unemployment dropped from 940,000 in September 1953 to 830,000 in summer 1954.[186] From 1953 onwards, employers in industry and agriculture in the southern and western parts of West Germany requested some degree of labour immigration.

Regulating the recruitment of labour became increasingly difficult. As employment was growing in West Germany, recruitment of labour in Germany by the French National Office of Immigration became more costly. Potential workers were moved to France, and then discovered that employment and housing conditions were no better than at home and requested to return to Germany with their families. As noted in October 1952 in the Interior Ministry: 'These quite frequent facts cause . . . serious problems. Not only do they mobilise our services for unnecessary tasks, but the French public bears the cost of moving and housing these foreigners.'[187] At the same time, the Prefect of Bas-Rhin stressed 'the considerable expense for the French community to move and house'[188] these uncertain migrants.

In parallel, the six member states of the ECSC were engaged in new negotiations. As the Korean War escalated in 1950, the U.S. government put forward the need for German rearmament. Appalled by this prospect, but forced to arrange it, the French government proposed to apply a method similar to that used with the ECSC and to create a European Defence Community, in which German rearmament would be monitored.[189] The Germans were ready to agree to the controls proposed by the French, but in exchange they wanted to promote their own economic plans in Europe. The West German government and the other governments engaged in the ECSC accepted the French plan but arranged to complete it with a Common Market, by creating a broader European Political Community.

In September 1952, the ECSC Common Assembly became the Ad Hoc Assembly responsible for drafting the Treaty for the European Political Community (EPC). Max Becker was a German delegate to this assembly. He came from the border region between Hessen and East Germany,[190] still deeply affected by unemployment and immigration from the East.[191] This made him particularly interested in emigration opportunities for Germans within Western Europe. In November 1952, Becker proposed the abolition of visas within the EPC.[192] This proposal was in line with German calls made in other forums at the time. As far as the definition of the Common Market was concerned, Italian delegate Lodovico Benvenuti, Under-Secretary of State for Foreign Trade in the De Gasperi government, proposed to link trade liberalisation with the liberalisation of migration. The debate in the Ad Hoc Assembly was politically weak and the final plan did not commit any member state. It was thus easy for Benvenuti in February 1953 to get both the free movement of goods and the free movement of persons included in the definition of the Common Market.[193] Finally, on 10 March 1953, before the Ad Hoc Assembly presented its plan, Becker managed to insert an article granting freedom of movement to anyone born after the EPC Treaty came into force, together with those who had served in the armed forces of the planned European Defence Community.[194]

The intergovernmental negotiations on the EPC began once the plan of the Ad Hoc Assembly was submitted, on the basis of this plan. In German diplomatic circles, head of unit Herbert Müller, in a note of 27 May 1953, commented on this plan to Carl Friedrich Ophüls, the head of division for international and supranational organisations in the Foreign Ministry *(Auswärtiges Amt)*. He supported the principle of free movement of persons in the plan and criticised the fact that it was originally only recognised for children and soldiers. He had a political approach to this plan and envisaged it within the framework of the relations with the East: relationships of open migration among Western Europeans would be an expression of solidarity and unity in the face of the Soviet Union.[195] In February 1954, in intergovernmental negotiations, the Germans took care to remind other delegates of the definition of the term 'German national' in the German Basic Law, so as to make sure that immigrants from the East would benefit from free movement. This notion indeed included German refugees from Eastern Europe.[196] More broadly, to express the unity of the Western Europeans in the face of the Soviet Union, German delegates, supported by Italian, Dutch, and Belgian delegates, proposed to recognise 'that by virtue of the principle of the free movement of persons, labour surplus in the Community [should] be dealt with as a common problem.' French and Luxembourg delegates opposed such a provision.[197]

The Italians also stressed the advantages of free movement: 'Only freedom,' they wrote in a note to their partners in February 1954, 'can allow . . . to completely satisfy the capillary capacity to absorb labour in economies as complex as those of European countries.'[198] These remarks echoed the problems of regulated recruitment faced by France. In this context, in January 1954,

> all the delegations agree on the fact that the definition of the Common Market must contain, as one of the basic elements, the principle of the

free movement of persons.... All the delegations agree that the principle expressed above is the final goal and that its realisation must be progressive.[199]

France accepted this principle, but it went hand in hand with a reserve according to which labour surplus could not be resolved satisfactorily in the framework of the Community of the Six.[200] The demand for foreign manpower remained too low to soothe French concern over the social outcome of free movement in France, while in 1953 and 1954 Belgium and France arranged to obtain a particularly low level of net immigration.[201]

Moreover, Belgian, French, and Luxembourg delegates highlighted the geopolitical problems of implementing the principle of free movement of persons. They argued that this principle should not threaten 'the national substance of member countries.'[202] For the Belgians and French, 'the application of the principle of the free movement of persons [could] never mean changing the national character of a given region.'[203] The French were still concerned by the cases of Alsace and Moselle, while the Interior Ministry reaffirmed at the end of 1953 the decree of 18 March 1946 in the face of the calls by the Chamber of Agriculture in Moselle to suspend it. Belgian and Luxembourg delegates also wanted to be able to exclude foreigners from free access to 'occupations related to public authority.'[204] Luxembourg delegates pointed to the small size of their territory in order to ask for special exemptions to protect the 'national entity' of the country.[205] For Luxembourg, annexed by Germany during the war, and for France and Belgium, which had been repeatedly occupied, German immigration was still a disturbing fact in some parts of their territories, as long as the flow of German migrants from Eastern Europe raised fears that German emigration to Western Europe could be substantial.

### Inference

In summer 1954, the French abandoned the plan of the European Defense Community, which they had themselves proposed. As a result, the two projects of the European Defense Community and the European Political Community, which were linked, failed. Nevertheless, by then the German strategy had led to the recognition of the principle of the free movement of labour. For the Germans, this strategy was particularly meaningful in the context of the Cold War. The economic growth and the demand for labour increased German bargaining power and constituted a positive context in which to dismantle protectionist procedures.

## Synopsis

From 1947 to 1954, the Western European bureaucratic migration regime caused multiple forms of tension between West Germany and Italy on the one hand and the other countries of Western Europe on the other. The French initiative to reshape the regime failed due to insufficient French resources, even in cooperation with other immigration states. To calm the acute tensions in Germany and Italy, reinforced by immigration from the East, the United States intervened to open up migration opportunities overseas for Europeans, despite German preferences for geographically nearby areas and temporary emigration. The weak demand for labour in France and Britain gave rise to trade-union opposition to growing immigration. The regime evolved towards a dual form, with the North-West on the one hand, and the central and southern parts of Western Europe on the other, characterised by labour markets in diverging conditions and by uneven migration opportunities. Yet West Germany, enjoying increasing resources, managed to promote the principle of the free movement of persons within the reduced framework of the ECSC and, despite its failure, the EPC.

2

# A NEW REGIME TAKING SHAPE, 1955–1964

From 1955 to 1964, under German influence, the migration regime in Western Europe underwent a profound change. Previous research examining this transformation has focused on the role of Italy, supported by the Commission. In this chapter, I show how this transformation of the migration regime in Western Europe was the result of renewed German strength linked to an increased demand for labour in West Germany. Regime change corresponded to German preferences: excluding colonial populations, subordinating migration opening up to increased labour demand in host countries, introducing mechanisms for labour-force rotation, and extending the regime among the Six to the rest of Western Europe.

## New German power

In 1955 the strength of Federal Germany's resources made it the main actor in unblocking migration negotiations. In this section, I will explain which foreign policy interests guided German strategy in the negotiations of the Treaty of Rome.[1] I will substantiate how West Germany opted for the reduced framework of the six ECSC member states to guarantee more rapid progress towards its key international objectives. I will show how this framework became central in the development of the European migration regime, concentrating the basic elements of change. Britain was not part of the Six and not an important migratory actor; consequently the British government lost any role in the definition of the European migration regime.

### German influence and interests

By 1954 the geopolitical concerns between Germany and its Western neighbours had declined. Germany was from then on firmly divided and had gained the confidence of its Western neighbours by cooperating over coal, steel, and defence. The new strategic environment among nuclear powers made it difficult to consider it a threat, even in the long term.[2] The French were ready to give up the project of the European Defense Community, which had been designed to control German rearmament more tightly. The Paris Agreements of 23 October 1954 recognised West German rearmament, its renunciation of atomic, bacteriological, and chemical weapons, along with its membership of NATO and the Brussels Pact. The Paris Agreements also settled the problem of the Saarland, due to return to Germany on 1 January 1957. West Germany became France's ally. After 1953 the French Interior Ministry did not reaffirm the exceptional measures to prevent German immigration in the three Eastern *départements* and finally repealed them in December 1957.[3] The weakness of the German presence in these territories facilitated this repeal. In 1957 in Moselle, Germans only accounted for 7,625 people out of a population of 769,388, of whom 86,664 were foreigners.[4]

At the same time German resources in the Western European migration system increased with the spectacular growth of its economy and a predictable shortage of labour. Unemployment, which had reached 11 percent of the active population in 1950, dropped to 7 percent in 1954 and then 5 percent in 1955. Near Germany's western borders, the unemployment rate was even lower with almost full employment in Baden-Württemberg (2.2 percent) and North Rhine Westphalia (2.9 percent). Only the geographical outlier Schleswig-Holstein had an unemployment rate of more than 11 percent. Moreover, since the average unemployment rate for men in West Germany was 1.8 percent, there was a shortage of male manpower, overrepresented among migrants.[5] At the same time, the prospects of an increase in the labour supply were low. Young cohorts entering the labour market in 1956 and 1957 were less numerous than before, due to a drop in the birth rate during the war, and the reintroduction of military service following the Paris Agreements.[6] Immigration from East Germany was volatile[7] and did not match economic cycles in either pace or composition. Besides, with the Hallstein Doctrine, which existed unofficially even before it was endorsed in December 1955, the West German government did not consider relationships with countries that recognised the German Democratic Republic. As a result, this government had no plan to formally recruit labour from Eastern Europe. In response to increased labour demand and in order to facilitate labour-market adjustments, it resorted, for geopolitical reasons, to the migrant workforce in Western Europe.

In November 1954, German Minister for Economic Affairs Ludwig Erhard justified immigration on the grounds that a shortage of labour would slow down West German economic expansion.[8] The DGB, the Industrial Union of Miners (IG Bergbau), and the Industrial Union of Metalworkers (IG Metall) were all hostile because mass immigration would reduce wages.[9]

The representatives of regions bordering on the East still hit by immigration and unemployment also expressed concern. The Christian Social Union (CSU) deputy Alois Niederalt, from Cham, at the border between Bavaria and the Sudetenland, declared in the Bundestag in December 1954 that 'the last German worker must have a job before we think of such things [as foreign immigration].' He pressed the government 'to do everything to encourage . . . our industry to go where there is still a workforce.'[10] Farming associations in Baden-Württemberg complained nonetheless of a shortage of labour, siphoned off by higher wages in industry.[11] In June 1955, the Labour Ministry gave in and announced that it no longer objected to hiring Italian workers in regions with a shortage of agricultural labour, but that this immigration had to be temporary, not accompanied by families, and should not lead to a lowering of wages or social benefits.[12]

A bilateral recruitment agreement perfectly in line with the migration regime of previous years was signed with Italy on 20 December 1955.[13] A note from the German Labour Ministry stated with relief that 'the agreement contains no indication of the number of Italian workers to be recruited. . . . In cases where there is a suitable German workforce, there would not be any recruitment of Italians.'[14] The Federal Institute for Occupational Placement and Unemployment Insurance (BAVAV) had to issue migrants with entry visas, residence permits, and work permits. These documents were issued free of charge, but work permits only lasted a year and were only valid for one employer.[15] To encourage families to remain in Italy, the agreement would pay family allowances to workers irrespective of the family's place of residence.[16]

Therefore, contrary to what has been claimed,[17] it was not its workforce needs that prompted West Germany to accept a transformation of the European migration regime. The German-Italian agreement of 20 December 1955 demonstrated that even the West German government, when it again resorted to immigrant labour, found the bureaucratic migration regime, with its potential for selective and temporary opening up, a satisfactory framework that could reconcile the internal pressures from employers and trade unions. The advantages of regulated recruitment still exceeded the costs. Negotiation on this agreement also showed that Italy had no plans to close its borders to Germany-bound Italian emigrants. Quite the reverse, the higher wages in West Germany and Italian unemployment, which peaked at almost 10 percent,[18] sustained Italy's long-term interest in emigration.

Even though the West German government was not ready to commit to new migration arrangements through bilateral agreements, it was willing to do so in a multilateral framework, where several actors would share adjustments caused by freer migration and which would allow for some German emigration. The

German strategy was dictated by the context of the Cold War. West Germany's territory amounted to half of German territory until 1937. East Germany was occupied by Soviet troops and Berlin was divided into four zones of foreign occupation. Central Europe was subject to Soviet power. On the eve of Chancellor Konrad Adenauer's visit to Moscow in September 1955, to negotiate German reunification, and even after the failure of the visit, West Germany had to build up its strength. To obtain Soviet concessions, the West German government needed to be able to demonstrate to the Soviet government that it was strong. For this it needed the unity of Western Europe. A note from the German Foreign Ministry for the session of the Bundestag Foreign Affairs Committee on 3 May 1955 stated that 'Europe cannot be successful in negotiations with the East unless it presents itself united. The FRG is particularly interested in this, in the prospect of German reunification.'[19]

In early June 1955, the foreign ministers of the six member states of the ECSC met in Messina, Italy, to discuss further collaboration after the failure of the European Defense Community. There, on 2 June 1955, German Foreign Ministry Secretary of State Walter Hallstein pointed out to his partners that 'European unification is . . . more necessary than ever if we are to consider relations of western countries with the East. . . . The Federal government . . . does not think that the current tension has really diminished.'[20] In a directive to his government, in January 1956, Adenauer reminded: 'If integration [of Western Europe] is successful, we can throw the weight of a united Europe into the balance . . . during negotiations on both security and reunification.'[21]

Yet the unity of Western Europe remained uncertain. After the accession of Italy and West Germany to the Western Union, it became the Western European Union, but it remained a loose framework.[22] In Italy, a powerful Communist Party benefited from unemployment and popular discontent. At the 1953 elections it won almost a quarter of the seats in Parliament. This development concerned Adenauer, who reported in his memoirs that in case of

> a great impetus to the Communist Parties in France and Italy . . . the idea of a united non-communist Western Europe would be finished. It was one of Soviet Russia's aims to do everything to prevent the creation of such a united Western Europe.[23]

An Italian default to the Western alliance would undermine the German position vis-à-vis the Soviet Union, as Italy and the other Mediterranean countries played a strategic role in the NATO security framework.[24]

On 2 June 1955 in Messina, Hallstein declared that 'the lack of unity in Western Europe gives the Soviet Union the hope and prospect of the more or less close

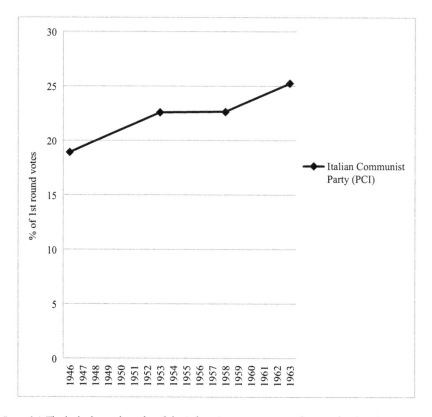

*Figure 2.1* The high electoral results of the Italian Communist Party: elections for the Chamber of Deputies (1946–1963)[25]

progress of world revolution.'[26] In his directive of 19 January 1956 Adenauer addressed his government:

> We must not expect serious concessions from the Soviet Union, as long as the division of Europe gives it the hope of drawing one state or another towards it, in order to break the cohesion of the West and to progressively bring Europe into its system of satellites.[27]

Free movement of labour among the Six would help reduce Italian unemployment and protect Italian workers against the 'poison' of Communism, according to German Labour Minister Anton Storch.[28]

West Germany also had to be in a position to absorb the migration flux from the East. German officials anticipated the continuance of the inflow of migrants from East Germany, linked to internal political shocks. Until February 1955, the Special Representative of the Council of Europe for Displaced Persons, Refugees, and

## A NEW REGIME TAKING SHAPE, 1955–1964

*Figure 2.2* The geostrategic vulnerability of West Germany in Europe in May 1955

Surplus Population, Pierre Schneiter, met successively with Adenauer, Hallstein, Storch, German Minister for Agriculture Heinrich Lübke, and Minister for Expellees Theodor Oberländer. On the basis of these meetings, Schneiter considered that an 'influx of refugees . . . [would probably continue] as long as the Iron Curtain separating the two worlds [would cut] Europe in two.'[29] Another shared expectation was that these migrants might create problems in times of economic recession.[30] In February 1955, Schneiter recommended to the Council of Europe organising intra-European movements to deal with the flux of refugees.[31] The federal government needed other Western European economies to maintain an opening up to the East and offer opportunities to these populations whatever the economic situation. The federal government was especially interested in offering such opportunities to the regular influx of qualified professionals from East Germany looking for skilled jobs that the West German economy could not always provide. Offering opportunities to the East German elite also helped undermine the Communist regime.[32]

A transformation of the Western European migration regime in a more open sense thus allowed Germany to reduce social tensions in Mediterranean Europe, preventing the defection of strategic allies. It allowed for an opening up of permanent opportunities for the waves of refugees from the East, even in the case of an economic downturn in West Germany. In this way, the West German government was in a position to harm the East German government by integrating emigrants when the latter was facing political crises. All these aspects worked to undermine the Communist regime in East Germany and the Soviet order in Central Europe.

To this end the West German government favoured the framework of the six member states of the ECSC after the failed attempts within the OEEC and the Council of Europe. In contrast to the latter, the ECSC included only one emigration country – the most strategically important, Italy – and most of the immigration countries. Migratory pressure was lower than in the OEEC, which could calm down the concerns of immigration countries regarding freer migration arrangements. The ECSC framework also avoided Britain, which was opposed to European integration. In Messina, Hallstein was 'convinced that the progress to realise [had to] be sought in the more limited framework of the Six, where only . . . close ties and solid forms of organisation [were] possible.'[33]

## The free movement of persons as a Community cornerstone

In Messina, the six foreign ministers wanted to restart negotiations on the Common Market begun for the failed EPC. The Benelux representatives adopted a limited definition of the term 'Common Market' as the 'progressive abolition of quantitative restrictions and tariffs.'[34] This was a step backwards with respect to the definition adopted in the EPC negotiations. The Benelux governments concentrated on the basics, without compromising on other issues in the negotiations. French reticence on the free movement of persons during EPC negotiations and the difficult negotiation on the application of Article 69 of the ECSC Treaty suggested that the free movement of labour was a dangerous issue. Italy took the same line, but suggested that the Common Market should 'cover all the economic and social life of the countries involved, without neglecting either the social domain or that of labour.'[35] This timid position was far from earlier Italian statements on the matter, because Italy wanted the negotiation to succeed, albeit limited to trade. In Messina, adopting deeper and new migration arrangements was a German proposal.

The German memorandum was drafted by the Foreign Ministry, together with the Ministry for Economic Affairs and other ministries. Adenauer ranked German foreign policy interests first.[36] The draft memorandum planned the 'progressive establishment of the free movement of labour among Community countries.'[37] The final memorandum agreed with other German ministries maintained the goal of a 'gradual introduction of the free movement of labour.'[38] On 2 June 1955 in Messina, Hallstein managed to get his counterparts to approve the plan for the free movement of labour in exactly the same terms as those of the German memorandum.[39] The final resolution of the Messina Conference referred to 'the gradual introduction of the free movement of labour.'[40] Unlike the German proposal, the six governments only committed to study this question, but it was deemed necessary for 'the implementation' of a Common Market.

After the conference, the six governments created an Intergovernmental Committee to study the Messina resolution. The German Ministry for Economic Affairs only then took the major role in representing Germany in the negotiations on migration affairs. German delegates supported the abolition of discrimination against German nationals in other Western European countries. More broadly, the Ministry was interested in a general principle of non-discrimination linked to nationality. This broader phrasing would include not only people, but also firms, which was likely to promote the establishment of German businesses in neighbouring countries. In August 1955, the Germans had a working group created to 'define the particular problems of the free movement of physical persons whose occupational activity was not a salaried job,'[41] that is, who were self-employed and not employees. The group accepted German demands 'to take into consideration all the people who [were going] or [were] abroad and who [wished] to exercise an independent profit-making activity.'[42] This included in particular German farmers, a large number of whom had migrated from Eastern Germany.

After the work of the Intergovernmental Committee was completed, the six members states set up an Intergovernmental Conference to draft the treaty for the European Economic Community (EEC). There the Germans followed up the issue of the principle of non-discrimination by submitting an article 'to set up, within the Community, the freedom of establishment of independent workers and companies of member states.'[43] These German calls intended to eliminate discrimination against German businessmen and farmers in neighbouring countries[44] and to help promote the expansion of German firms in Europe. The EEC Treaty contained a general principle of non-discrimination that guaranteed full equality to nationals of other member states in economic life, enabling them to 'perform all legal acts in the same conditions as nationals.'[45]

Finally, the Germans managed to get into the Treaty the plan that they had defended for several years to cope with the shortage of vocational training positions in West Germany: the exchange of young workers.[46] Belgium, supported by France, accepted it, but opposed the German proposal to give grants to promote the exchange of young workers.[47] German support for this plan was no longer for the same reasons as in the early 1950s, because German demography had changed, but the West German government still favoured such programmes, considering that the mobility of young people was an important end in itself. This objective was part of the German political plan to reinforce concord among the countries of Western Europe.

### Inference

The increased resources of West Germany in the Western European migration system changed the structure of this system and allowed the West German government to give impetus to the transformation of the then prevailing international regime. A more open regime was to avoid the defection of strategic German allies and to allow the German government to maintain an opening up to inflows from East Germany, thus undermining its Communist government. West Germany dominated the first migratory negotiations among the Six, and also integrated measures in the EEC Treaty to promote the establishment of independent workers and the penetration of foreign markets by German companies.

## Excluding colonies

The first feature of the new migration regime between the Six was its limitation to European populations. Earlier studies examined the exclusion of Algerian workers, explaining this in terms of Italian demands.[48] This section highlights the different views of the French and West German governments in order to explain how the negotiations that led to the exclusion of colonial populations unfolded.

### The Paris Compromise

In the Treaty, migration arrangements included both the 'free movement of workers' and the 'right of establishment' for independent workers within the Common Market. In the negotiations on what those arrangements should include, a first and major point of contention had to do with Overseas France. It included first its Overseas Departments (*départements d'outre-mer*, DOM), which were possessions deeply integrated with France (Algeria, French Guiana, Guadeloupe, Martinique, and Réunion). French law referred to other possessions in Africa and elsewhere as Overseas Territories (*territoires d'outre-mer*, TOM).

France's partners opposed the free movement of labour for inhabitants of Overseas France. During the preparation of the Messina conference, in late May 1955, the German Labour Ministry called on the German Foreign Ministry to make sure that 'extra-European possessions of member states remain outside the planned [and] progressively established . . . freedom of movement.'[49] This became the position of the German government. Belgium and Italy followed suit.[50] This position was due to the sheer number of people involved, along with the large differences in the living standards of these populations compared to European workers. The French government had to recognise that 'in applying Treaty measures on the free movement of workers . . . problems of adaptation could arise for other member states as regards labour from Algeria and the DOM and that of the TOM.'[51] While war had broken out in Algeria, over 1 million Algerian unemployed were ready to emigrate. In early 1955 there were between 250,000 and 300,000 Algerian workers in France, but only 150,000 to 200,000 were regularly employed.[52] The migration potential towards other European countries in the case of open migration arrangements was therefore high.

This problem was one of the main reasons for a conference of heads of government gathered in Paris on 19 and 20 February 1957. French Prime Minister Guy Mollet proposed the following compromise. The Common Market would cover the entire territory of the French Republic, except Overseas Territories, thus including Algeria and the other DOM. The free movement of workers and the right of establishment would not immediately apply to the DOM, but only within two years, after a unanimous vote in the Council.[53] A note from the German Foreign Ministry spoke of 'difficult, hard negotiations in Paris.'[54] Nevertheless, the basic political question of equality of rights among French citizens and territories led the Germans to finally accept the French compromise in Paris.

## The non-application of the Paris Compromise

In the last phase of Treaty negotiations, France's partners already started interpreting the compromise in the strict sense. In the planned article dealing with the free movement of labour, beneficiaries were initially supposed to be 'national workers' of member states. Algerians and the inhabitants of other DOM with French nationality were thus to benefit from free movement as per this single article, as long as they were on metropolitan territory. To prevent this, the delegations deleted the term 'national' in 'national workers' of member-states.[55] The inclusion of Algerians and other DOM French citizens could only occur through a unanimous decision of the Council of Ministers of the Community, as per Article 227, which repeated the Paris Compromise.

Yet in the months after the Treaty came into force, the continuation of the war in Algeria undermined France's negotiating position. In the Treaty, member states set up a Commission to implement Treaty provisions. It included nine commissioners from the various member states. French Commissioner Robert Lemaignen presented a document to the Council of the Community in December 1958, which recognised: 'It appears politically difficult to include Algeria. . . . In agreement with governmental experts, we have temporarily given up preparing measures for Algeria.'[56] According to Article 227 of the Treaty, the Council was supposed to adopt the conditions for the free movement of labour from Algeria and other

French DOM before 31 December 1959, but this did not occur. In France in September 1960, the Labour Ministry solicited the Prime Minister so that Algerian workers be integrated into the first Council regulation designed to implement free movement of labour among member states.[57] This too, did not occur.[58]

After independence in 1962, Algerian nationals lost any entitlement to the free movement of labour and the question remained pending for those of the other DOM. In the Council in 1963, France pushed for the adoption of an interpretative declaration so that the exclusion of Algeria from the treaty provisions related to the DOM would not prejudice 'future relations between the Community and Algeria.'[59] France wanted to keep open the option of a migration agreement between Algeria and the Community, so as to absorb growing Algerian immigration to France within a broader framework. Maintaining good relations with Algeria was also a major concern for France as the French army was using the Algerian Sahara for nuclear testing and French oil companies were also active there. Nonetheless, a migration agreement between Algeria and the Community never materialised.

As far as the inhabitants from the TOM were concerned, the February 1957 negotiations in Paris led to Article 135 of the Treaty, which provided that workers from Overseas 'Countries and Territories' would be entitled to freedom of movement in member countries through 'subsequent conventions [requiring] unanimity of member states.' The notion of Overseas Countries and Territories (OCT) included French TOM, former French territories that remained associated to the Community, and other dependent territories with a special relationship with another member state. In contrast to the provision for Algeria and the other DOM, the article for OCT contained no obligation or deadline. No measures in this domain ever materialised. French attempts to create migratory opportunities for its overseas workforce thus failed due to the opposition of its partners, driven by their fear of mass immigration of low-wage labour.

## The right of establishment: an asymmetrical migration agreement

Besides the free movement of workers, the Treaty included provisions for the right of establishment for independent workers and firms, following German moves on these issues. Once again, one of the first questions discussed was the application of such provisions overseas. In this field, the member states agreed on greater opening, but created asymmetric opportunities for European and overseas populations. France and Belgium's partners wished to give their nationals and companies access to the vast resources of Overseas France and the Belgian Congo. In October 1956, the French and Belgian governments jointly argued that only investments overseas by member states could generate a right of establishment there for their nationals.[60]

The compromise established by Article 132 of the Treaty provided that the Treaty chapter on the right of establishment should apply both to European and overseas populations across all the Common Market and the OCT when such chapter would be activated. In parallel, the member states signed and annexed to the Treaty a Convention for the association of the OCT with the Community for five years. It provided that member states were to 'promote the social and economic development of [those] countries and territories' (Article 1). In exchange, Article 8 of this Convention asserted the right of establishment for the nationals of all member states in the OCT (and not the other way round), and planned that the Council would define the application of such right during the first year of the Convention's application. In this way, special procedures emerged for the establishment of member-state nationals in the OCT that differed from those for the establishment of nationals of the OCT in member countries, regulated only by the Treaty chapter. The Convention justified these special procedures by the contributions of member states to the development of the OCT.

As a result, in a declaration of 23 November 1959 the Council provided for more lenient conditions for the migration of Community nationals into the OCT, mostly then French TOM. Visas were abolished for stays of less than three months, and expulsion could only be justified on the grounds of public order, public safety, or public health. Taxes paid to local authorities in order to obtain or renew identity documents or residence permits were abolished.[61]

A Council directive of the same day created a right of establishment for Community nationals in the OCT and the DOM.[62] The content of the directive reflected France's partners' willingness to exploit the agricultural resources in these territories through a reduced and targeted form of emigration. The directive extended the right to exercise the profession of land surveyor to citizens of other member states in most OCT and DOM. This profession was strategic for exploiting forests and agricultural resources in general. In the Economic and Social Committee (ESC) of the Community, the German winegrower Richard Matuschka Greiffen-Clau, president of the German Winegrowers' Association (*Deutscher Weinbauverband*),[63] drew attention to the presence in the member states of 'young forestry workers keen to help develop African forests.' The winemaking interests that he defended meant not only forestry exploitation, but also deforestation in order to develop viticulture overseas. A French member of the ESC, Youssef Oulid Aissa, Director of Agriculture in the General Government of Algeria, opposed these demands.[64]

This directive of 23 November 1959 planned that in 1960 the granting of land concessions was to be extended to citizens of other member states in the Malagasy Republic, French Somaliland, New Caledonia and dependencies, as well as Dutch New Guinea. In French Guiana, this applied to 'agricultural and breeding concessions.'[65]

France thus granted migratory opportunities for Europeans overseas, allowing nationals and companies of other member states to migrate to French territories to exploit natural resources, in exchange for their investment in development. The negotiation had created an asymmetrical situation. On the one hand, there was this right of establishment for member-state citizens in the OCT and the DOM, regulated by the Declaration and the Directive of the Council of 23 November 1959. On the other hand, there was a right of establishment for the inhabitants of the OCT and the DOM in the member states that still had to be implemented with the activation of the relevant Treaty chapter. This activation had not yet occurred.

Moreover, this chapter only ruled on the establishment of independent workers and firms. France had recognised the abolition of short-stay visas, free residence permits, and a limited risk of expulsion for citizens of member states in the OCT and the DOM in the Declaration of 23 November 1959, and not in the directive of the same day. The exclusion of these provisions from the directive was meant to prevent them being considered as necessary features of the right of establishment.[66] In the negotiations between the member states on the definition of the right of establishment, which OCT populations should receive, 'No agreement could be reached on the question of whether the right of establishment set out in the Treaty [contained] provisions on entry, residence, and expulsion.'[67] Without these measures the right of establishment was unlikely to create migratory opportunities for OCT or DOM inhabitants. The migration potential of these territories was not that of independent workers or enterprises, but of people without capital.

The independence in 1960 of most OCT affected the measures previously agreed. Newly independent states were unhappy with the asymmetrical migratory opportunities the Treaty and its annexed Association Convention had created. According to the German delegation in the Council, only one newly independent state continued to apply in May 1961 the directive of 23 November 1959.[68] As the Association Convention was limited to five years' duration, a new convention was to be negotiated to maintain the association. On 20 July 1963 the states of the Community signed the Yaoundé Convention of Association with the new independent states in Africa, referred to as the Associated African and Malagasy States (AAMS). Article 29 specified the conditions of a supposedly more reciprocal right of establishment within the association.

On the one hand, the article maintained that

> in each Associated State, nationals and companies of every Member State shall be placed on an equal footing as regards the right of establishment and provision of services, progressively and not later than three years after the entry into force of this Convention.[69]

This meant granting French treatment in associated countries for the nationals and companies of other member states. On the other hand, more reciprocity between

European and African populations was supposed to derive from the subsequent subparagraph of the same article.

> Nationals and companies of a Member State may benefit from the provisions of the first sub-paragraph, in respect of a given activity, only insofar as the State to which they belong grants similar advantages for the same activity to nationals and companies of the Associated State in question.[70]

This provision created a biased form of reciprocity. In April 1964, the West German representation to the Community specified in a verbal note to the Commission that it interpreted this to mean that member states were 'free to decide themselves to what extent they wish to grant rights of establishment to nationals of the AAMS.'[71] Indeed the new Convention allowed the member states to decide whether to extend the right of establishment to their citizens and their companies in the associated countries, by recognising or not this right to AAMS nationals on their territories. But whenever a member state of the Community recognised a right to the AAMS, Article 29 implied that the latter should recognise reciprocity to the former. The agreement was thus unequal: the member states could eliminate the right of establishment in sectors likely to offer migratory opportunities to AAMS populations — at best agriculture or small-scale trading if they had access to credit in the host country — and could apply it only to the sectors linked to the exploitation of resources in the associated countries, such as mining and large-scale land exploitation.

## The continued exclusion of (former) colonies

The failure of Community negotiations on migration meant that France had to shoulder the growing migration pressure from the Maghreb and sub-Saharan Africa alone.[72] In the relations between France and its former colonies, freedom of movement was indeed still in force. Citizens of newly independent states were not required to hold a residence permit or a work permit in France.[73] This situation threatened to create excessive immigration, and the government took steps to restrict the influx and to make it dependent on local labour demand. A convention with Mali signed on 8 March 1963, effective as of 1 May, made access to French territory subject to presenting a work contract approved by the French Labour Ministry, together with proof of accommodation and payment of a deposit to pay for the worker's repatriation.[74] Similar conventions were signed with Mauritania on 15 July 1963 and Senegal on 14 March 1964.[75]

This was the situation when negotiations started for Britain's first application for membership of the Community. Britain was in a similar position to France, and faced large flows of postcolonial immigration. Between 1951 and 1961, the number of immigrants from the Caribbean, India, and Pakistan to Britain doubled to 541,000.[76] In the accession negotiations, the Commission questioned British representatives on how to differentiate British subjects from the colonies and the Commonwealth in order to grant migratory opportunities in the Community exclusively to British subjects from Britain.[77] The discussion remained unsettled when accession negotiations ended after the French veto to British membership in January 1963. Like France, Britain was involved in a parallel legislative process meant to restrict the influx of postcolonial immigrants. The 1962 Commonwealth Immigration Act introduced obligatory work permits for Commonwealth subjects and subjects of British colonies holding passports issued by a colonial government rather than by the British government.[78]

### Inference

The first feature of the new migration regime that emerged in the period 1955–1964 was thus its limitation to European populations at the expense of overseas population in colonies or former colonies of member states. Asymmetrical immigration opportunities were envisaged in overseas countries for Europeans in the form of the right to establishment. These features of the new regime reflected German preferences.

## Tailoring opportunities to needs

The new migration regime created more opportunities for the European workforce. West Germany and France basically shaped the conditions of labour immigration in the new regime. I will explain in particular that the priority for migrants from other Community countries was not the result of Italian or Commission requests, mitigated by a Benelux compromise, as had been previously argued.[79] It succeeded as long as it was in the French interest.

### The West German labour market

Without German support, no more open migration arrangements would have occurred. Article 48 of the Treaty stipulated that 'the free movement of workers shall be assured within the Community by the end of the transitional period at the latest,' that is, within twelve years. When negotiations started, Italian emigration in Europe had been overwhelmingly directed towards France and Belgium, where large Italian communities attracted more Italian immigration. France was reluctant to accept additional inflows, as higher birth rates in previous years meant an increased supply on the labour market as of 1960, while increased productivity was likely to cause a drop in demand.[80] As West Germany was the main champion of a more open migration regime among the Six, the other immigration states wanted the West German labour market to absorb the largest share of any additional migration flows created by more open arrangements.

The situation of the West German labour market stabilised the environment of the negotiation. Demand for foreign labour was increasing and the number of job offers by employers for each unmet request by workers went from 1.1 in October 1959 to 2.2 a year later. In Baden-Württemberg, this number even reached 83 in 1960! In 1961, the German employment office (BAVAV) planned hiring 150,000 foreign workers, including 100,000 Italians, 30,000 Greeks, and 20,000 Spaniards.[81] Within the Council of the Community, the Group on Social Questions (GSQ) was mainly in charge of negotiations. To ensure that Italian migration would be redirected towards West Germany, in February 1961 French delegates wanted to avoid member states 'slowing down the commitments they [had] made with . . . Articles 48 and 49' of the Treaty through recruitment in third countries.[82] France supported a declaration of intent by member states on giving priority to member-state labour over that of third countries, in order to boost the use of Italian labour by West German firms instead of Greek or Spanish labour.

German Labour Minister Theodor Blank declared to his counterparts in the Council in May 1961 that 'The Bundestag, the Bundesrat, professional associations, and German trade unions'[83] were all hostile to the principle proposed and believed that it overstepped the Treaty framework, since a Community priority would slow down labour recruitment for the German economy. Blank tried to reassure his partners by specifying that the West German economy not only absorbed a growing number of Italian immigrants, but that the share of Italians in total immigration to West Germany had increased. Out of 123,000 foreign workers in 1958, 25,000 were Italian, and by 31 March 1961 out of 400,000 foreign workers, 170,000 were Italian. Nonetheless, French and Belgian Labour Ministers Paul Bacon and Léon Servais maintained their commitment to a Council declaration on Community priority.

The intervention of the president of the Commission, Walter Hallstein, was decisive to overcome Blank's resistance. Exceptionally, it was Hallstein who explained Germany's position to its partners in the Council in June 1961.[84] He had contacted the Minister for Foreign Affairs Heinrich von Brentano and Chancellor Adenauer to make the German Labour Minister cede on this politically salient issue of Community priority. Article 43 of Regulation 15 of 16 August 1961 finally stated: 'The member states . . . will try hard . . . to fill available jobs by priority . . . with workers from member states . . . before resorting to workers from third countries.'[85] French Labour Minister Paul Bacon expressed a 'wish that the text of the regulation [would] actually [encourage] the free movement of workers in the Europe of the Six.'[86]

Soon afterwards, labour needs expanded in most Community countries. Labour immigration in France, which had only managed to surpass 50,000 a year in the first half of the 1950s, increased to 200,000 a year as of 1962. In West Germany, labour immigration increased almost twelvefold, from 31,600 in 1956 to 360,500 in 1961, stabilising at around 430,000 as of 1964.[87] The Italian unemployment rate plummeted to 4 percent in 1963.[88] Italian emigration was directed mainly towards West Germany, where wages were higher.[89] The French turned away from a rigid Community priority given the hostility of French farmers, and agreed with the Germans on a flexible commitment.[90] In July 1962, Councillor General of the Bas-Rhin Théo Braun considered in the Economic and Social Committee of the Community that 'if finding 100,000 workers for the grape harvest in France, [meant] procedures such that the necessary labour would never arrive [in time] before the grapes [were] lost,' then employers would resort to a workforce from a third country without respecting the Community priority.[91] The second regulation dealing with the free movement of labour in the Community, Regulation 38/64 of 25 March 1964, only referred to 'providing by priority to the greatest possible extent available jobs to citizens' of member states. The phrase 'to the greatest possible extent' opened the way to many different interpretations.[92] The West German labour market had a stabilising effect, along with the growing demand for labour elsewhere, and other immigration states followed West Germany to define a more open migration regime.

## Individual migration to respond to job offers

In their reciprocal relations, member states relinquished collective and administrated migration. There were 94,148 assisted Italian immigrants in 1960 in West Germany, as against only 2,852 free immigrants. In 1962, there were only 76,742 assisted immigrants against already 88,260 free immigrants.[93] Free migrants were those who had found work without the help of Italian or German placement services. The director of the employment office in Lörrach, Baden-Württemberg, Hausin, considered that the extension of free placement for Italian labour in previous years had not caused any problems. According to him, the free entry of Italian workers to West Germany would soon become the rule.[94] In 1966, only 8 percent of Italian workers immigrating to West Germany did so on the basis of official recruitment programmes, against 69 percent of Greeks and Spaniards and 80 percent of Portuguese.[95]

To guarantee free movement, labour-importing member states challenged the need for exit visas on the passports of Italian émigrés.[96] With this requirement, the Italian government was able to suspend emigration to the Belgian mines after the coalmining tragedy in Marcinelle, which killed 262 people in August 1956, most of them Italian immigrant workers.[97] Employers in other countries of the Community complained against this requirement. The president of the French delegation to the Permanent Conference of French and Italian Chambers of Trade and Industry of the Border Region, Bonjean, echoed this in January 1962.[98] Article 2(1) of Regulation 38/64 stated that member states were obliged to grant workers 'the right to leave their territories to practice a paid activity on the territory of another member state ... on the simple presentation of an identity card or valid passport.'[99]

As regards the regulation in destination countries, as early on as the first negotiations in 1955, the French government wanted immigration to take place 'on the condition that [workers had] found employment beforehand.'[100] In the Intergovernmental Committee after the Messina conference, the French delegation already reported the risk of an influx of workers to the Paris region. To prevent this, Article 48(3) of the Treaty stated that the free movement of workers entailed the right 'to accept offers of employment actually made.' In 1961, Regulation 15 of the Council – the first implementing regulation for free movement – authorised migrant workers to take up the jobs that no local worker had accepted three weeks after notification of the vacancy by the employer.[101] Regulation 38/64 abolished any time criterion and made issuing work permits automatic, but authorised immigration states to keep a time criterion of up to two weeks in regions or industries with a labour surplus.[102]

Consequently, with Regulation 38/64, labour migration became generally free among the Six in 1964, but workers had to present proof of a prior offer of employment. Partly as a result of this easier access, the Italian emigration flow became mainly oriented towards Europe and ever less towards intercontinental destinations. In the 1960s over 80 percent of Italian emigrants remained in Europe, whereas until the 1950s this proportion was only 50 percent.[103]

## Selective bias

Beyond predominant international considerations, the new migration arrangements among the Six were easier to implement because they facilitated the arrival of a highly sought-after workforce. A few of these arrangements directly favoured the movement of skilled workers. Article 5 of Regulation 38/64 made the two-week exemption inapplicable for workers who had received a job offer based on their skills.[104] For the exchange of young workers, Article 50 of the Treaty provided that joint programmes would 'concentrate efforts on young people who already held a qualification and who [wanted] to go abroad to perfect [their skills], that is, trainees.'[105] Despite its origins in the lack of training capacities in post-war West Germany, this measure thus ended up benefiting only already-trained young workers.

More generally member states also considered Community workers to be on average more skilled than third-country workers. In the words of a Council of Europe report, 'Italian labour [was] particularly valued by the other members of the Western community.'[106] Among all the emigration countries of the

Mediterranean basin, Italy had the most developed industrial sector; consequently its workforce was the most likely to have experience with industrial work or mechanised agriculture. Furthermore, a Commission report on the social condition of migrant workers in 1960 cited the better adaptation of some nationalities, given their geographical and linguistic proximity: the Dutch and even the French in West Germany, and Italians in South-East France.[107] In February 1964, French Labour Minister Gilbert Grandval admitted that 'given its central situation and training, Community labour [enjoyed] a significant natural advantage.'[108] Thus as a group of neighbouring industrialised countries, sometimes with similar languages, Community states had an interest in their respective labour force.

## Immigrants and the local labour force

The new regime was defined in such a way that migrants were not likely to threaten local workers' core concerns. First, it aimed at preserving the wages of local workers. Article 48(2) of the Treaty forbade immigrant workers to accept any form of payment lower than the one currently in force. As immigrants were often willing to accept lower wages, it was important to guarantee that this rule was enforced. In the Economic and Social Committee, Belgian trade unionist Louis Major wanted to encourage public funding of labour unions' social services in immigration countries, because these services played an important role in controlling the conditions in which immigrants worked. As he declared, 'labour unions make sure that migrant workers have the same rights as national citizens . . . and should not be exploited during their period of adaptation.' The Commission subsequently recommended that member states finance social services for migrant workers via the labour unions. This was to prevent migrant workers from having contacts exclusively with the social services of their country of origin, less concerned with the risk that immigration would undercut wages in destination countries.[109]

Second, the regime guaranteed that immigrants were underrepresented compared to local workers. By May 1961, the Commission had proposed that the Council extend to Community migrants the right to be elected to firms' joint committees. German Labour Minister Theodor Blank defended the German Law on Firms (*Betriebsverfassungsgesetz*), which granted this right exclusively to German citizens meeting the conditions to be elected members of the Bundestag.[110] According to political scientist Kenneth A. Dahlberg, this position was due to the pressure of the DGB, which feared that Italian workers would be elected to firms' joint committees with the votes of Greek and Turkish workers.[111] Such foreign coalitions may have supported conditions likely to increase employment and undercut German wages. In 1963, the French supported the Germans on this issue, and argued that members of workers' representative bodies might 'reveal [firms'] industrial secrets.'[112] In the Council, the German and French Ministers, Blank and Grandval, were able to ensure that the right of eligibility was recognised for Community workers if they had worked in a company for at least three years, in comparison to one year for national workers.[113] This allowed companies to ensure the loyalty of foreign workers and made international industrial spying more difficult. Moreover, it allowed the representation of only the most integrated immigrant workers.

The argument of the possible disloyalty of foreigners also led to the exclusion of Community workers from public administration, as per Article 48(4) of the Treaty. The outcome was that opportunities in the public service were preserved for local workers or professionals. This exclusion yet did not affect the 'nationalised and paragovernmental companies,'[114] which the Bundestag had made clear when it ratified the Treaty.[115] In the same vein, Article 55 excluded activities relating to 'the exercise of public authority' from the right of establishment.

## A more limited right of establishment

Alongside the relaxed measures for the movement of employed workers, establishment as craftsmen, or small-scale traders was the main channel of upwards mobility for employed migrant workers in destination countries. Yet the right of establishment for independent migrant workers was applied sparingly. In 1962, the German craft sector included 720,000 businesses, a third of which consisted of just one person in 1956. The politically influential Central Association of German Crafts (*Zentralverband des Deutschen Handwerks*) defended this economic sector; in 1960 and 1961 Chancellor Adenauer and Minister for Economic Affairs Erhard attended its annual meeting and each year Erhard opened the International Arts and Crafts Salon in Munich.[116] Craftsmen feared that the establishment of foreigners would cause an increase in products offered and a drop in income. For this reason, in the timetable to apply the right of establishment among the Six, craftsmen, retail traders, and the professions were deemed sensitive sectors and not affected by the first measures adopted.[117]

Initial measures for establishment were also modest in the agricultural sector. France was the European country with the largest amount of cultivable land. In 1955 it already hosted 41,000 foreign farmers, two-thirds of whom were from the Community, especially Italy and Belgium.[118] In West Germany farmers expelled from Eastern Germany were seeking a chance to set up anew. In 1964, 160,000 German farming families were still trying to obtain their own farm or a larger farm. In a five-year plan for 1959–1964, the German government had earmarked DM 2.5 billion to reinstate farmers.[119] The French fear was then that the right of establishment in agriculture would lead to considerable immigration and a rise in land prices. Henri Canonge, Secretary General of the National Confederation of Mutuality, Cooperation, and Agricultural Credit in France, expressed this concern in the Economic and Social Committee,[120] pointing to land purchases 'made by companies or individuals with substantial financial means.'[121] Meanwhile, French farmers were already experiencing difficulties. Land consolidation (*remembrement*) forced a drop in the number of farms, and the arrival of repatriated farmers from Algeria increased the total agricultural population in France.

With the extension of the right of establishment in agriculture, France called for compensation under the Common Agricultural Policy (CAP), which had by then become a major priority for the French government.[122] In the Economic and Social Committee, Canonge linked French approval of the general programme proposed by the Commission to abolish obstacles to the freedom of establishment to the timetabled implementation of the CAP.[123] As a result of French concerns, the measures adopted in the agricultural sector on the right of establishment were initially limited to land abandoned or unfarmed for more than two years,[124] and persons who had worked as farm employees in the destination country for two years without interruption.[125]

### Inference

With the more open migration regime within the Community, migrants could take up offers of employment and automatically receive a work permit without undergoing a regulated recruitment procedure. A series of mechanisms guaranteed that such immigrants would carry no risk for local workers. More importantly, the vast labour demand in West German stabilised this regime. Developments were lower for establishment as independent workers, where the German economy did not play such a stabilising role.

## Preventing family migration

In the context of the additional opportunities for the migrant workforce within the Community, the new regime also dealt with family migration. In this section I present the contrasting positions of France and West Germany on this issue and develop the general historiography of European Integration by showing how this cleavage was accommodated by French concessions to obtain the CAP.[126]

### A line of cleavage

Family allowances for migrant workers were a key instrument for states to shape flows of family migration, by maintaining families in the country of origin or not. West Germany, the Netherlands, and Luxembourg had high population density, exacerbated by immigration from the East in the case of West Germany. This led to tension on their housing markets. To resolve these tensions, the Netherlands had to build 70,000 extra housing units a year.[127] In these countries, family allowances were low, in order to stabilise population growth. In 1955, they amounted to the equivalent of USD 5.95 for a family with three children in West Germany and USD 11.29 in the Netherlands, against USD 59.70 in France. Because they wanted to discourage family reunion for immigrant workers and because their family allowances were low, West Germany and the Netherlands backed the complete transfer of family benefits abroad. In the mid-1950s, thanks to bilateral agreements, they paid the full amount (Luxembourg almost the full amount) of family benefits to Italian workers when the family resided in Italy.[128]

France, by contrast, had a pro-natal policy to compensate for the population losses of the two wars and for its low population density compared to other European countries. In order to attract families, the amount paid when the migrant's family lived abroad was cut by more than 60 percent in comparison to the amount paid when the migrant's family lived in France.[129] Alongside family allowances, French birth and maternity benefits were only granted to parents whose children had French nationality.[130] This meant that migrant parents were urged to take up French nationality to pass it on to any children born in France, which encouraged parents to settle there. Besides demographic objectives and the fact that French family benefits were high, there was a third reason why France was reluctant to pay its benefits abroad. After 1945 France had been the main immigration country in Europe. Consequently, by the 1950s it was the hardest hit by requests for the exportation of benefits, based on rights acquired by migrant workers. The difficult situation of the French balance of payments meant that France was usually against transferring benefits abroad, whereas West Germany, the Netherlands, and Italy, which had experienced emigration after 1945, backed such transfers.

## France negotiating for lower transfers

These preferences determined negotiating positions. Following Article 69 of the ECSC Treaty, the Six negotiated a convention on the social security rights of migrant workers. To limit its commitments, France promoted the principle of territoriality in these matters, which meant that the cost of benefits would return, at least in part, to the social security institutions of the country on whose territory the beneficiaries lived.[131] Other long-standing countries of immigration among the Six, Belgium and Luxembourg, backed the French position.[132] Initially France managed to accommodate certain aspects of the Convention to its preferences. As the country that paid the most and received the least from the others, it was in a strong position. The Convention on the social security of migrant workers, signed by the six governments in December 1957, provided that family allowances paid abroad would be those of the worker's country of employment, but would not exceed those of the worker's country of origin, which were generally lower.[133] The Convention also specified that for France the amount of family allowances transferred to another country would be that usually transferred to families living outside metropolitan France, which was lower than that paid to families in France.[134]

To affirm the principle of territoriality and to promote family reunification, France also pushed for a two-year limit on the payment of family allowances abroad. It justified this as 'an exemption . . . for workers whose families had to live temporarily in the country of origin [due to] a lack of immediately available suitable housing.'[135] In order to secure German support, in July 1957 France accepted to pay invalidity pensions for German miners for the time they had worked in France, which ran counter to the principle of territoriality. The question of the two-year limit on the payment of family allowances abroad was raised at the same meeting when France made this concession. German Labour Minister Anton Storch then declared, 'If need be, backing the French proposal.'[136] As this created an incentive for family reunion and exacerbated housing market tensions, Storch finally managed to get French consent for a three-year time limit, instead of two. The same time limit was set for the reimbursement of illness and maternity care abroad.[137] Finally, birth allowances were not dealt with in the Convention and France maintained the condition of French nationality.[138] The Convention signed on 9 December 1957 became thereafter one of the first regulations of the Community, Regulation 3 of 25 September 1958,[139] and the three-year limit became effective when it came into force on 1 January 1959.[140]

Financial rather than demographic criteria shaped France's position on unemployment benefits for Community migrants who left the country after becoming unemployed. France and Luxembourg opposed transferring unemployment benefits abroad, pointing out that their unemployment insurance regimes were not contributory and consequently did not create individual entitlements.[141] Their partners agreed to let France and Luxembourg limit the payment of unemployment benefits abroad to skilled workers in the coal and steel sectors. This restriction would apply reciprocally to French and Luxembourg migrants in the rest of the Community. In contrast, all migrants of other member states would receive their unemployment benefits abroad. Member states also agreed that any entitlement to the unemployment benefits of the country of immigration would end four months after leaving that country.

France was even more isolated when it proposed reducing the rates of unemployment benefits for migrants. Countries of immigration were reluctant to pay these benefits abroad because payment had to be accompanied by a control on unemployed workers. All immigration countries agreed that the unemployed worker's destination country should bear a percentage of the unemployment benefits, so that the country that controlled the unemployed worker had an interest in the cost of benefits. Most countries agreed that the country of last employment should only bear 85 percent of the cost of unemployment benefits. Yet during the negotiations on the Convention in January 1957, French Secretary of State for Labour and Social Security Jean Minjoz managed to cut this rate to 60 percent.[142] This rate was too low and created a technical problem. Most cases were Italian migrant workers returning to Italy after becoming unemployed. The Italian unemployment insurance scheme had not received any contribution from these workers while they were employed, so that it had to pay them unemployment benefits at its own expense.

During negotiations on the transformation of the Convention into Regulation 3, France's new Gaullist government was determined to limit payments abroad and launched a general offensive on social security issues in June 1958. The French even asked whether the benefits – linked to the rates previously discussed – were those of the country of last employment or of residence, which were often much lower.[143] France was isolated and had to cede. Regulation 3 provided that France and the Netherlands would temporarily apply a 60 percent rate, instead of the normal 85 percent rate. This rate would rise to 70 percent after five years and reach 85 percent after another five years.[144] Thus France's preferences were accommodated only in the form of a temporary exemption.

In summer 1958 the offensive of the new French government also affected benefits for frontier and seasonal workers. France wanted to exclude these workers from the scope of Regulation 3.[145] The first reason was that most frontier or seasonal migrants within the Community worked in France. On 31 December 1958 France had 47,069 Belgian frontier workers, 8,108 Belgian seasonal workers, and 37,000 Italian seasonal workers. By comparison, on 30 September 1959 there were only 5,367 Community frontier workers in West Germany.[146] France therefore had to shoulder most of the cost, and was in a better position to impose its position. The second reason for the French position was that if frontier workers were included in Regulation 3, France would have to extend the privileged treatment of Belgian frontier workers to other Community frontier workers in France. With France in such a strong position, the other governments had to accept French demand, but member states agreed to regulate later, in another regulation, the rights of these frontier and seasonal workers.[147]

## Financial flows and migration flows

The different preferences of governments and the resulting agreement in Regulation 3 accounted for the major differences in the transfers of social security benefits abroad by the various countries in the following years.[148] By the first half of the 1960s West Germany and France had similar populations of Community immigrants. Yet when it came to healthcare benefits paid in Italy on behalf of Germany or France, there were only 6,237 cases for France in 1961, against 90,686 for Germany. In 1964, healthcare benefits paid in Italy to families of migrant workers amounted to 394.2 billion Belgian francs on behalf of Germany, against 89.5 on behalf of France. In 1961, Germany paid family allowances to 47,925 families in other Community countries; meanwhile, France was transferring family allowances under Regulation 3 to 14,670 children in other Community countries, that is only to around 6,000 families. The respective amounts in Belgian francs were 294.3 billion for Germany and 46.9 billion for France. Despite a similar stock of Community immigrants, the transfers made by West Germany were therefore much higher than those made by France and this was the result of the former's greater readiness to transfer benefits abroad.

Of the 35.6 million French francs of family allowances that France transferred in 1962 to other Community countries, under Regulation 3 or bilateral agreements, 25.2 million went to children of Belgian frontier workers, 4.4 million to children of German frontier workers, and only 5.3 million to children of Italian migrant workers. The transfers for frontier workers were calculated under bilateral agreements. The privileged treatment for Belgian frontier workers was linked to the large demand for a francophone workforce in North-East France. There was also a French national interest behind the transfers to the families of Belgian frontier workers, and this is why France was reluctant to extent such treatment in other cases. The effect of these transfers of family allowances was indeed to encourage natality in Southern Belgium and, as a result, to reinforce the francophone community in the country. The policy was efficient: while only 40 percent of Belgian frontier workers in the Netherlands had family dependents, this figure rose to 60 percent for Belgian frontier workers in France.

Financial transfers were powerful instruments to shape actual migration flows: as a result of the different levels of family benefits transferred abroad by France or West Germany, there were different levels of family migration flows to both countries. In 1962 a Commission report stated: 'Their family more frequently accompanies Italian workers in France than Italian workers in Germany. . . . It seems . . . that the countries granting higher family allowances attract large families.'[149] In line with the preference of the respective governments, few families of migrant workers in West Germany migrated to Germany, while the opposite was taking place in France. The agreement in Regulation 3 of 1958 explained these differences. This pattern also shaped workers' migration flows. Between 1958 and 1963, most Italian migrant workers went to West Germany when staying inside the Community. As their families had remained in Italy, two-thirds of all Italian emigrants returned to their homeland after migrating during this period and 80 percent in the five-year period starting in 1964. The proportion was below 50 percent in the 1946–1951 period, partly due to the family policies of France and Belgium.[150]

## Greater opportunities to export social security benefits

Despite France's initial success in limiting payments abroad, the regime shifted under German influence towards greater opportunities for migrant workers to get their benefits exported. This shift first affected the three-year time limit secured by France for the export of healthcare and family allowances for the families of immigrant workers. This three-year limit was supposed to apply as of 1 January 1962, that is, three years after Regulation 3 came into force on 1 January 1959. The increasing shift of Italian migrant workers towards West Germany was reducing French financial interest in this issue. The Germans and the Dutch also presented their housing problems to justify a new extension of the time limit.[151] When the Italians raised the question and it was discussed at the Council meeting of 18 December 1961, French Minister of Agriculture Edgard Pisani – who championed French interest in the Common Agricultural Policy[152] – represented France at the meeting and took care of the question. He worked for concessions on social issues.[153] On 29 December 1961, the West German government, which then held the presidency of the Council, finally managed to extend the three-year limit in a six-year limit.[154]

When the Council started discussing a new regulation for frontier and seasonal workers in 1962 and 1963, as per the earlier commitment made, French Labour Minister Gilbert Grandval accepted the abolition of the six-year time limit for these workers.[155] Yet he opposed any change in the arrangement regarding the level of family allowances. He stated that the family allowances transferred could not exceed the level provided by the legislation of the country of residence. French family allowances transferred to Italy should still not exceed the level of Italian allowances, which were much lower.

As far as unemployment benefits for frontier and seasonal workers were concerned, most border regions in immigration countries were then experiencing strong economic growth. The drive to attract the neighbouring workforce led to favourable arrangements to export unemployment benefits for these workers. Employers in North-West Germany experienced such a shortage of labour that they were keen to keep their Dutch workers when they were partially unemployed. In February 1963, German Labour Minister Theodor Blank explained in the Council[156] that this region had industries where unemployment periods frequently occurred. Such a situation affected textile industries, where business depended on the seasons and on fashion. The West German government was willing to keep Dutch workers as long as possible for German employers and therefore accepted paying unemployment benefits for a longer period for frontier and seasonal workers.[157] To attract and keep frontier workers, even France and Luxembourg agreed to apply Community measures on unemployment benefits to all frontier workers, while until then Regulation 3 had only bound them to apply these measures to skilled workers in the coal and steel sector.[158] Yet they kept the limitation for seasonal workers.[159]

In July 1964 the Council completed the shift towards greater opportunities to transfer benefits by abolishing the six-year time limit for the export of family allowances.[160] This took place before 1 January 1965, when that limit would first have come into effect. On the one hand, the French retreat was due to the growing importance of West Germany in Community migration by the mid-1960s. This reduced France's financial burden. Italian immigration to France had collapsed to the extent that France had an incentive to guarantee the same advantages as Germany to attract immigrant workers. On the other hand, France was keen to cooperate with its partners in its attempt to promote the CAP.

In parallel to all these negotiations, member states continued implementing the formal opening up of the European migration regime they had agreed to in the Treaty of Rome. They arranged for the broad right of residence for Community migrants that this opening entailed. With Council Directive 64/220 of 25 February 1964, which recognised a right of residence for providers and recipients of services for the duration of those services, the right of residence was almost general.[161] During preparatory discussions, Dutch delegates pushed to exclude recipients of common services, but other delegates opposed this restriction.[162] As a result, simply renting accommodation could confer a right of residence. Member states also agreed that the right of residence should extend to the entire territory of each country and not be limited to a particular region, as was potentially the case earlier on.[163] Furthermore the definition of family was broad, including spouse, children under the age of twenty-one, and any other relatives dependent on the worker and their spouse.[164] The right to family reunion was nevertheless subordinate to the criterion of having 'normal' housing in the host country,[165] which would allow certain states, particularly the Netherlands, to limit family reunion in practice.[166]

Overall, this broad residence right was consistent with the principles of the migration regime that Germany was ready to sustain. It was a migration regime between countries with a strong degree of diplomatic cohesion, and therefore unwilling to deport their reciprocal nationals by force.

### Inference

The new migration regime in the Community was formally open and included a number of mechanisms to shape actual migration flows and take care of each state's financial and demographic concerns. With their high population density and pressure on their housing markets, the Netherlands and West Germany were reluctant to encourage family immigration whereas France was, having a lower population than the other large Western European countries. Rules were therefore not unified and Germany exported its family allowances widely, while France did not. Nevertheless, France had growing difficulties maintaining its position and the trend was towards the arrangements sustained by West Germany. It was a regime that favoured the movement of active persons and maintained families in origin countries through financial incentives.

## Spreading the regime

This new migration regime offered unprecedented opportunities for migrants from less developed regions, particularly in Italy. By doing so, it reduced social tensions and created a cohesive environment around West Germany. Yet, while limited to the Six it only tackled a part of Western Europe's social problems and sources of disunity. In this section, I will show how immigration states led by West Germany strove to manage the migration tensions threatening the cohesion of Western Europe on a regional basis.

### Supporting the less developed countries of Western Europe

The project of a more open regional migration regime at the Western European level still generated important concerns. Among countries of immigration, Switzerland still opposed long-term immigration. As a node of communication at the heart of Europe, it could easily import labour where it was needed in construction, tourism, and agriculture. During the second part of 1954, of the 115,859 work permits issued to migrants in Switzerland, 59,158 were for seasonal workers and 19,380 for frontier workers, that is almost 70 percent.[167] Less than one-third of permits were issued to migrant workers likely to settle in the country. Even for them, their contracts were only renewed for a limited time in order to avoid long-term settlement. In December 1955, the Swiss delegate to the OEEC, Gérard Bauer, expressed Swiss concerns about the size of the foreign population in Switzerland: 15 percent of a total population of 4 million. Bauer raised the 'political problem' this situation created for a 'federal' state with 'three languages.'[168] Large-scale Italian immigration was likely to challenge the linguistic homogeneity of cantons and the balance between the three main linguistic groups. In Britain, the unions opposed the immigration of unskilled labour in many sectors: construction, parts of the textile industry, some coalmines, and livestock breeding. They justified this by stressing that part-time work and low wages had become widespread.[169] Like the Netherlands, Britain referred to its shortage of housing to exploit the exceptions provided for in the 1953 Decision of the OEEC on the movement of labour.[170]

Even among countries of emigration, Portugal maintained policies that ran counter to the principles of an open migration regime. To prevent Communist and pro-democratic contagion, the Portuguese government required entry visas for OEEC nationals, and under the principle of reciprocity, the latter imposed the same requirement for Portuguese nationals.[171] This was also a way for the government to limit emigration opportunities in Europe for Portuguese citizens, while it wished to orient the emigration flow towards the colonies that Portugal strove to maintain overseas.[172] In the same vein, the price of a Portuguese passport,

USD 7.50, was the highest among OEEC states, if we exclude passports costing USD 11.20 issued by a few Swiss cantons, which were nonetheless valid for five years. The two-year validity of the Portuguese passport meant that its annual cost was by far the highest of all OEEC member states.[173]

The positions of these actors did not help resolve migratory tensions in Western Europe. In Mediterranean Europe, population growth, the mechanisation of agriculture, and the slow pace of industrialisation generated a sizeable population seeking emigration opportunities. In the late 1950s, 30,000 people could emigrate from Greece annually, and 100,000 from Italy.[174] One side effect of the more open migration regimes developed in some parts of Western Europe was the reduction of the use of external labour, at the expense of countries such as Greece and other U.S. allies, for which emigration was a condition of domestic political stability.[175] At the end of 1956, the Greek government called on the U.S. government to help extend migratory outlets for Greeks, including towards nearby countries, by linking migratory and trade liberalisation within the OEEC.[176]

In December 1956, the U.S. government submitted a plan to the OEEC for a free market for labour extended to all of Western Europe.[177] The Swedish ambassador to the OEEC, Ingemar Hägglöf, rallied to this suggestion and approved 'the creation of a free market taking in all of Europe.' Regardless of this support, the British delegate, Edward Redston Warner, declared that his government would 'by no means agree that it [might be] possible to . . . put [the U.S. proposals] into practice.' The plan was ditched. In 1961, the OEEC became the Organisation for Economic Co-operation and Development (OECD), and integrated Canada and the United States. By then, the U.S. government, along with its Canadian counterpart, was unwilling to change its immigration policies and enter into open migration arrangements with European countries. As a result, not only did it stop promoting such projects in the OECD, but also the United States and Canada did not even take part in the decision on the freedom of movement of labour negotiated in 1953 within the OEEC, and then continued within the OECD.[178]

In such a context, immigration states within the Community acted to open migratory outlets to populations of Mediterranean Europe, while their employers were ready to step up recruitment of foreign labour. West Germany, France, Belgium, and the Netherlands on the one hand, and Greece, Spain, Turkey, and even Portugal on the other, signed multiple bilateral recruitment agreements.[179] While in 1954, the remittances of Greek emigrants accounted for 14.2 percent of imports and 2.8 percent of national revenue, by 1962 they had reached 21.9 percent of imports and 4.7 percent of national revenue. By comparison, the figures for Italy in the same period went from 3.3 and 0.5 percent to 9.0 and 1.9 percent, respectively. Greek emigration rose from around 20,000 people a year in the 1950s to 100,000 in 1963. West Germany absorbed the lion's share of these migration flows. While two-thirds of Greek emigration was overseas in the 1950s, the percentage of emigration towards West Germany leapt from 11 percent in 1959 to 70 percent in 1964.[180] From then on Turkey also considered emigration as a way to accelerate modernisation in agriculture and the industrial sector, thanks to the expertise of return migrants. Work permits for Turks in West Germany grew from 15,000 in 1962 to around 63,000 in 1964.[181]

The West German government played the leading role in shaping migratory relations between the Community and Greece and Turkey. On 9 July 1961 in Athens, Greece and the Community signed an Association Agreement. It provided that the free movement of workers 'as per . . . the Treaty establishing the Community' and the right of establishment of the Treaty would be applied between the Community and Greece, but without setting a timetable.[182] Similarly, the Community and Turkey signed an Association Agreement in Ankara on 12 September 1963. This specified in Article 12 that 'the Contracting Parties [agreed] to be inspired by . . . the Treaty establishing the European Economic Community to realise gradually the free movement of workers among them.'[183] No timetable was set, and unlike the Greek case these measures would not necessarily be the same as those agreed among the Six. Greater precautions were taken with Turkey due to its demographic explosion: it had a population of over 30 million growing at an annual rate of 3 percent, whereas Greece had a population of only 8.5 million and weak demographic growth. Yet on the same day that the Ankara Agreement was signed, Turkey obtained an exchange of letters between the parties referring to Article 12, in which they agreed to 'study the problems of labour in Turkey from the preparatory phase.'[184] The preparatory phase in the Ankara Agreement referred to the first five years after the entry into force of the agreement.

With these bilateral and association agreements, West Germany backed by the other immigration countries of the Community replaced destination countries overseas by offering migratory opportunities to less developed Western European countries. This was a way to stabilise strategic countries in the Cold War. As a consequence of economic development in Europe and the greater importance of intra-European migration, the role of the Intergovernmental Committee for European Migration (ICEM) in managing European emigration and development became less important. From then onwards Western European countries were able to manage migratory tensions regionally, without resorting much to Western organisations for overseas emigration. The number of migrants transported by ICEM peaked in 1956 at over 130,000, without counting Hungarian refugees,[185] but then fell to under 100,000 in 1960 and thereafter. ICEM remained active mainly to transport migrants from Eastern Europe.

## Absorbing immigrants from Eastern Europe

The absorption of migrants from Eastern Europe was Germany's final aim for a Western European migration regime likely to maximise German preferences. A swift absorption of these migrants could help undermine Communist regimes in Eastern Europe. The Hungarian crisis revealed the role that Western migratory cooperation could play in complicating the management of political crises by Communist governments in Eastern Europe. Following the political troubles in Hungary, the number of Hungarians seeking asylum in Austria increased dramatically as of 4 November 1956. By 31 December, around 160,000 Hungarians had arrived in Austria. Between 6 November and 31 December 1956, the ICEM evacuated directly 42,045 Hungarian refugees from Austria and assisted the transport of 40,797 others. The United States ranked first among the countries of destination, receiving around 19,000 people shortly after the Hungarian uprising. West Germany received around 11,000, Switzerland over 10,000, France over 8,000, and Canada over 7,000.[186] In 1959, of the 180,000 Hungarian refugees who had arrived in Austria in the wake of the Hungarian crisis, 160,000 had emigrated: 82,000 went overseas and 78,000 remained in Europe.[187] Without Western cooperation, Austria would have had to close its borders to these migrants. In welcoming as many Hungarians as possible, Western states made the suppression more costly for the Hungarian government, which thus lost a significant part of its population, and stimulated future unrest in Eastern Europe by rewarding those who had taken part in the uprising. However, the Hungarian crisis also showed that Western Europeans were not able to achieve these results alone, that is without U.S. support.

To overcome this dependency, West Germany and France supported the creation of a European Resettlement Fund for Refugees from Eastern Europe. As early as December 1955, German Minister for Foreign Affairs Heinrich von Brentano invited his counterparts in the Committee of Ministers of the Council of Europe to take part in 'this grand gesture of European solidarity.'[188] West Germany favoured permanent European institutions to deal with Eastern migrants and to facilitate rapid international action in the case of a sudden influx. The other member states of the Council of Europe who accepted the proposal and adopted the Fund's statute, on 16 April 1956, were the countries of immigration and donors of North-West Europe – France, Belgium, and Luxembourg – and the countries bordering the East and dealing with the flows of Eastern migrants and with surplus populations – Italy, Greece, and Turkey. West Germany belonged to both categories.[189] The loans that the Fund granted went to building housing and setting up vocational training facilities to ease migrants' integration. These loans already amounted to USD 12 million in early 1960.[190]

From 1959 onwards, as migration tensions within Western Europe declined thanks to rising migration to West Germany, Western European states deepened their cooperation in absorbing immigrants from Eastern Europe. Gradually, most Western European countries adhered to the 1951 Geneva Convention on the status of refugees. By 1959, only the outliers Spain, Portugal, and Turkey had not joined.[191] In addition, within the Council of Europe France and West Germany championed a European Accord on the abolition of visas for refugees, signed on 20 April 1959 and effective on 3 September 1960. Under this Accord, refugees who were legally resident in one of the participating countries enjoyed a right of residence of less than three months in other participating countries. Only a travel document issued in accordance with the Geneva Convention by the regular country of residence was required.[192] This was a major step to create westward migration opportunities for refugees, thus alleviating the burden for the countries bordering Eastern Europe. The first countries to ratify the Accord were West Germany and France, together with the Benelux countries,[193] followed by the Scandinavian countries.

In May 1960, to facilitate access to jobs for migrants from Eastern Europe, and despite British reserves,[194] the OEEC Council recommended OEEC member states to issue visas freely and deliver work and residence permits more easily to refugees recognised as such in other OEEC countries.[195] In a common declaration on 25 March 1964, the member governments of the Community also committed to consider favourably granting work permits to people recognised as refugees under the Geneva Convention and resident in another Community country.[196] West Germany thus managed to secure French support to develop a migration regime opening up opportunities for migrants from Eastern Europe at a Western European level. This was strategic in absorbing migrants from Eastern Europe, in particular during political crises there, and support pro-Western feelings in that region. Nonetheless, this cooperation did not grant Eastern European migrants rights identical with those of Community migrants.

### Spreading elements of the regime beyond Western Europe

Finally, the six members of the Community negotiated to spread some elements of their regime in their relations with countries outside Western Europe. To cope with tensions on its housing market and its infrastructure, the West German government was even ready to export family allowances for immigrants from outside the Community.[197] West Germany, supported among the Six by Italy, the Netherlands, and Luxembourg, promoted this principle in the International Labour Organisation (ILO), where a convention on the equality of treatment for nationals and non-nationals in social security was under negotiation.[198] Densely populated countries like West Germany, the Netherlands, and Luxembourg favoured temporary rather than long-term immigration. Italy wanted to prevent third-country immigrants from appearing cheaper by having fewer social security rights than Italian immigrants. France was isolated in Europe on this issue, but found the support of overseas countries favouring long-term immigration. In June 1962, an Australian representative in the negotiations, Henderson, stressed that many

European countries were interested in temporary opportunities for immigrant workers, but that the Australian government favoured the assimilation of immigrants. Immigrants in Australia had to be naturalised before being entitled to long-term social security benefits, which gave them an incentive to take up Australian nationality.[199]

In the final text of the convention, the principles promoted by West Germany prevailed. The signatory states committed to guarantee entitlement to family allowances for children resident on the territory of another signatory state, but only 'in the conditions and subject to limits to be established through a common agreement among the interested members.' Signatory states also committed themselves to design instruments to maintain rights for invalidity, old age, and survivors' pensions acquired in the different national legislations to which a migrant had contributed.[200] Thus, at the ILO level, West Germany and other European states encouraged principles similar to those developed in Western Europe.

Beyond the objective of creating temporary immigration flows, this stance was related to the West German government's concerns about the rights acquired in Central Europe by German citizens before their expulsion to West Germany in the aftermath of the war. In parallel to the Social Security Convention on Equality of Treatment for Nationals and Non-nationals, ILO member states also negotiated a recommendation. In this negotiation, on 19 June 1962, U.S. delegate Doherty called to allow the beneficiaries of any social security benefits to enjoy their entitlements without being penalised by circumstances beyond their control, such as the policies of their country, or by the fact that they had changed nationality or residence. West German labour delegate Bernt Heise supported this proposal on behalf of labour members, and the West German government carefully refrained from voting.[201] This proposal was to allow Germans who had fled Central Europe after the Second World War to receive German old age pensions for which they had acquired rights in their countries of origin. Until then, U.S.-German coordination seemed to have worked well enough so that Eastern European governments had not realised such implications of the text.

On 22 June, during the last review of the recommendation before final approval, Soviet representative Mikhail Semyonovitch Lantsev declared that this constituted 'interference in the domestic affairs of states' and that it would have 'serious repercussions,' forcing many countries to vote against the Recommendation. He argued that this would mean that countries that had supported a war against Nazism would have to pay benefits to individuals who were their enemies. This position was supported not only by Czechoslovakia, Romania, and Belorussia, but also by Mali and Nigeria, which refused to 'pay benefits to their former colonisers.' Despite the coalition between Eastern states and newly independent states, this point and the Recommendation were adopted.[202]

## Inference

In line with the interests of the Western camp in the Cold War, a regional management of migratory tensions in Western Europe developed beyond the Community thanks to the influence of West Germany. This management could alleviate social tensions in Greece and Turkey, which had the prospect of being integrated in the regime of the Community. Regional cooperation also aimed at facilitating the movement and settlement of migrants from Eastern Europe to the West, which was critical to undermine Communist regimes in Eastern Europe. German and French interests also converged to safeguard rights acquired by their nationals in territories outside Western Europe.

## Synopsis

From 1955 to 1964, a new migration regime was therefore taking shape not only among the Six, but also at a Western European level. This occurred under German influence, as West German economic growth helped in managing the greater part of additional migratory and financial burdens generated by the regime. This contribution placed the West German government in a pre-eminent position for defining the regime: limiting opportunities to European populations, making such opportunities dependent on the rise of labour demand, keeping families in the country of origin, and extending opportunities to Greece, Turkey, and immigrants from Eastern Europe. In this configuration, France generally followed, also due to the financial concessions made by West Germany to the European Development Fund for French former colonies and in the Common Agricultural Policy for French farmers.

# 3

# A SHRINKING DYNAMIC, 1965–1973

In this chapter, I will show that from 1965 to 1973 West Germany continued to develop a new migration regime in Western Europe, but that this evolution was slowed down by a growing divergence with France. I will show how progress towards free trade for industrial goods in the Community and German reluctance to grant more concessions to France in the field of the Common Agricultural Policy meant repeated French obstruction in the domain of migration.[1] I will show in particular how France managed to maintain the barriers to immigrants in independent occupations. I will also describe how the nature of immigration to France and West Germany diverged in this period. Greater international openness resulted in a higher degree of labour unrest in France. I will explain how, in this context, France and West Germany continued opening up to Community migrant workers, but how this was subject to the interests of their national workers and how the dynamic expanding the regime to third countries slackened.

## Uncoupling forces

The divergence between France and West Germany was partly due to the different levels of political tension surrounding immigration, linked to the different nature of their immigration flows.

### Flows and tensions

In the 1960s, the number of immigrants in Western Europe increased dramatically, from around 1.8 million in 1960 to almost 4.5 million in 1974.[2] Over 52 percent of them were in West Germany, where 2.35 million foreign workers accounted for 10.8 percent of the active population in September 1972.[3] Admittedly Community immigration became secondary as immigration from third countries shot up from 38 percent of total inflows in Community countries in 1960 to 65 percent between 1965 and 1968 and 80 percent in 1969.[4] Long-distance migration flows to North-West Europe from the furthest periphery of Western Europe, Africa, and Asia took significance during this period. Within this long-term trend, we can observe the impact on migration flows of the successive steps to open the Community migration regime. The opening up of the migration regime in the Community thus contributed to the general increase in immigration flows. After Regulation 38/64 of March 1964 came into force, the number of new entries of Community immigrant workers in West Germany increased by over 40 percent between 1964 and 1965, from 153,390 to 216,448.[5] The share of Community migrants in the total immigrant labour force in the Community rose from 40 to 50 percent in 1967. It rose again from 20 to 25 percent after Regulation 1612/68 of 15 October 1968 on the free movement of labour came into force.[6]

Meanwhile, immigration started to generate more acute tension in France than in West Germany. In France, immigrants came mostly from outside the Community; they were less skilled and poorer than in Germany. Lower wages in France made the country less attractive to Italian migrants. In 1965, 203,064 Italian workers entered West Germany, while only 18,043 entered France.[7] The share of Community immigration in total immigration to France fell from around 65 percent in 1958 to only 10 percent in 1965, and even 3.4 percent in 1969.[8] By contrast, linguistic proximity and agreements between France and its former colonies favoured expanding immigration from North and West Africa. In 1969, the number of Algerian workers moving to France rose from 257,650 to 352,530.[9] These immigrants were less skilled than Italians. In France, Community immigration consisted of 45 percent of skilled workers and 12.5 percent of overseers or foremen, whereas non-European immigration involved 75 percent of specialised labourers, and only 23 percent of skilled workers and 2 percent of overseers or foremen. The differences in living standards between France and migrants' countries of origin were also high: the gross domestic product (GDP) per capita ratio was 1:2 with Spain in 1974, 1:2.5 with Portugal in 1974, but around 1:11 with the Maghreb countries in 1973.[10]

Immigration also became an autonomous process in France. Employers frequently bypassed the official recruitment channels to find cheap immigrant labour. According to the economist Georges Photios Tapinos, by 1968 82 percent of immigrant workers entered France outside these channels.[11] Besides those recruited by employers in their country of origin, a growing numbers of immigrants arrived as tourists without a job, found an employer, and were regularised later on.

In West Germany, the situation was the opposite. Immigrants came mostly from Italy, Greece, Spain, and Turkey. The GDP per capita ratio between these countries and West Germany revealed less disparity than in the French case: 1:1.5 with Italy, 1:2 with Greece and Spain, and 1:6 with Turkey in 1974.[12] Immigration was tightly related to the evolution of labour demand. The 1967 recession highlighted the important turnover of immigrant labour, and its weak downward impact on wages. Industrial production dropped by 3 percent in 1967.[13] In just a year, from the end of June 1966 to the end of June 1967, the number of Italian workers in West Germany fell by 31.4 percent, from 399,200 to 274,000. In the same period, the number of Greek workers fell from 196,200 to 146,800, and that of Spanish workers from 185,300 to 129,100.[14] In addition, the demand for labour in West Germany outstripped supply. The number of unfilled jobs reached 625,000 in late February 1969 and the gap between labour supply and demand became a 'substantial problem to be resolved' in the words of German Labour Minister Hans Katzer.[15] The demand for labour was especially high for skilled metalworkers, electricians, and workers in the building sector. Meanwhile, there were only 107,800 unemployed workers at the end of October 1969 in West Germany, accounting for only 0.5 percent of the active population.

As a result, tensions caused by immigration differed sharply in France and West Germany. In France, unskilled immigrant labour supply could downgrade work. In the words of an official in the International Labour Office, W. R. Böhning:

> Employers may completely redesign their whole production process to adjust it to the kind of immigrant labour available . . . If, . . . semi-literate farmers from underdeveloped countries can offer no industrial skills at all, they can still be put into a work place where no more than a repetitive manual movement is required.[16]

It is also likely that the relative poverty of newcomers and the disconnection between the evolution of immigration and labour demand were responsible for stagnating or even decreasing wages among French workers. In the hierarchy of wages, the ratio between the threshold of the top decile and the top of the bottom decile increased by 13.5 percent from 1959 to 1966 (from 3.7 to 4.2).[17] In only four years, between 1963 and 1967, the ratio of salaries of senior executives to workers' wages increased by almost 10 percent (from 4.2 to 4.6).[18]

This explains why immigration – even Community immigration – became a contentious issue among French workers in the following years. In May 1969, a communication from the secretary general of the *Confédération générale du travail* (CGT) to the president of the Council of Ministers pointed out that the free movement of labour should never 'be considered as a way to resolve existing unemployment in some regions of the Community' and that 'member states and employers [should] not use migrant workers as competing labour or to undermine trade union action.'[19]

Immigration did not have the same impact on wages in West Germany, but the national infrastructure was overloaded. Despite efforts to rein in family reunification, it increased. The ratio between the number of returns and the size of the foreign population declined steadily, apart from a sharp increase during the 1967 recession. It fell from 50 percent in 1963 to 29 percent in 1969 for Italians, and from 22 percent to 11 percent for Turks.[20] Immigration meant a rising demand for education and housing.[21] Nursery schools were overloaded and had long waiting lists.[22] To protect the 40 million tenants in West Germany from 'abuse' and from the 'intolerable consequences of the housing market situation,' as stated in a German note to the Commission in 1967, on 4 November 1971 the Bundestag adopted a law to cap rent increases and architects' fees.[23]

In the mid-1960s, tensions in Switzerland also made the prevailing regime unstable. Looking at flows, Switzerland seems a very important country of Italian immigration. Yet, looking at stocks, the number of Italians almost remained constant in the 1950s and 1960s. Swiss authorities indeed granted mostly only short-term permits, so that the Italian migrants going to Switzerland were forced to return to Italy regularly. Half a million Italians accounted nevertheless for two-thirds of the foreign population in Switzerland and 10 percent of the total population.[24] The Italian government managed to negotiate an agreement with the Swiss government that provided for family reunification and authorised Italian immigrants in Switzerland to move from one canton to another after a given period of residence. It should have been ratified in early 1965. Yet the agreement met with opposition in the Lower House of the Swiss Parliament, which wanted to protect the stability of the Confederation and prevent the Italian-speaking population from increasing in the French-speaking and German-speaking cantons.[25]

## The onset of the closure to immigration

All these tensions resulted in new forms of closure. Switzerland acted first, contradicting the provisions of the unratified agreement with Italy. A first decree came into force on 15 February 1965 and doubled the forces stationed at the Swiss border to turn back immigrants.[26] In the first twenty-four hours 1,300 immigrants were refused entry.[27] A second decree was adopted at the same time by the Minister for Economic Affairs, Hans Schaffner, and the Minister for Justice, Ludwig von Moos: it planned a 5 percent cutback of the foreign workforce by all companies between 1 March and 30 June 1965. Around 40,000 immigrants, including over 25,000 Italians, had to leave the country. A new reduction of 5 percent was scheduled for 30 June 1966.[28] Although larger geographically and economically than Switzerland, Italy was unable to retaliate against this unilateral closure by the Swiss government that ran counter to a newly signed, but unratified, agreement between the two countries.

The French government also took new steps to curb increasing labour immigration. It imposed a two-week waiting period for Community nationals before taking up offers advertised by French employers. Regulation 38/64 still allowed for such restrictions in areas where immigration was likely to depress wages or create unemployment. France applied the restriction to all unskilled office and retail employees throughout the country.[29] Initially it also covered all manual jobs, but as of 1 April 1965, the French government only applied the restriction to manual jobs in Lower Normandy, Brittany, and Pays-de-la-Loire. Furthermore, the French government used the restriction for all shipyard areas in Western and Southern France, where labour conflicts were particularly acute: Lorient-Pont-Scorff-Hennebont, Saint-Nazaire-Nantes, La Rochelle-La Pallice, Port-de-Bouc, La Seyne-sur-Mer, and Toulon. Finally, French workers in the industrial areas of central France enjoyed the same protection: Châteauroux, Montluçon-Commentry, and Nevers-Fourchambault-Imphy.

The tensions on the French labour market came to a head in the worker uprising in May 1968. The first serious strike started in 1967 at the Saviem factory in Caen, in Lower Normandy, triggered by an increase in the pace of production. In the weeks that followed, strikes spread to La Rochelle and Saint-Nazaire. Industrial action at Sud-Aviation in Nantes sparked the general strike of May 1968. The areas that the French government had tried to protect from Community immigration were thus precisely those where the May 1968 strikes started. In order to put a halt to the downward pressure on wages and deteriorating working conditions, union demands focused on increasing the minimum wage. The first point of the Grenelle Agreements on 27 May 1968 provided for a hourly minimum wage increased to 3 French francs and abolished the lower levels of the minimum wage that still applied in provincial France.[30] Where the minimum wage was lowest, this amounted to a nominal increase of around 50 percent[31] and a real increase of around 40 percent.[32] In comparison, the basic level of the minimum wage had only experienced a real increase of 23.5 percent from its creation in 1950 to 1967, that is an average annual real increase of 1.25 percent.[33] The law of 2 January 1970 adopted the recommendations of the Grenelle Agreements and created a new type of minimum wage (*salaire minimum interprofessionnel de croissance*, SMIC). The new regulation was based on the principle that the minimum wage and the average wage should not diverge.[34]

In the following years the French minimum wage continued to increase, and employers lost their incentives to hire cheap unskilled immigrant workers, who found it increasingly difficult to find a job in France. Taking the changing circumstances into consideration, the French government negotiated a Franco-Algerian agreement shortly after the Grenelle Agreements. This reduced the number of Algerian workers allowed to enter French territory to take up employment to a maximum of 35,000 a year for the period 1969–1971, despite the fact that the immigration flow was then much higher.[35] A new agreement for 1972 and 1973 capped this limit at 25,000. The government hoped that the real number of entries would converge gradually towards these levels. Excluding Community immigrants, the share of immigrants entering the country without a job and regularised later on fell from 82 percent in 1968 to 44.3 percent in 1972.[36]

Hostility towards immigrant workers, and even against Community workers, persisted in France. In December 1972, the French Parliament debated the abolition of the condition of French nationality to take up employment in the sector of maritime navigation. This was a necessary step to adapt French law to the provisions of the Treaty of Rome, which should have been fully effective as of January 1970. Communist members of Parliament opposed the abolition, even if this would mean violating the Treaty.[37] In parallel to these debates, the trade unions CGT and CFDT (*Confédération française démocratique du travail*) opposed the reform by calling an all-out strike that paralysed French ports.[38] The Parliament rejected proposals by the government on this matter in December 1972 and December 1973. Even Senator JosephYvon, from the liberal and pro-European party *Républicains indépendants*, shared the CGT position. He represented the seaport of Lorient, where sailors were mobilising against the intended reform.[39] After these failures, the Commission took France to the Court of Justice of the Community. In its judgment of 4 April 1974, the Court declared France guilty of non-compliance with the free movement of workers in the sector of maritime transport. France eventually complied with the Treaty with a circular of April 1975.[40] This affair revealed the underlying tension against the immigration of Community workers in France.

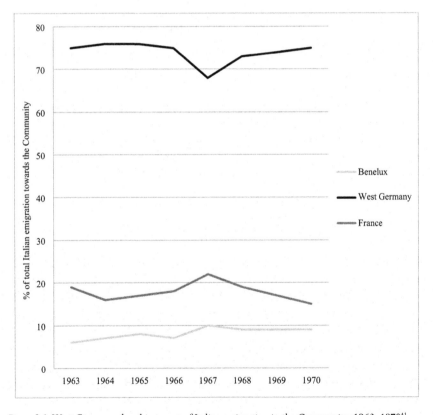

*Figure 3.1* West Germany absorbing most of Italian emigration in the Community, 1963–1970[41]

Given the situation in France, it was even more important that the West German economy stabilise the Community's open migration regime. Throughout this period, it absorbed around three-quarters of Italian emigration within the Community. Despite overloaded infrastructures, the West German government took no steps against immigration. It did not resort to the protection allowed by Regulation 38/64 and, from May 1964 onward, employment of Community immigrants remained unrestricted throughout West Germany.

### Inference

Disconnection between immigration levels and the evolution of labour demand, African immigration willing to accept low-paid jobs, which France absorbed single-handed, resulted in French workers' opposition to any type of immigration. In response, the French government shifted towards a restrictive immigration policy and was also forced to sidestep some provisions of the Treaty of Rome on the free movement of labour.

## Controlling immigrant workers

The French government was not willing to give in to the most radical union demands. Instead, by 1968 it had come up with a new immigration strategy. Given that Community immigrants in France were few and did not accept low-paid jobs, the French government was ready to work with the Germans and not to obstruct the implementation of the Treaty of Rome. In this section, I will show that this negotiation revealed nevertheless French efforts to tailor immigration flows to the interests of French workers, beyond what the West German government had anticipated.

### Attracting a trained workforce

Employers appreciated Community immigrant workers. This was obvious in West Germany. In 1967, during the drop in the recruitment of foreign workers, German employers opted for the Italian workforce, with 57,000 workers hired out of a total of 90,000 immigrant workers. Almost two-thirds of those hired were Italian immigrant workers.[42] In 1968, the central employment office of North Rhine-Westphalia reported that 'the greater part of Italians ... find work almost without exception.'[43] It is likely that such choices rested on the consideration that Italian workers were on average more skilled than other immigrant workers from non-industrialised countries. By hiring workers from other industrialised countries, employers could expect them to have some training in industrial work. Indeed, when Britain was about to join the Community in 1971, German employers asked their government to hire 200,000 British workers.[44]

The new French immigration policy stemmed from similar preoccupations and aimed at transforming immigrants' countries of origin. The government was willing to maintain the number of European immigrants, who generally took up higher-paid jobs. The Franco-Portuguese Protocol of 29 July 1971 kept the annual entry quota of Portuguese workers in France at 65,000.[45] In addition, the government wanted to increase Community immigration. In the Community Council of Ministers, the French Minister for Social Affairs, Joseph Fontanet, expressed his regret that the number of Italian migrants coming to work in France was constantly decreasing. He spoke of a tenfold reduction in a few years, from 60,000 to 6,000 a year.[46] In early 1968, the French government took steps to recruit more Italian workers.[47] The French were ready to drop the last forms of protection against Community workers. In the negotiations for Regulation 1612/68 on the free movement of workers, which replaced Regulation 38/64, the French accepted that measures limiting the employment of foreigners would no longer apply to Community nationals,[48] and work permits would be abolished by late December 1969.[49]

With other immigration countries, France was also ready to go beyond Regulation 38/64 by authorising Community migrants to search for work in their territories, dropping the requirement of a job offer 'actually made' before migrating. In February 1968, French delegates in the Council declared that a 'measure that would bind the right of admission to member-state territory to the prior condition of having a job, would challenge the principle of the free movement of workers.' France was in favour of free access for Community immigrant workers and their families with only their national identity cards or passports, but with a three-month limit during which migrants had to look for work, after which they could be expelled.[50] These positions prevailed in the official interpretative declarations on Regulation 1612/68 and its complementary Directive 68/360 on the free movement of labour, which the Council adopted on 15 October 1968.[51]

French Minister for Social Affairs Maurice Schumann even proposed that 'member states examine with the Commission all the options to fill, in priority, existing vacancies with Community workers, so as to reach a balance between labour supply and labour demand at the Community level.'[52] On 15 October 1968, the Council adopted an interpretative declaration stressing 'the importance of guaranteeing a compensation of job demands and job offers at the Community level in the most effective conditions possible.'[53] The various French positions were part and parcel of a new immigration policy. Despite certain radical union demands, the French government promoted the Community's open migration regime as a way to increase Community immigration, considered less harmful for the wage level of local workers in France. During this period Community immigration to France increased to around 8 percent in 1972.[54]

The West German government used this French policy to get the French welfare system to pay unemployment benefits to Community migrants. Since the negotiations on the social security of migrant workers within the Community in 1958, West Germany had been the main country exporting unemployment benefits and consequently attracted the migrants most interested in this export. By the late 1960s, West Germany exported unemployment benefits to around half of the 100,000 Italian workers returning to Italy on average each year. This amounted to between DM 5 and 8 million a year.[55] The agreement reached in 1958 had been that France and Luxembourg would export unemployment benefits only to skilled workers in the coal and steel sectors, with the same limitation applying to French and Luxemburg migrant workers in other countries.[56] In autumn 1968, in the Council the Germans indicated that 'the Bundesrat had invited [the] government to insist on the inclusion without exception of the French unemployment regime in the Regulation [on the social security of migrant workers] to give it its full meaning.'[57] Once again, France was ready to reach an agreement.[58]

In exchange for their participation, the French negotiated a reduction of the maximum duration of payments of unemployment benefits abroad, which the 1958 agreement had set at four months.[59] In January 1969, French delegates in the Council asked for a limit of two months.[60] In April 1969, French and German delegates agreed on three months.[61] The Germans had become more reluctant to spend for workers no longer available for German employers. German employers were interested in keeping the few unemployed Community immigrant workers available; they had already been employed and had useful training for German firms. From the summer 1969 onwards, the West German government asked that availability to the employers of the previous employment country should be a general condition for the payment of unemployment benefits. In November 1969, the Council agreed on a four-week period, before leaving the country, during which Community workers receiving unemployment benefits had to remain available to the employers in the country of last employment.

Regulation 1408/71 of the Council of 14 June 1971 included these provisions and replaced Regulation 3 of September 1958 to determine the social security of migrant workers within the Community. With this new regulation, the governments of immigration countries also accepted that unemployment benefits paid in other countries would be calculated according to the laws of the country of employment, which was generally more favourable for unemployed migrants.[62] Payment of unemployment benefits abroad could take place when the unemployed migrant worker returned to their country of origin or when they moved to another country in the Community to look for work.[63] While Regulation 3 had maintained a range of different situations, this new regulation defined a uniform regime for the payment abroad of unemployment benefits.

In the second half of 1971, the Germans called into question the agreement previously reached on the payment abroad of unemployment benefits. The West German labour market was extremely tight and employers were in dire need of labour. German delegates within the Council reported the dissatisfaction of German employers with current arrangements and called for keeping Community unemployed migrants available for German employers as long as they were receiving German unemployment benefits.[64] In the last instance, the Germans had to give up their demands, which went against provisions they had just accepted in Regulation 1408/71. German delegates officially declared that they regretted that their proposal had been rejected, as it would have promoted 'the priority of Community member-state workers in the labour market.'[65]

The Germans were therefore attached to Community immigrants, but this attachment was subordinated to their participation in the labour market. Inactive immigrants likely to become a burden were still not welcome, and this is why Germany and the Netherlands called for an expulsion option for the unemployed who had not found a job and had become dependent on public assistance. In April 1968, German delegates within the Council considered that applying for public assistance was a sufficient ground for expelling an unemployed foreign worker no longer entitled to unemployment benefits.[66] This line of reasoning prevailed in the Council. With Regulation 1612/68 member states could expel immigrants unemployed for more than three months before they became entitled to public assistance.[67] The regime thus favoured the immigration of active persons, but did not entail rights to social assistance in the country of immigration. This was in line with German preferences.

## An occupational status subject to the interests of the local workforce

Beyond their policy to attract Community workers, the French government pushed for an occupational status of Community workers likely to preserve the interests of local workers. The opposition of local workers to immigration in various sectors and acute labour conflicts more generally, which culminated with the wave of strikes of May 1968, contributed to such positions. The Commission proposed that Community workers be entitled to join firms' committees under the same conditions as national workers. German delegates within the Council highlighted the role of these bodies in companies jointly managed by workers and employers. It called for 'special conditions . . . before granting [Community workers] complete equality of treatment in this domain.' German delegates referred to the 'sometimes secret elements . . . brought to the attention of staff representatives.' It called for three years' residence in the country of employment before granting Community nationals this right of eligibility.[68]

Even though French companies also feared industrial espionage, the French did not support the Germans on this issue. French Minister for Social Affairs Maurice Schumann wanted to recognise the right of eligibility to Community nationals under the same conditions as French nationals. This position reflected trade union demands. The CGT opposed any discrimination against Community workers as far as trade union rights were concerned.[69] The aim was to integrate migrants into trade union action. For financial reasons Schumann nevertheless requested that nationals of other member states should not take part in the management of 'public services' as some trade union representatives might have to in France. Germany was isolated and the French position prevailed. Regulation 1612/68 recognised the right of eligibility of Community workers, without special conditions, within companies, but foreign representatives could not be involved in the management of public services.[70]

In this case, the subordination of the status of Community workers to local interests helped improve their status. In other cases, it reduced their opportunities. French companies in the building sector were concerned about competition from other companies in the Common Market providing services in France but with lower labour costs. These French companies used the Permanent Committee for the Study of the Problems Created by the European Common Market in the Building Industry[71] to express their concerns. The Committee was dominated by the French: its headquarters were in Paris and its president, Henri Courbot, was a member of the board of the National Council of French Employers (*Conseil national du patronat français*, CNPF) and president of the French Union of Public Works Companies.[72] The Committee concentrated on preventing companies in the sectors of building and public works from operating under the regulations of their country of origin even when providing short-term services in other countries. The most important regulations in this sense were social security law and 'collective conventions on conditions of pay and duration of work.'[73] In France, social security contributions paid by employers on top of wages were high. Operating in France under the regulations of their country of origin could therefore give foreign companies a significant competitive advantage over French firms in terms of labour costs. The French government took up these demands and called in the Council for 'removing competitive distortions.'[74]

As the country in which a significant proportion of the provision of services would occur, France had influence in these matters. In line with French preferences, Community legislation provided that each state was free to impose national regulations on wages and working conditions to all paid workers on its territory, including in the case of short-term provisions of services. Yet as far as social security law was concerned, an opposition emerged between the French and the Germans. The German government wished to open up opportunities for German companies in the Common Market. Not paying French high social contributions to enjoy a competitive advantage in France was not the Germans' main concern. Having to adapt to foreign social security legislation would simply mean the sort of bureaucratic complexity that would deter most companies from providing services anywhere abroad. German delegates in the Council consequently declared themselves in favour of the greatest possible freedom.[75] This opposition led to a status quo, which satisfied German views. Regulation 1408/71 simply maintained the provisions of Regulation 3 on this matter. Social security law of the country of origin could be applied to any worker posted abroad by their company to provide services in the Community, on condition that the job did not last more than twelve months.[76]

France acted more successfully in tailoring the occupational status of Community workers to the interests of local workers in the field of recognition of qualifications. In the early 1970s the French government started developing conditions of qualifications for access to a number of professional occupations, but without recognising foreign qualifications. In December 1972, French Transport Minister Robert Galley tried to reassure workers and their representatives in Parliament to accept the freedom of movement for Community migrants in the sector of maritime navigation because 'the French government does not recognise, and does not intend to recognise, equivalence of foreign qualifications.' As a result, he stressed, such a freedom would not 'have great consequences in practice.'[77] In December 1973, French Transport Minister Yves Guéna decided to impose the requirement of a diploma for all sailors aboard French ships, whereas formerly qualifications had only been required for officers and sailors under the age of twenty-five.[78] Qualification requirements in sensitive sectors and the non-recognition of foreign qualifications reduced the opportunities of Community migrants and protected the local workforce.

France also used the national defence argument to differentiate the status of local and Community workers. The Commission proposed to abolish all nationality-based discriminations for Community workers. In the Council, the French wanted to exclude 'provisions on the protection of secrecy in companies dealing with military defence.'[79] This could guarantee privileged employment for French workers in French military industry. France's influence as a country of immigration steered its partners to accept its demand, registered on 15 October 1968 as an interpretative declaration of Regulation 1612/68.[80] In the sector of maritime navigation the national defence argument also required some members of crews to be French. As Gaullist Deputy from Finistère Gabriel Miossec stated in the National Assembly in December 1972:

> The radio officer may have to transmit and receive messages dealing with national defence; as regards the captain, he has an important role as a civil official and exercises extensive prerogatives in keeping order and observing any breaches of law committed on board.[81]

In a variety of ways, France thus managed to define a status for Community migrants that maintained the employment opportunities and wage levels of its own workforce in cases where immigrants might constitute a threat.

### Inference

The new regime was the result of a power play between France and West Germany. The tensions created by African immigration in France from the mid-1960s until the mid-1970s sparked a renewed preference for Community labour with its geographical proximity and economic similarity, making it less of a threat for local wage levels. Nevertheless, France arranged a status for Community migrants so that they could not affect French wages and employment in sensitive sectors. The regime thus guaranteed a control of immigrant workers.

## On population settlement

As migration flows within the Community matured, governments faced not only questions associated with labour immigration, but increasingly questions related to immigrants' settlement and families' immigration. I will show which were the instruments states used to regulate the settlement of migrants and how they used them in the context of the Community migration regime. I will also emphasise the prevalence of West Germany's immigration concerns in accounting for the new direction taken by the regime.

### Exporting social security benefits to maintain families in the countries of origin

In the migration regime within the Community, social security provisions became the main instruments used by states to regulate the extent of family reunification and permanent settlement. In 1967 there were 1 million Community migrant workers. With their families, they amounted to a population of 3 million.[82] Western European governments had different preferences regarding the migration of family members. Belgium and France still supported family reunification in immigration countries. The Belgian government welcomed family immigration in order to stem Wallonia's population decline. The Belgian Royal Order of 12 July 1965 set up a Consultative Council on Immigration. When the new body was inaugurated on 20 December 1965, Belgian Labour Minister Léon Servais declared: 'In addition to being essential for the development of our economic life, immigration also exerts a compensatory effect on our country's demographic situation.'[83] France shared Belgium's concerns. In July 1968, French Minister for Social Affairs Maurice Schumann stated in the Council of Ministers of the Community: 'The time has come to consider migrants from Community member states not as a supplementary workforce, but as a permanent population.'[84]

In contrast, the West German government considered that the immigration of workers' families would exacerbate the problems of infrastructure in Germany. By 1967, West Germany had become the most important country of Italian emigration, with 360,000 Italians working there as against only 340,000 in France.[85] In addition, flows went mostly towards West Germany; the importance of the Italian population in France was the result of previous inflows. Through Community regulations or bilateral agreements, the West German government granted Italian migrants privileged rights to export social security benefits. In 1969, while Italians accounted for 45 percent of migrant workers in West Germany, 90 percent of West German social security transfers abroad were paid to Italy.[86] The same year, West German social security was paying 88 percent of benefits for the families in Italy of Italian migrant workers in the Community.[87] This situation considerably enhanced West German influence over social security negotiations in the Community.

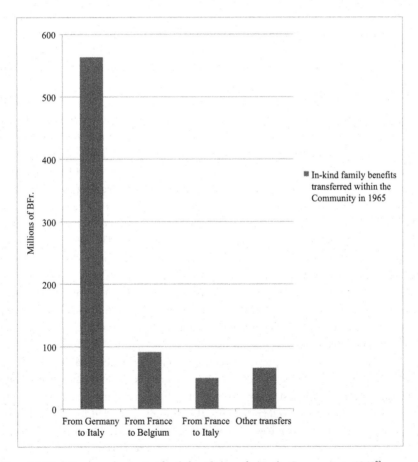

*Figure 3.2* West Germany dominating family benefits transfers in the Community in 1965[88]

German policy intended to encourage families to remain in Italy instead of seeking reunification in Germany. It was a success and the ratio of returnees to the Italian inflow for a given year peaked at 88 percent in the period 1964–1969.[89] In practice, Italian social security paid benefits to families and was later reimbursed by German social security. With these transfers the German government was interested in shaping the migration flow, not in helping Italian social security institutions. It was careful to prevent gains for these institutions. The Germans calculated the refunds to Italian social security precisely. Under Regulation 3 of 1958, the social security scheme of the country of employment refunded benefits for illness and pregnancy up to 75 percent of the amounts of these benefits in the country of residence. The welfare authorities in that latter country were responsible for supplementing up to 100 percent, which involved them in controlling the costs. In the 1969 Council negotiations for a new Regulation, the Commission was proposing a complete refund by the welfare scheme of the country of employment. Italy and the Netherlands – emigration countries within the Community – supported this proposal.[90] Italian delegates pointed out that it was unreasonable to make the welfare scheme of the country of residence responsible for a part of the benefits, because social contributions were paid entirely in the country of employment.[91]

In April 1969, German delegates estimated that a refund of 100 percent would exceed the real costs borne by the welfare system of the country of residence. It stressed that in the Italian case the standard amounts would be calculated on the basis of the national average cost, while 90 percent of Italian emigrants to West Germany came from the South of Italy, where the average cost of benefits was lower. According to German delegates, a refund of 75 percent of the standard amount covered 'without doubt' real costs.[92] German policy on refunds was not the result of any open-handedness towards the Italian social security scheme; it was quite simply driven by German immigration policy goals. The French were still anxious to limit payments abroad and supported the Germans and their position prevailed in the new Regulation 1408/71 of 14 June 1971, which provided for refunding 'as close as possible to actual expenditure.'[93] The interpretative declaration of this provision, reported in the Council minutes, stated: 'Taking into account all the elements requiring adjustment, a refund of 80 percent of the average cost is as close as possible to actual expenditures.'[94]

The main line of opposition between governments concerned family allowances. Belgium and France ran expansive demographic policies and their family allowances were the highest in the Community. Therefore, if they had to pay family allowances abroad, they preferred to pay the amounts provided for by the law of the family's country of residence.[95] This allowed them to reduce their payments abroad and encouraged family reunification on their territories. Furthermore, if some of their workers emigrated, their families had an interest in remaining in order to receive higher family allowances. By contrast, densely populated countries had lower levels of family allowances. Although willing to encourage the families of their immigrant workers to stay in their country of origin, they were not ready to pay allowances which were higher than those provided for in national law.

Regulation 3 had provided that the amount of exported family allowances would be the same as in the worker's country of employment, but no more than that of the family's country of residence. The Commission officially transmitted a proposal for a new social security regulation to the Council on 6 January 1966. This was a time of major crisis for the Community. France had stopped attending Council meetings after 30 June 1965, to protest against the slow implementation of the Common Agricultural Policy and the extension of majority voting within the Council.[96] In this tense period, called the 'empty chair' crisis, the Commission was trying to deal leniently with the French. Its proposal opted for French preferences and provided for the payment of family allowances at the rate of the family's country of residence. When the Council started negotiating this point in January 1969, well after the 'empty chair' crisis, immigration states with lower family allowances – Luxembourg, the Netherlands, and West Germany – rejected the Commission option. This would mean they would have to pay family allowances abroad that were higher than what could be covered by workers' contributions.[97] A solution without the agreement of West Germany, the main immigration country, which paid the bulk of family allowances abroad, was simply not feasible. The German and Dutch governments defended the principle of the country of employment to set the amount of family allowances, rather than that of the country of residence. In this, they had the support of the Italian government.[98]

In October 1969, the French defended the principle of the country of residence in the Council, arguing that the high level of family benefits in France was the product of a 'pro-natal policy.' France was ready to pay 'migrant workers and their families on its territory all the family benefits provided for by law,' but refused to pay benefits which would have a demographic impact in other countries.[99] French delegates did not explain that this pro-natal policy, dating back from the interwar period and reinforced after the Second World War, had been decided to stem France's population decline in comparison with Germany and Italy. When ministers met in the Council on 24–25 November 1969, the French minister found himself isolated.

The Dutch government then assumed the presidency of the Council and proposed to apply the principle of the country of employment to calculate the amount of exportable benefits. The Council agreed on this solution, along with a temporary exception for France, which would continue to apply the law of the country of residence. The agreement planned that the Council would 'before 1 January 1973' make a new examination of the entire problem 'to reach a uniform solution for all Community member states,' namely, to put an end to the exceptional solution for France.[100]

Besides family allowances, when it came to childbirth allowances, France was clear that it did not want to export them and entitlement was conditional on the child having French nationality.[101] The Council finally allowed states to exclude these benefits, as long as the exclusion was notified immediately in the agreement. West Germany, the Netherlands, and Italy did not make any exclusion, whereas Belgium and France excluded childbirth allowances from the scope of the agreement.[102] Meanwhile, bilateral measures between Belgium and France provided for reciprocal entitlement to childbirth allowances for Belgian and French nationals.

In this way France was able to save its demographic policy for a while and its application to Belgium. It aimed at increasing natality in France and the French-speaking part of Belgium, the home of most Belgian immigrants to France. Yet France had failed to promote the principle of the country of residence at the Community level when exporting family allowances. The French could continue to apply this principle, but with exceptional provisions, subject to re-examination. Even the French exclusion of childbirth allowances from the agreement was achieved as an exception. The migration regime within the Community thus tended towards exporting benefits under the law of the country of employment, in line with German preferences.

Yet the Council did not respect the deadline of 1 January 1973 for the abolition of the French exception on family allowances so as to reach a uniform solution. In July 1972, the Italians reminded the Commission that it was responsible for submitting a proposal to the Council to re-examine the exceptional solution for France. The Commission referred to the approaching enlargement of the Community to Britain, Ireland, Denmark, and, Norway, due to take effect on 1 January 1973. The Commission preferred not to respect the deadline and negotiate a solution with the new member states.[103]

## The potential for settlement

Under the Community migration regime, states used mostly positive financial incentives via social security benefits in order to shape migration flows. The use of other instruments gradually declined. The German administration demanded high fees for issuing residence permits as part of its policy to limit the permanent settlement of immigrants. As the risk of permanent immigration became higher in the mid-1960s, West German authorities sharply increased the price of permits. Regulation 38/64 and its accompanying Directive on residence authorised this practice. For the Directive on residence accompanying Regulation 1612/68, the Commission proposed that residence permits be issued free of charge or at a price not above that charged to nationals.[104] In the Council in March 1968, German delegates tried to oppose this plan. They emphasised that these revenues were important for the budgets of German local authorities. Soon after the downturn of 1967 and the decline in foreign employment in West Germany, France was worried by signs of a possible return to migratory protectionism in West Germany. Thus the French defended the Commission proposal to 'prevent member states [from hindering] the free movement of workers by demanding high taxes for issuing residence permits.'[105] Even though France was then ready to increase, in principle, the recruitment of Community workers, a turn to protectionism in West Germany would make the open migration regime of the Community untenable for France. To reassure other governments, German Secretary of State for Labour Ludwig Kattenstroth finally accepted the Commission proposal on 29 July 1968.[106]

Another instrument to limit immigrants' settlement was the condition of having 'normal housing' prior to family reunification. The Germans and particularly the Dutch had resorted heavily to this instrument. To justify it in European circles, the Dutch pointed to their housing shortage: building programmes, they said, could not keep pace with the increase of population.[107] In the Council session of 29 July 1968, French Minister for Social Affairs Maurice Schumann proposed to maintain the use of this instrument, under the condition that the requirement of normal housing should not lead to discrimination between national workers and Community workers.[108] This position prevailed.[109] Until then, equal access to housing for Community migrant workers in the Netherlands was conditional on one year's employment in the Netherlands and on holding a work contract for an additional year. Regulation 1612/68 abolished these conditions as a result of the agreement in the Council preventing discrimination.

In 1968, the definition of family members of employed workers was also extended. Regulation 1612/68 included children of a worker's spouse, under the age of twenty-one, who were not dependent on the latter, and basically recommended admitting all family members who had ties with the worker.[110]

When it came to immigrants' right to remain, the West German government had to demonstrate more openness than what suited a narrowly defined German interest. The Treaty of Rome had provided that, exceptionally, it was up to the Commission directly, and not the Council, to rule on the question of immigrants' right to remain.[111] This right applied to workers reaching retirement age or with a permanent invalidity arising from a work accident. To limit foreign settlement in West Germany, German diplomats in European circles initially wanted this right to be conditional on five years' uninterrupted residence and five years' paid activity at least in the previous ten years.[112] French experts considered it sufficient to demonstrate the reality of employment and two years' residence. This position matched the French national regulations at the time, which granted Community workers an automatically renewable residence permit valid for ten years after two years' residence. The Benelux states supported the German position. Belgium was interested in the settlement of young active immigrants but had a restrictive position on the right to remain and asked for four years' employment. In the case of retirement, the Netherlands and Luxemburg, like Germany, demanded five years' employment.[113]

The Commission did not need formal Council approval because it was empowered by the Treaty provisions. The fact that France did not support West Germany was enough for the Commission to establish a broad right to remain. The Commission dealt with this matter in Regulation 1251/70 of 29 June 1970. In the case of retirement, the right to remain in a country was dependent on having had a job there for the previous twelve months and having resided there continuously for over three years. In the case of permanent work invalidity, the right was acquired after having resided continuously in the country for over two years.[114] The West German government had to accept the direction taken by the Commission. First, it was unwilling to weaken the Community's legal order, which gave authority to the Commission.[115] This order was the basis of Western Europe's stability, which Germany promoted. Second, a limited right to remain, even though desirable from the point of view of German immigration preferences, would have caused serious diplomatic concerns. The forced expulsion of old or invalid people present on German soil for several years would have had potentially damaging diplomatic repercussions. Creating a stable and cohesive international order in Western Europe explained German support for the Community's open migration regime.

By the early 1970s, such a stable and cohesive international order in Western Europe had become an even stronger objective for France and West Germany. Pan-European negotiations with Eastern European countries started in 1973 in the Conference on Security and Cooperation in Europe (CSCE). That same year, the Arab-Israeli war triggered a major international crisis. To achieve successful negotiations with Arab and, even more importantly, with Communist governments, France and West Germany needed the cohesion and the support of Western Europe. This support was particularly important to arrange greater migratory opening towards Eastern Europe in those negotiations.[116] In this context, the Community's migration regime took on a more political outlook. The question of assimilating nationals of other member states to citizens of the host country emerged. At the Copenhagen Summit of 14 December 1973, the heads of state and governments of the nine members of the Community adopted a declaration on European identity. One year later in Paris, they decided to set up a working group 'to study the conditions and the deadline to attribute to citizens of the nine member states special rights as members of the Community.'[117] As France and West Germany were trying to enhance the international role of the Community to influence negotiations with the Soviet Union and Arab states, plans to grant political rights to migrants of other member states became part of the comprehensive plan for diplomatic cooperation and unity among the Nine.[118]

## Inference

The question of the permanent settlement of Community immigrants in destination countries caused frequent disagreements between France and West Germany on the exportation of social security benefits, the cost of residence permits, family reunification, and the right to remain. The disagreement over the exportation of family benefits set countries with a high population density (West Germany and the Netherlands) against countries with expansive demographic policies (France and Belgium). The West German position prevailed, with the application of the law of the country of employment to calculate family allowances, but France obtained a temporary exemption. Yet the West German government yielded to the requests of its partners on the formal obstacles to settlement. In so doing, the government demonstrated its commitment to support the open migration regime of the Community and to reinforce the cohesion of Community's member states. This had come to matter much more in the face of rapidly changing conditions in Eastern Europe and the Middle East.

# Closed independent occupations

In parallel, from the mid-1960s the gradual implementation of the provisions of the Treaty of Rome started to impinge on occupational groups which were more closed and protected than employed workers, and affected by the free movement of labour. Independent workers still accounted for a sizeable part of the workforce, including farmers, retail traders, and the professions. France remained the most likely country of immigration for these workers. In this section, I will show how these occupational groups managed to limit the establishment of foreigners.

## Opening up in agriculture

Opening up to establishment in agriculture took place despite the opposition between urbanised countries looking for outlets for their agricultural populations and France, which had the largest amount of cultivable land. French farmers feared that immigration would lead to higher land prices, increase agricultural production, and decrease agricultural prices. Mechanisation and land consolidation (*remembrement*) had already caused a difficult situation. The number of farms in France had collapsed and many farmers were looking for land. When consolidation was in full swing, from 40,000 to 50,000 farms disappeared in France each year. The total number of persons working in agriculture fell by more than 30 percent in the 1960s in France, from 4,189,000 in 1960 to 2,898,000 in 1970. At the end of the decade, 2,301,000 were farm managers and family associates, and 597,000 worked as paid farm labourers, so that most of the agricultural workforce consisted of independent workers and their families. In January 1966, a report by the European Parliament identified two risks when extending the right of establishment in agriculture: increases in land prices in the 'main host country,' France, and a 'massive increase in production' leading to falling prices for agricultural products.[119] The rapporteur, René Tomasini, was a Gaullist member of the French National Assembly from Normandy. The other report writer was Kléber Loustau, a socialist member of the French National Assembly from Sologne. Both echoed the concerns of French farmers.

In the other countries, many farmers were looking for land abroad. In 1970, there were still 2,406,000 people working in agriculture in West Germany and 3,683,000 in Italy.[120] In the mid-1960s, Community nationals, mainly Belgians, acquired an average of around 15,000 hectares of agricultural land a year in France.[121] They often received financial aid from their governments to resettle abroad, which was likely to cause an increase in land prices in France. In West Germany, the society for establishment abroad (*Auslandsiedlungsgesellschaft*), helped finance the emigration of German farmers.[122] A German directive of 1 October 1964 still planned budgetary resources for the Minister of Agriculture to promote emigration.[123] The *Istituto di crediti per il lavoro italiano all'estero* in Italy[124] and the *Rijkskredietgarantieregeling* in the Netherlands[125] had similar functions. In April 1967, French delegates in the Council expressed concerns about the impact of such credits on land prices.[126] In March 1968, German and Dutch delegates agreed to abolish these credits.[127]

The abolition of the credits was supposed to be compensated by access to credit institutions in the destination country, on an equal footing with local farmers. Indeed, discrimination based on nationality had to be eliminated in line with the provisions of the Treaty of Rome. The Council negotiated a directive on the access to credit for farmers from other member states, which it finally adopted in spring 1968. As French delegates in the Council alerted, 'in [French] rural circles,' this negotiation aroused 'some apprehension motivated basically by the financial consequences that [the] entry into force [of such measures] would have for the mutual funds whose resources [were] already considered insufficient.'[128] These reactions did not bode well for the effective application of the directive and equal access for immigrant farmers to agricultural credit. In addition, until the mid-1960s, French nationality was required to be a director, representative, or auditor of an agricultural cooperative company.[129] It was also required for the advantageous loans granted to young farmers setting up their first agricultural venture.[130] Such discrimination had to be eliminated with the gradual implementation of the Treaty of Rome, but it meant that the agricultural sector in France was still a very national one, in which foreigners were hardly represented.

In European circles, the French demanded a safeguard to prevent foreign establishment in agriculture during periods of adversity. In October 1969, in the

Economic and Social Committee of the Community, Henri Canonge raised this point. As Secretary General of the *Confédération nationale de la mutualité, de la coopération et du crédit agricole* (National Confederation of Mutual Funds, Cooperation and Agricultural Credit), he represented French agricultural interests. French trade unionist Maurice Bouladoux and Vice President of the *Centre national des jeunes agriculteurs* (National Centre for Young Farmers) Hilaire Flandre also backed his point. They warned that even in the absence of Community provisions, measures to safeguard farmers would be applied in practice and that it was worth 'planning an appropriate Community procedure rather than risking that at some point the Directive [would] not be respected by a member state.'[131] The French then threatened that the agreement would not be applied in practice.

That demand for a safeguard against the right of establishment in agriculture failed. The French government gave it up, because it was ready to find an agreement with its partners in agriculture. The Common Agricultural Policy had turned out to be the most important item of expenditure in the Community budget and it benefited the French agricultural sector enormously.[132] The remarks of French agricultural representatives simply augured ill for the non-discriminatory application of the right to establishment in agriculture in France. Despite this uncertainty, the sector was one of the independent occupations that opened up the most thanks to Community measures.

## An intermediary situation in the retail trade

As far as the migration of retail traders was concerned, protectionist pressures in France and the inability of the West German economy to stabilise an open migration regime in the sector resulted in a contrasted situation. On 15 October 1968, the Council adopted Directive 68/363 on the right of establishment in the retail trade, but this piece of legislation did not apply to all groups. Tobacconists were the first to raise objections. Within the Council, French and Italian delegates highlighted the public monopoly for this occupation in their countries. In France, tobacconists carried out administrative duties. They were responsible for collecting the special tax on cars by selling tax stickers to the public. They also sold tax stamps, and acted as post offices in rural areas. French delegates put forward the provisions of Article 55 of the Treaty of Rome, which exempted activities that involved 'exercising official authority' from the right of establishment.[133] As a result, the right of establishment, negotiated in 1968, did not apply to tobacconists throughout the Community.[134]

Itinerant traders, hawkers, and pedlars could not migrate freely within the Community either.[135] In their case, German protectionist concerns were decisive. The German federal law organising small crafts allowed the authorities to refuse the permit of itinerant retail trader to any person unable to provide proof of their place of domicile or residence. As the French pointed out in the Council in

May 1972, this included 'nomads, gypsies, Romany people without a well-defined economic trade.'[136] Most gypsies and nomads in Western Europe lived in France: around 145,000, against 30,000 in West Germany in 1965.[137] These nomad populations were often of French nationality and the West German government was willing to keep them out of German territory. Beyond the grounds of public order highlighted by German delegates in the Council in May and June 1972, it also had the effect of eliminating competition from cut-price retail traders.

Generally speaking, when groups succeeded in putting forward a higher public interest associated with their occupation, they managed to limit foreign establishment. A public health requirement thus protected optical, acoustic, and orthopaedic professions in France, Italy, and Belgium.[138] In the Council, German, Dutch, and Luxembourg delegates were unsuccessful in their requests for the recognition of diplomas and the coordination of conditions of entry to these occupations.[139] In occupations where rules differed from one country to another, transitional measures made establishment in another country conditional on the exercise of the activity for a set duration. These transitional measures were supposed to disappear once the professions had been coordinated.[140] Yet member states opposed the Commission's call to carry out this coordination before 1 January 1970 – the deadline set in the Treaty of Rome to implement all its provisions. Member states even rejected any deadline for the abolition of transitional measures.[141] Small retailers, hoteliers, and caterers in immigration countries were thus able to limit foreign competition by postponing *sine die* the application of the right to establishment.

The right to set up as an independent worker turned out to be more useful for migrants who had first worked as employees in the destination country than for independent migrant workers. This right opened up opportunities for upward social mobility by setting up their own businesses. This was the effect of the first directives in the small craft sector adopted in the first half of the 1960s. In the mid-1960s, the most rooted foreign population from other member countries resided in France. The Council Directive of 7 July 1964 on establishment in the small craft sector was followed by a 38 percent increase in the number of permits granted to Community nationals, with 1,517 permits issued in 1965. These were issued in the main regions of Italian immigration: the Nice area and the rest of Provence, the Greater Paris area, Rhône-Alpes, Lorraine, and the North.[142] Half the foreign craftsmen or tradesmen from the Community working in France were in the building sector.[143]

In the years that followed, France was slow to apply the subsequent directives on the right of establishment as independent workers. This was the main country where immigrants would use this right and the number of potential beneficiaries created difficulties. In spring 1968, the French government still had not abolished the requirement for a special identity card for Community traders. The Germans complained about this situation in the Council in June 1968.[144] The Commission considered starting infringement proceedings against France.[145] This situation shows that when the French had to provide the bulk of professional opportunities for Community migrants, the regime hardly opened up. The strongest resistance to establishment, however, came from the professions.

## Closed professions

The professions included lawyers, insurance brokers, doctors, chemists, veterinarians, and technical professions such as engineers and architects. The provisions of the Treaty of Rome implied that these independent workers should also be able to migrate and set up their business in other Community countries. The national regulations of these professions were often technical, making negotiations among member states difficult. To start negotiations, the Council decided to focus first on the case of architects. In June 1967, a note from the Economic and Social Committee referred to architects as a 'test case.'[146] In January 1970, Italian delegates in the Council considered the directives on architects as the 'first group of directives to deal with the professions,' which would set a 'precedent . . . valid for all future directives.'[147] This casuistic approach consisted in negotiating a single case in depth in order to discover general principles that could be applied to other professions. With 269,000 doctors in the Community, the medical profession also included large numbers of people,[149] but the issue was too complex to be used as a basis for negotiations. Given the importance of the building sector, the economic stakes were high in the architects' profession. Finally, the architects' profession did not involve the exercise of public authority, unlike the profession of lawyers.[148] The profession included large numbers of people across the Community. This is why negotiations started with architects.

In Belgium, France, and Italy, there was an Association of Architects (*Ordre des architectes*), where admission was necessary to take up this activity. Admission was based on qualifications certified exclusively by university training.[150] In the Netherlands and West Germany, an alternative way to access the profession had developed following the destruction at the end of the war and the subsequent housing shortage. Technical schools, where the admission did not require university entry level, offered three years' training in architecture, leading to the exercise of the profession.[151] These were the *Voortgezet Bijzonder Onderwijs* (VBO) schools in the Netherlands and the *Fachhochschulen* in West Germany.[152] In 1973 Germany had 120,000 engineers in architecture from these schools, against 25,000 university-trained architects.[153] Eliminating this alternative way to access the profession of architect in order to coordinate national regulations within the Community would have led to a sharp drop in the number of architects, an increase in construction costs, and a worsening of the housing shortage in West Germany and the Netherlands.[154] In addition, in these countries, engineers in architecture represented an important interest group, eager to exploit the new opportunities offered by the right of establishment in the Community.

In Belgium, France, and Italy, recognising German and Dutch architects trained in technical schools created serious concern.[155] In January 1968, the Italian member of the Economic and Social Committee Virgilio Dagnino argued that

> instead of spending four or five years at the university, students [would prefer] to attend a technical school in another member state where they [could] obtain a technical qualification in architecture; then, . . . they [would return] to their own country, to practice the profession of architect.[156]

In this way students would bypass university training and choose the easier access route into the profession. This would undermine the barriers to entry in the profession, giving rise to an increase in the number of architects and, consequently, to a drop in their income and status.

Two groups of countries ended up defending opposing views in European circles. On the one hand, Belgium, France, and Italy, and on the other hand, West Germany and the Netherlands. In January 1968, the German member of the Economic and Social Committee Maria Weber, director of the department of professional training at the DGB, emphasised that in other countries university-trained architects had repeatedly managed to increase the duration of training required to join the profession, to five years in Italy and seven in Belgium and France.[157] At a time when a growing number of young people attended universities, such restrictive regulations limited the number of new architects and preserved the income and status of those already established.

At this point a Liaison Committee of Architects of the Common Market emerged to exert pressure on the negotiations.[158] It was dominated by French architects: its delegate general was the French architect Jacques Barge, and the secretariat of the Committee was entrusted to the *Conseil supérieur de l'ordre des architectes* in Paris (the French Association of Architects). It consisted exclusively of university-trained architects from all the Community countries. In October 1969, they argued that the Committee defended high-quality architecture and pointed out the public interest of architecture to the president of the Commission, claiming that 'architectural forms . . . [marked] a country for centuries.'[159] By 1971, the Council was trying to find an equivalence to allow German and Dutch engineers in architecture to benefit from the right of establishment. At its meeting in Brussels on 29 January 1972, the Liaison Committee of Architects and all its national delegations unanimously voted a motion condemning the turn taken by the negotiations in the Council. The signatories were apprehensive of any opening up of the domain of architecture 'to other professional categories.'[160] French delegates in the Council took up this position, which led to a halt in Council negotiations in early 1972.

## The Court's intervention

Yet Article 52 of the Treaty of Rome had provided that 'restrictions on the freedom of establishment of nationals of a Member State in the territory of another Member State [should] be abolished by progressive stages in the course of the transitional period,' which had expired on 31 December 1969. The lack of results in Council negotiations created legal uncertainty.

In 1974, the Court of Justice of the Community had to rule on a case dealing with one of the most closed professions: lawyers. In Belgium, the law of 25 October 1919 had reserved the exercise of the profession of lawyer to persons of Belgian nationality. This was a way to prevent German lawyers from defending the German state in cases related to the German occupation during the First World War.[161] Dutch national Jean Reyners obtained his Doctor of Law degree in Belgium in 1957. In 1970, he requested to be admitted to the Belgian bar, but the Belgian Council of State rejected the request on the ground of his nationality. Reyners filed a complaint on the basis of Article 52 of the Treaty. The Belgian Council of State asked the Court of Justice of the Communities whether Article 52 could be applied directly since the end of the transitional period, and whether Article 55 of the Treaty, which excluded activities relating to the exercise of public authority from the right of establishment, applied to the profession of lawyer.[162] The Belgian Association of Lawyers took sides in the case, considering that Article 55 excluded the profession of lawyer from the right of establishment.[163]

The German government took the opposite view. As companies were increasingly internationalising their activities, German lawyers in other countries were strategic to facilitate the expansion of German companies. They could advise them best on the differences between the German legal system and the local legal system. In its opinion on the Reyners case, the German government highlighted this growing internationalisation and concluded: 'In the future [companies] will have to make greater use of the assistance of lawyers from other member states.'[164] As a result, the German government supported the direct application of Article 52 since the end of the transitional period, and argued that Article 55 only related to the activities of lawyers actually participating in the exercise of public authority, and not to the entire profession.[165]

In its ruling on 21 June 1974, the Court found that Article 52 was directly applicable since the end of the transitional period. As regards Article 55, the Court considered that it only referred to those parts of an occupation actually participating in the exercise of public authority. When these parts were detachable from the rest of the activity, the entire occupation could not be excluded from the right of establishment.[166] The Court's judgment matched not only German views at the time of the case, but also the agreement during the negotiation of the Treaty. This agreement already emanated from the strategy of the German government to eliminate discrimination based on nationality in Western Europe, in order to favour the expansion of German companies in neighbouring markets.[167]

The Court's ruling was highly influential in speeding up the application of the Treaty provisions. From then on, Community retail traders or independent workers were no longer required to carry special permits. Yet member states could continue to insist on the differences in training and qualifications in order to refuse the right of establishment. The mutual recognition of qualifications and the coordination of entry conditions and professional practices were still necessary.[168] As Italian jurist Alberto Trabucchi stressed at the time, the Court's clarifications were, above all, useful for the children of migrant workers who received training in the immigration country without having its nationality and who tried to be self-employed.[169]

### Inference

By the mid-1970s, the right of establishment was still limited, as a result of frequent oppositions between France, often supported by Belgium and Luxembourg, and West Germany, often supported by the Netherlands. The fact that migratory flows of independent workers were not overwhelmingly directed towards West Germany but were mostly directed towards France limited the capacity of the West German government to support the open migration regime it had successfully developed for wage-earners. French farmers threatened, in practice, not to let Community farmers join mutual credit unions. Retail traders managed to avoid foreign competition when they could refer to a public monopoly or a higher public interest. French architects and Belgian lawyers lobbied for the closure of professions by citing different training requirements between member countries. The Court's clarification in *Reyners v. Belgian State* in June 1974 was instrumental in abolishing the specific authorisations required for foreigners in the case of Community nationals. Nevertheless, this ruling did not question the obstacles to the right of establishment related to the recognition of qualifications and the coordination of conditions of access and exercise.

## Ending regime spread

During this period the area where the divergences between France, West Germany, and from then on, Britain reached a peak was on the question of migrants from outside the Community. In this section, I will show that the open migration regime stopped spreading beyond the limits of the Community. Each of the three big states in the Community favoured openness towards different regions, but none of them, not even West Germany, had the ability to stabilise an open migration regime with any of these regions. The preferences of major countries when it came to immigration from outside the Community, I will explain, were incompatible, as their resources were insufficient.

## Facilitating the recruitment of workers

In the first place, immigration states within the Community were able to agree on more openness towards external migrants by weakening the Community priority. In October 1967, Belgian metallurgist Georges Velter argued in the Economic and Social Committee that such a priority should not hinder the recruitment of foreign workers, but should only improve the movement of Community workers.[170] In 1968, the Germans and the French agreed on this principle in the Council.[171] The French were anxious not to create obstacles to the recruitment of seasonal labour for the grape harvest.[172] In the first nine months of 1967, of the 96,577 seasonal labourers in the Community, 95,643 were in France, of which 92,076 worked in agriculture. A total of 92,034 out of the 96,577 came from outside the Community.[173] Regulation 1612/68 still included a Community priority, which provided for the exchange of job offers before approaching workers from third countries. But this legislation allowed exceptions for specialised workers, teams of seasonal workers, and workers from border regions.[174] This last exception favoured the recruitment of Austrians in West Germany and Spaniards in France.

Italian workers were the main losers with this less rigid Community priority. In a memorandum of 24 June 1971, the Italian government expressed concern that in 1969 and 1970 the proportion of Italians among immigrant workers in the Community had collapsed to 17 percent.[175] Italian delegates in the Council regretted that immigration states were not even applying the elements of Community priority in Regulation 1612/68. They called for employment services in immigration states to assist Italian workers, and for member states and the Commission to consider ways to prioritise member-state nationals for available jobs in the Community.[176] The Italian government tried to help Italian workers obtain in priority job opportunities in North-West Europe. Yet immigration states had emphasised the costs associated with Italian requests. As early as July 1970 in the Council, Labour and Employment Ministers from Belgium and France, Louis Major and Joseph Fontanet, had stressed the higher cost of finding Italian workers. Major had declared that it was 'almost impossible [to] find' Italian workers to fill available jobs.[177] As Italian emigrants were fewer and as living standards in Italy increased, it became increasingly costly for employers in immigration countries to find Italian workers. The Community priority remained weak as a consequence. Immigration states were ready not to create Community restrictions for their employers hiring third-country workers, but, as I will now turn to explain, they could not agree on further openness towards any precise third countries.

## The countries of emigration to West Germany

This state of affairs even applied to countries of emigration to West Germany, which had previously received prospects of inclusion in the Community's open migration regime. This had happened for Greece with the Athens Agreement of 1961. Furthermore, bilateral agreements linked Greece with the countries of North-West Europe. By 1965, the number of Greek workers employed in the Community had risen to 200,000.[178] Bilateral agreements made no provision for illness and family benefits for family members who had remained in Greece and for the export of cash benefits to workers returning to Greece.[179] For the period 1966–1970, the Greek government decided on a programme of economic development based on short-term emigration movements towards industrialised countries. The plan was to arrange cash remittances and the return of expertise for industrialisation in Greece. Nevertheless, far from more migratory cooperation with the Community, the military *coup d'état* in April 1967 led to the suspension of the Association Agreement, challenging Greek plans for development through emigration.

Like Greece, Turkey had signed an Association Agreement with the Community in Ankara in 1963 and, like the Greek government, the Turkish government was ready to foster emigration to promote economic development. In 1965, Turkey's population reached 31 million, growing by 800,000 annually, at a rate of almost 3 percent. Economic growth could not absorb demographic growth. The number of unemployed or underemployed workers in Turkey, which approached 1.5 million in 1962, was bound to increase. To negotiate the implementation of the Ankara Agreement, the Community and Turkey set up an Association Council, assisted by an Association Committee. In the July 1965 meeting of the Association Council, Turkish ambassador Oğuz Gökmen contended his country's 'basic objective [was to] export Turkish manpower.'[180] This was to be both 'the start of the realisation of Turkey's social integration within the Community,' and 'a positive factor in the balance of payments.' He expected that the number of Turkish workers abroad would reach 500,000 in 1972. In 1965, they were only 160,000, of whom three-quarters worked in West Germany.[181] In December 1965, Turkish delegates to the Association Committee anticipated a total of USD 1,584 million in remittances over the period ending in 1972.[182]

To back these demands, the Turks pointed to the geopolitical importance of Turkey for Western Europe. In September 1965, at the request of Turkish representatives, the Consultative Assembly of the Council of Europe adopted a recommendation stressing Turkey's geopolitical importance, at the 'crossroads' of a 'very sensitive region,' and pressed 'member governments to pay particular attention to the problems of development in Turkey.'[183] In February 1966, the Commission of the Community supported Turkish plans. It considered that the magnitude of unemployment and underemployment in Turkey could well upset 'economic and social equilibrium' and threaten 'the national political equilibrium, along with an international political equilibrium.'[184]

On 12 September 1963, an exchange of letters between Turkey and the Community had complemented the Ankara Agreement. Referring to the provisions of the agreement on migration, this exchange of letters had planned a rapid study of labour problems in Turkey.[185] In July 1965, anxious to preserve the privileged access of Italian workers to the West German labour market, Italian Foreign Affairs Minister Amintore Fanfani opposed Turkish demands in the Association Council to start negotiations on migration issues immediately.

Initially, the West German government was ready to reassure its partners. German Secretary of State in the Ministry for Foreign Affairs Rolf Otto Lahr was aware of Turkey's geopolitical importance. He replied to Fanfani that there were then 1.3 million foreign workers in West Germany, 'among whom the nationals of one of the six Community member states naturally occupy, and rightly so, the first place.' After alluding thus to the importance of Italian immigration in West Germany, he went on to stress that the West German economy still had hundreds of thousands of vacant jobs and that its goal was to increase the number of foreign workers. He concluded: 'Under these conditions, the problem presented by the Turkish delegation should not cause major difficulties and . . . the interests of Turkey could certainly be accommodated to a certain degree by the Community without this damaging anyone.' West Germany began its rapprochement with Turkey with a bilateral agreement that came into effect on 1 May 1966. It guaranteed equal treatment for Turkish and German workers in and outside West Germany for sickness insurance, accident insurance, and pension insurance: the benefits could be transferred abroad and the rights acquired would be maintained abroad.[186]

Yet when the Community had to take a position on the Turkish request to immediately start negotiations on migration issues, the cyclical downturn of 1966 and 1967 had already hit the West German labour market. In May 1967, Turkish delegates in the Association Committee expressed their concern about the drop in Turkish emigration to the Community.[187] Community delegates informed Turkey that 'on the basis of the provisions of the Agreement then applicable it [did] not appear possible to take any concrete measures' for Turkish immigration.[188] The position of the Community thus referred only to the provisions of the Agreement and not to the exchange of letters, which thus did not lead to measures facilitating Turkish immigration to the Community.

With demographic pressure in Turkey and tension on the French labour market, even the momentum of Germany's economic recovery in the late 1960s could only give Turkey a minimal prospect of progress towards freer immigration to the Community. After coming into effect on 1 December 1964, the Ankara Agreement provided for a five-year preparatory phase, which could be extended. With a one-year delay, on 23 November 1970, Turkey and the Community signed the

Additional Protocol. It put an end to the preparatory phase and opened the transitional phase, during which the provisions of the agreement were to come into effect. The transitional phase was not supposed to exceed twelve years, but in the Additional Protocol the Community arranged that the free movement of workers with Turkey would be realised between the end of the twelfth year and the end of the twenty-second year after the coming into force of the Ankara Agreement, that is possibly four years after the normal end of the transitional period.[189] Article 36 of the Additional Protocol nevertheless gave Turkey a clear prospect of inclusion: 'The free movement of workers between the member states of the Community and Turkey will be realised progressively in accordance with the principles set out in Article 12 of the Association Agreement.'[190] Article 39 of the Additional Protocol also dealt with social security measures, but only for Turkish workers migrating between the territories of the member countries of the Community, and not between Turkey and the Community.

Admittedly the strength of the West German demand for labour helped achieve Turkish emigration goals: the number of Turkish workers in the Community reached 450,000 in early 1971. Most of them migrated under bilateral agreements between West Germany and Turkey.[191] But migration policies in North-West Europe were gradually starting to move away from their liberal attitude of the previous decade in the face of rising immigration from less-developed countries.[192] In March 1971, the Joint Parliamentary Commission between the Community and Turkey recommended that Turkey 'put an end to the activity of unscrupulous traffickers' who brought Turkish migrants into the Community 'as fake tourists . . . thwarting the prescribed immigration procedures.'[193] British accession to the Community did not favour Turkish demands either. During a debate in the House of Lords in October 1971, David Hennessy, Baron Windlesham, Minister of State at the Home Office, spoke out against granting freedom of movement for Greek and Turkish workers 'as long as economic conditions in Turkey and Greece do not get any closer to those in EEC countries.'[194] The opening up of the migration regime between the Community and countries of emigration towards West Germany was thus minimal during this period. The same was true for migrants from former British and French colonies.

## The migrants from former colonies

In April 1968, the French requested in the Council that French Overseas *départements* (DOM) finally be included in the scope of Regulation 1612/68. Article 227 of the Treaty had initially provided for the inclusion of these territories in the free movement of workers scheme by 31 December 1959. The Italians expressed their opposition, arguing that the deadline in Article 227 meant that the inclusion could no longer be arranged. Following decolonisation, French Overseas Departments at that time only included Guadeloupe, Martinique, French Guiana, and Réunion. The populations living there had full French nationality. For these reasons, the other partners of France accepted the request.[195] On 15 October 1968, Decision 68/359 of the Council applied Articles 48 and 49 of the Treaty to the DOM, thus providing for the free movement of workers.[196] As far as the social security of migrant workers provided for in Article 51 of the Treaty was concerned, the first Community regulation on this matter (Regulation 3) had already integrated French from the DOM in 1958. Because the DOM then also included Algeria, Regulation 109/65 of 30 June 1965 abolished the mention of Algeria in Regulation 3. Finally, for the sake of clarity, Decision 71/238 of the Council on 14 June 1971 repeated that the DOM benefited from Article 51.[197]

As far as the relations with the former French colonies in West Africa were concerned, the Yaoundé Convention of 1963 had established an unequal migratory agreement. Limited to the right of establishment, the agreement authorised the Europeans to select the sectors in which they wished to apply this right.[198] Senegal tried to extend the agreement to define the sectors of application. The Senegalese government wanted a general abolition of visas for Senegalese nationals in Europe. The government abolished visas for all Community nationals on the basis of Article 29 of the Convention and demanded reciprocity. Following the Yaoundé Convention, an Association Council and an Association Committee had been created for the negotiations between the Community and the Associated African and Malagasy States (AAMS). As German and Italian business interests in Africa were increasing, German and Italian delegates to the AAMS Council declared themselves ready in September 1965 to interpret the right of establishment in Article 29 as including visas.[199] Their capacity to select the sectors in which the right of establishment of the Yaoundé Convention would be applied meant that they could in any case oppose the immigration of AAMS nationals despite this abolition. The Benelux states, however, opposed it. The Senegalese ambassador in Brussels, Médoune Fall, brought the matter to the AAMS Association Committee in 1967 and deplored Belgium's stance. Belgium's permanent representative to the Community, Joseph van der Meulen, stressed that the Yaoundé Convention had not 'expressly bound the signatory states to adopt a determined attitude on the issue of visas.'[200] Given the strong links between France and Senegal, the French insisted that the Belgian government find a solution. Finally, in March 1968, the Belgian representative in the Association Committee announced the abolition of visas for Senegalese nationals for stays of less than three months in Belgium, as of 1 April 1968.[201] Yet this decision did not change the meaning to be attached to the provisions of the Yaoundé Convention.

On the other hand, the Senegalese government wanted to keep in sensitive sectors restrictions on the establishment of Community nationals, except French nationals. In the Council of the Community, the Italians complained to their partners about a case in which Senegalese authorities refused an Italian national permission to open a bar in Dakar, while French nationals normally received licences in this economic sector.[202] Such practices ran counter to the provisions of Article 29 and Senegal did not manage to obtain changes to the Yaoundé Convention to allow them. Generally speaking, Senegal, albeit supported by France, did not manage to change the asymmetric migration arrangements between African countries and the Community.

Besides the right of establishment of the Yaoundé Convention, Article 135 of the Treaty of Rome was intended to create opportunities in Europe for migrants from West Africa, but it went unheeded. Restrictions also prevailed with the Maghreb countries. As cooperation agreements were under negotiation with these countries, the Council decided in May 1972 that these agreements 'should not contain any measures planning the free access of nationals of [these] countries to the Community labour market [or even] the free movement of these workers within the Community.'[203] The door of the Community remained closed for African immigrants and the rising tension on the French labour market largely contributed to this outcome.

British accession to the Community did not modify this trend. British nationality was reformed in parallel to accession negotiations in the sense of a closure to immigration from the colonies. The 1968 Commonwealth Immigrants Act and the 1971 Immigration Act limited the right of entry to Britain for British subjects.[204] People with British nationality with a right of abode in Britain were referred to as 'patrials.' After 1971 patrials included (a) persons who had acquired British nationality by birth, adoption, naturalisation, or registration in Britain; (b) the children or grandchildren of persons who had acquired British nationality for the reasons cited under a); and (c) British nationals who had been admitted to settle in Britain and who had lived there regularly for an uninterrupted period of five years.[205] Immigration to Britain for British nationals who were not patrials was regulated with quotas.[206] The definition of patrials allowed to prevent the greater part of potential migrants from former British colonies or independent Commonwealth states from entering Britain as immigrants.

These restrictions happened in parellel to requests by other European states in the context of the negotiations for British membership of the Community. In November 1971, in discussions within the Council, Dutch delegates called for the right to free movement to be limited to British nationals born in Britain. As the German Basic Law provided for a broad definition of 'national,' including East Germans, German delegates were slightly more open and regarded the evolution of British nationality law positively. They accepted to extend the right to free movement to all patrials and would even consider the incorporation of those British nationals outside Britain included in the annual quota of 13,600 set for immigration to Britain from the colonies. The French were less inclined to ask Britain for restrictions. France was initially looking for partners to open the doors of the Community to immigrants from its former colonies. Consequently French delegates to the Council stated that each state should be free to define its own nationals.[207] Yet, faced with the failure to opening up the Community to migrants from former French colonies, and with worsening tension on the French labour market, France finally sided with the German and Dutch position and called on Britain to exclude migrants from colonies from the free movement of workers in the Community.[208] On 3 December 1971, British delegates in the accession negotiations made a Declaration on British nationality that limited the definition of the term 'national,' in Community treaties and related acts, to patrials.[209] This declaration was annexed to the accession treaty of 22 January 1972.[210]

### Inference

From this period onwards the European migration regime stood out for the way it differentiated between Community and non-Community migrants and the absence of common rules to deal with the latter. Despite the goals of Germany, France, and Britain to incorporate migrants from certain regions to promote their security and influence, the geographical incompatibility between these goals brought negotiations to an impasse. The lack of openness at the Community level led to restrictive immigration policies at the national level in most Western European countries, as immigration from surrounding less-developed countries started to increase.

## Synopsis

From 1965 to 1973, growing divergence between the main countries of immigration influenced the evolution of the European migration regime. France was ready to reorient its immigration policies to favour Community immigration, but regularly disagreed with West Germany regarding the status of immigrant workers, their social security rights, and, above all, the right of establishment for independent workers. This opposition was the outcome of the different tensions triggered by immigration on French and German labour markets, of differences of demographic pressure in the two countries, and of the importance of organised independent professions in France. In relations with countries outside the Community, the regional preferences of the main member states of immigration differed due to their colonial history and geographical positions. Even the expansion of the German labour market was not enough to get other member states to accept migratory opening with Turkey. All in all, German preferences had continued to prevail during this period due to Germany's economic and financial resources, leading gradually to a more open migration regime in Western Europe.

# 4

# A PROTECTIONIST STATUS QUO, 1973–1984

Starting in 1973, the drop in the demand for labour and demographic decline in West Germany led to a redefinition of West German preferences and an overall absence of change in the previously established regime. From 1973–1974 to around 1984, the migration regime within the Community remained stable. Community migrants did not figure much in public policies for workers, and negotiations on migration of populations came to a halt. In contrast, immigration states in Western Europe severely restricted inflows from outside the Community. Developments in Community cooperation were limited to trying to achieve closure to migrants from outside the Community. Only the expansion of the Community migration regime to the Mediterranean countries of Western Europe mitigated this closure. Greece, Spain, and Portugal successively joined the European Economic Community.

## A stop to immigration and selective enlargement

The first break with the previous period was the closure, decided at the national level, to immigration from outside the Community. This did not call Community rules into question. As a result, the share of Community migrants among all migrants within the Community increased in the 1970s. This shift constituted the context of the accession negotiations to the Community migration regime of Greece, Turkey, Spain, and Portugal. In this section I will illustrate the relations between economic and geopolitical interests in the treatment of migratory issues during accession negotiations.

### National closures to immigration

In West Germany, the decline in the demand for goods and services led to a decline in the demand for labour. In this situation, immigration might have created a drop in wages or higher unemployment. In September 1973, the German government increased the tax paid by employers hiring foreign labour. In November, it completely halted immigration from outside the Community.[1] From 1 April 1975 onwards, it limited the access of foreigners to 'overloaded areas' (*überlastete Siedlungsgebiete*), which embraced twenty-four cities and districts, including Frankfurt, Mannheim, Stuttgart, and Munich.[2] In the three years following September 1973, the number of foreign workers in West Germany fell by 500,000, or 20 percent, to 2.1 million.[3] By the end of December 1981, it had further declined to 1.8 million.

In Britain, the 1971 Immigration Act meant that the government stopped issuing work permits to unskilled or partially skilled workers from outside the Community, except those working in hotels and livestock farming.[4] In France too, the government restricted immigration. On 5 July 1974, a memorandum from the Secretary of State for Immigrant workers, André Postel-Vinay, suspended the immigration of

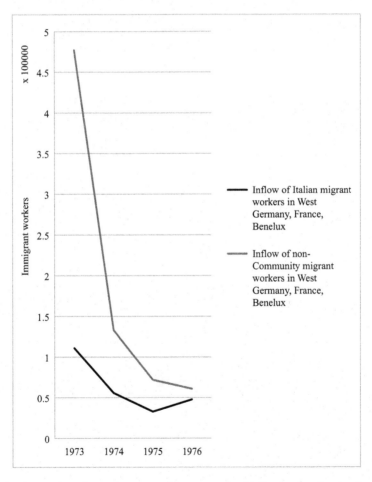

*Figure 4.1* Convergence of extra-Community immigration with intra-Community migration after 1973[5]

workers for an unspecified period. On 9 July, a memorandum put a cap on family immigration. On 9 August, an additional memorandum specified that the provisions of the memorandum of 9 July also applied to 'families of Algerian workers and nationals of countries in sub-Saharan Africa, formerly under French rule.'[6]

These measures only affected migrants from outside the Community. As a result, the number of immigrants from Mediterranean Europe, apart from Italy, collapsed and there was a convergence between the volume of migration flows within the Community and from outside the Community after 1973 (see Figure 4.1).

The share of Italian immigration in Western Europe increased, from 17 percent in the early 1970s to 45 percent in 1980.[7] This mostly resulted from the security the Community's open migration regime created for Italian emigration. The main country of Italian immigration outside the Community, Switzerland, applied stricter policies after 1973, as it was not bound by the Community regime. In 1977, the population of Italian workers in the Community reached 620,000, compared to 235,000 in Switzerland.[8]

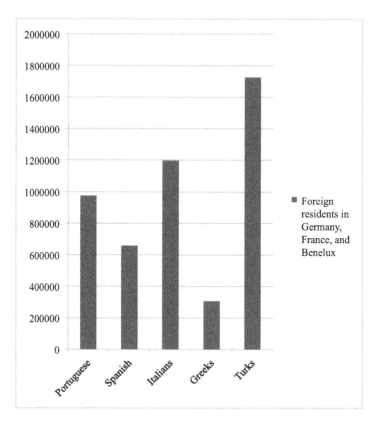

*Figure 4.2* Foreign residents from Mediterranean Europe in Germany, France, and Benelux in 1980[9]

In contrast, migrant workers from outside the Community accounted for the bulk of the closure. In 1973, still, 31,479 Portuguese workers entered West Germany and 20,692 entered France, out of a total Portuguese emigration of 79,517. By 1976, the legal immigration of Portuguese workers had fallen to 1,787 to France and to fewer than 800 to West Germany.[10] There were 46,234 Spanish entries to West Germany in 1973, and 13,140 to France. There were only 5,049 to West Germany in 1979 and 655 to France in 1980. The number of Spanish residents in France went from 618,079 in 1973 to 424,692 in 1980. In West Germany, there were only 179,952 Spanish residents left on 30 September 1981, that is 117,069 fewer than in 1979.[11]

For countries of emigration this meant that the incentive to join the Community was stronger, especially after the 1973 enlargement to Britain had increased the size of the Community labour market. The potential pressure in an open migration regime played an important role in the outcome of the accession negotiations for each country. The population of immigrants from each country already living in the Community was a key indicator in determining the migratory potential.

This potential was the most limited for Greece, higher for Spain and Portugal, and the highest for Turkey (see Figure 4.2).

## Greek membership

After the 1967 military coup in Greece, the migratory agreements with countries of North-West Europe had been suspended. Annual Greek emigration to West Germany was virtually decimated, from 91,500 in 1969 to 9,600 in 1973. Total Greek emigration amounted to only 27,000 in 1973.[12] After 1973, the number of Greeks employed in the Community continued to fall, from 280,000 in 1973 to 150,000 in 1978.[13] Most of them lived in West Germany. When the military junta collapsed in 1974, it was essential to arrange a future for the country beyond the alternative between Communism and dictatorship. This could only happen by generating enough support for liberal pro-Western parties in Greece, which meant resolving social problems by offering Greeks opportunities in Western Europe. For these reasons, Western European states agreed to open negotiations on Greek membership of the Community.[14]

As far as migration issues were concerned, the limited migratory pressure from Greece facilitated those negotiations: in 1978, the country counted only 9.4 million people, with a weak demographic growth of 0.7 percent.[15] As the main destination for Greek emigration, West Germany was prepared to support an enlargement of the migration regime of the Nine to include Greece. In early autumn 1978, the Germans nevertheless called for a 'sufficiently long' transitional period that could 'be extended if necessary.'[16] The Greeks then asked for a similar transitional period for the freedom of establishment and the free provision of services involving member-state enterprises, but this did not alter the German position.[17]

The Germans also cited their own financial problems: they were less willing to make payments abroad, and suggested waiting before guaranteeing Greek workers the same treatment as Community workers when it came to exporting family benefits.[18] The Act of Accession for Greece provided that the free movement of labour would only come into force as of 1 January 1988, with similar transition periods applying for the liberalisation of trade and of capital movements. The provisions of Regulation 1408/71 regarding social security benefits were also not applicable until December 1983, which meant a three-year transitional period. This outcome corresponded to German preferences.[19]

## Questioning the Association Agreement with Turkey

As far as Turkey was concerned, France opposed attempts to extend the rights of social security for Turkish migrant workers in the Community. Article 39 of the 1970 Additional Protocol to the 1963 Association Agreement only covered migration within the Community, and not between Turkey and the Community. In February 1974, the Commission advocated to extend the scope of this article, in spite of its wording, otherwise it would 'only cover the very limited number of Turkish workers [circulating] within the Community and would exclude . . . the hundreds of thousands of Turkish workers who only [worked] in a single member state.'[20] The Commission's request failed in the face of French opposition.

Furthermore, Article 36 of the Additional Protocol provided for the gradual realisation of the free movement of labour between Turkey and the Community between 1 December 1976 and 1 December 1986. On 16 July 1976, in the Association Committee, the Turks asked what measures the Community planned to take after 1 December to honour this commitment.[21] On 24 July 1976, in Ankara, the Community representatives stressed the 'problems [posed by] the presence of so many migrant workers in regions where they [were] settled,' 'the . . . employment situation,' the 'restrictive immigration policy' that the member states had been 'forced' to adopt. As a result, the Community representatives considered that 'the realisation of the objective pursued [would be] a difficult task.'[22] The weak demand for labour in West Germany in those years, but also the risk of Turkey reaching almost eighty million inhabitants by the end of the century, underpinned this wariness.[23]

The Association Council between Turkey and the Community adopted Decision 2/76, which came into force on 20 December 1976. It provided the framework of a first four-year phase, starting on 1 December 1976, in the supposed gradual realisation of the free movement of labour. The decision only codified the practices in force for Turkish workers in the member countries. After three years' work, Turks had the right to take up a new job, but in the same profession, the same branch of activity, and the same region. After five years' work they had free access to all types of paid employment.[24] However, a safeguarding clause curbed these provisions in the event of disturbance, or even a threat of disturbance to a member-state's labour market that 'could entail serious risks for the standard of living or employment, in a region, branch of activity, or occupation.'[25] The member states' sole concession was to 'make every effort' to give priority to Turks when recruiting workers outside the Community.[26] Yet even this measure was subordinate to the 'international commitments of each of the parties.' Danish delegates declared in particular that this priority did not affect Denmark's prior commitment to the Nordic labour market and British delegates stated that the same applied to Britain's prior commitment to workers from the Commonwealth.[27]

For the second phase, Decision 1/80 of 19 September 1980 came into force on 1 December, but made almost no changes to Decision 2/76. The main exception was the reduction from five to four years of the time after which a Turkish worker was entitled to 'free access to any paid employment of their choice.'[28] Decision 1/80 kept the three-year regular residence time limit in Decision 2/76 for family members of Turkish workers reunited in the destination country to take up job offers. As far family benefits were concerned, Decision 3/80 of the same day made no mention of their export. The Commission even regretted the absence of 'provisions . . . to guarantee the payment of family allowances to workers whose families [resided] in a member state other than that of the employing country,' despite the provisions of Article 39 of the Additional Protocol.[29]

Postponing the implementation of the free movement of labour did nothing to improve Turkey's economic perspectives. In 1980, the economy fell into recession; the unemployment rate rose to more than 20 percent and inflation reached 100 percent. Economic problems only reinforced political instability, while political violence had left 5,200 dead in Turkey between 1978 and 1980.[30] The army set up a military government on 12 September 1980. France and West Germany seized this opportunity to introduce obligatory visas for Turkish nationals as of 5 October 1980. The West German authorities demanded that Turkish workers hold a visa for each entry to, or transit through, its territory.[31] Between 1976 and 1982, ten member states of the Council of Europe introduced visa obligations for Turkish nationals.[32] On 13 October 1980, the Permanent Delegation of Turkey to the Community objected that the measures taken by France and West Germany were 'without any legal basis.'[33] Indeed, Article 41 of the Additional Protocol stipulated that the contracting parties would 'refrain from introducing between themselves any new restrictions on the freedom of establishment and the freedom to provide services.'

The recession that followed the second oil shock made Germany's position even more restrictive. On 1 June 1981, German Minister of Foreign Affairs

Hans-Dietrich Genscher wrote to the president of the Commission, Gaston Thorn, recognising 'the great importance that relations with Turkey [had] in the global framework of the politics of the Western Camp.'[34] The geopolitical interests that led West Germany to grant special treatment to Turkish labour were nevertheless offset by domestic political concerns: 'The federal government,' Genscher added, 'can only continue to develop cooperation with Turkey in the framework of the Association, in conditions that also safeguard its [own] basic interests. These are primarily at stake in the social domain.' He specified: 'The situation on the labour market and the worsening problems of integration resulting from the growth of the foreign population mean that, as of 1986, we cannot grant Turks a general right to take up employment in the Community.' Despite the interruption of recruitment in 1973, the Turkish population in West Germany had continued to grow through family reunification and births. It increased by 15.3 percent in 1979/1980, and reached 1.5 million on 30 September 1980, among which more than one-third were under the age of eighteen. In March 1981 the unemployment rate for Turks in West Germany was 9.4 percent. Genscher then asked the president of the Commission to present proposals to 'reconsider the measures on free movement in the association conventions with Turkey' before December 1981.

On 30 September 1981 Gaston Thorn replied that Article 12 of the Ankara Agreement only referred to 'drawing inspiration from' the articles in the Treaty of Rome on the free movement of labour, which gave the Community 'to handle the case elements allowing to take into account [West Germany's] specific difficulties.'[35] Yet, Thorn's analysis avoided reference to the more precise provisions that the Community had accepted in Article 36 of the Additional Protocol. The agreement with Turkey on the free movement of labour came to an end on 20 July 1984 in Brussels, during a meeting of the Association Committee. Turkish delegates called for the implementation of a third phase of the free movement of workers. Community delegates only stipulated that Decision 1/80 remained applicable. Turkish delegates pointed out 'that it [was] incumbent on the two parties to draw the consequences of this unjustified development, the Turkish delegation reserving the right to examine the situation thus created.'[36] In November 1986, a few days before the deadline set in Article 36 of the Additional Protocol, Turkish Minister of State for Relations with the Community Ali Bozer officially recalled the text of that article: 'Freedom of movement for workers between Member States of the Community and Turkey shall be secured . . . [by the end of] the twenty-second year after the entry into force of' the Agreement of Association. He unsuccessfully referred to Article 31 of the Vienna Convention on the law of treaties, specifying the way to interpret their wording: 'A treaty shall be interpreted in good faith in accordance with the ordinary meaning to be given to the terms of the treaty in their context and in the light of its object and purpose.' Turkey was too dependent on the Community and lacked resources to retaliate.

## The slow accession of Spain and Portugal

While the Community violated its commitment with Turkey, Spain and Portugal were taking steps to join the Community. Also for those countries, the willingness to limit Communist influence was a factor underlying the opening of the Community's labour market.[37] In their case, the migratory pressure was not comparable to that of Turkey. In 1976, the ratios of gross domestic product (GDP) per capita were much tighter: 1 to 1.8 between Spain and France and 1 to 2.8 between Portugal and France. The growth of a Spanish middle class in the 1960s and 1970s limited the risk of large-scale migration of unskilled workers.[38] This does not neglect the importance of potential Spanish migration. Spain's population totalled 36,351,000 in 1977. In 1978, 900,000, or 8 percent of the active population, were unemployed. The accelerated shift of the workforce away from the countryside and the reduction of emigration opportunities had magnified unemployment.[39] There were still 435,000 Spanish workers in the Community in 1976, without counting family members, creating a pole of attraction for further migration.[40] The 100,000 Spanish seasonal workers who travelled to France annually would also rapidly increase labour supply in the Community if they were allowed to take up job offers in the same way as French workers.[41]

The Community took into account

> the importance of [the Spanish] population, its . . . high rate of unemployment, work and pay conditions [in Spain], the prospects of development of the structure of its active population, as well as the existing or potential migratory movements from Spain.

Considering also 'the present situation and the risks of aggravation . . . on the [Community's] labour market,'[42] it called for transitional measures on the free movement of workers between Spain and the Community. Furthermore, in September 1984 in order to limit financial commitments, West Germany asked that allowances for the families of Spanish and Portuguese workers be calculated in the transitional period, on the basis of the laws of the country of residence and not the country of employment.[43]

The Accession Treaty of Spain and Portugal to the Community, signed in Lisbon on 12 June 1985, provided that Articles 1–6 of Regulation 1612/68, along with Directive 68/360 were not applicable until 31 December 1992.[44] This was the same seven-year transition period after accession as for Greece. After five years, that is, from 1 January 1991, the Council could take new measures. The Treaty also set a period of three years after membership, until 31 December 1988, during which family allowances of Spanish and Portuguese workers would be calculated according to the law of the family's country of residence.[45] As this measure was likely to create an incentive for reunification in the country of employment, the Accession Treaty limited this possibility. Family members of Spanish or Portuguese workers joining them in another country after the Treaty was signed could only be employed after three years' residence. This condition was to be reduced to eighteen months on 1 January 1989, and abolished on 1 January 1991.[46]

### Inference

From 1973 onwards, the Western European migration regime became closed to immigration from outside the Community. The regime opened up only to the extent that the countries of emigration of Mediterranean Europe were able to join the Community's open migration regime. The objective of immigration states to limit increases of labour supply made these negotiations more or less difficult depending on the importance of migratory pressure from various countries. For Greece, Spain, and Portugal, the limited migratory pressure did not create major obstacles to admission to the Community's open migration regime, yet arranged after a seven-year transition period. In the case of Turkey, large migratory pressure explains why this country was not integrated into the open European migration regime, despite the commitment previously adopted in the Association. Geopolitical interests mattered both for Greece and Turkey, but at the time they were unable to counterbalance domestic protectionist pressures against immigration.

## Protecting the national workforce

Even though member states maintained the migration regime unchanged within the Community, the new protectionist stance indirectly affected migratory opportunities within the Community. Labour market tensions in immigration countries led to decisions to increase the minimum wage at the national level, which led to fewer opportunities for unskilled migrants. As regarded skilled workers, the lack of recognition of qualifications and university degrees was also a barrier to migration. Finally, exceptions and breaches of Community rules increased sharply during this period.

### Increasing the minimum wage

France drastically reformed its unskilled labour market in the 1970s. Labour supply had outstripped demand throughout the 1960s, and the arrival of unskilled immigrants had become a threat for the wages of local workers. Large increases in the minimum wage were a radical measure to protect wage levels. The law of January 1970 reformed the French minimum wage and provided that it would be indexed not only on inflation, but also on the increase of the average wage and on the growth of GDP. As a result of both this new regulatory framework and constant pressures from French unions, the French government granted large increases of the minimum wage beyond inflation each year. The minimum hourly wage thus rose from FFr 2.06 in the areas where it was the lowest in the first months of 1968, to FFr 20.29 for the whole country in December 1982. At constant prices, the total minimum cost of labour almost tripled in less than fifteen years.[47]

In Denmark, there was no legal national minimum wage, but unions and employers' organisations were able to agree on such a minimum wage. The Union of Commerce and Office Employees had agreed on a monthly minimum wage of DKr 4,000 with the Employers' Organisation.[48] In 1976, a social conflict broke out involving immigrant workers from the Community undercutting the minimum wage. Hertz Rent-a-Car Corporation was not a member of the Employers' Organisation and thus not bound by the agreement between the union and this organisation. Around thirty of its workers in Denmark were nevertheless union members. Hertz paid monthly wages of DKr 3,600. Its workers asked Hertz to raise wages to the minimum wage level. After the company refused, the union called a strike. This multinational corporation found immigrant workers to replace striking workers. Danish authorities were in principle ready to support the union and refuse work permits to immigrant workers. They could not do this for Community migrant workers, who did not need a work permit. Moreover, as the minimum wage was not based on law, and as Hertz was not part of the Employers' Organisation, it could continue to pay wages of less than DKr 4,000. Community immigration could thus undermine union action, leading to a downward convergence of wages to the level in other Community countries.

Danish Social-Democrat Deputy Ole Espersen raised the question in November 1976 in the European Parliamentary Assembly. In this forum, the representatives of richer countries in the Community opposed those from poorer countries. For the former, the free movement of workers in the Community increased labour supply and led to lower wages. Danish Socialist Deputy Jens Maigaard pointed out that, among Danish workers, those who suffered as a result of the 'dogma of the free movement of workers' were 'the worst paid workers on the Danish labour market.' In contrast, Italian Communist Deputy Silvio Leonardi declared that 'the Italian Communist Party is in favour of the freedom of the movement of workers within the Community, which it considers one of its basic principles.' The Assembly and the Commission finally agreed to condemn the use of the free movement of workers to bypass national employment standards and to undermine local unions' actions. The Assembly pointed out the 'consequences of such practices for the social peace in the Community.'[49]

Minimum wage increases in destination countries thereby protected the wage levels of local unskilled workers. Nevertheless, the rigidity of the labour market created by a higher minimum wage meant an increase in unemployment when there was a drop in labour demand or an increase in labour supply. Trade union demands for a higher minimum wage in France only declined when unemployment reached alarming proportions, and when the minimum wage corresponded to the wages that unskilled local workers wished to protect.[50] As most immigrant workers were unskilled, employers had no particular incentive to hire them without the capacity to pay them lower wages. As a result, after the second oil shock, even immigration from the Community declined. The number of Italian residents in France collapsed by one-third in the 1980s, from 375,300 in 1980 to 253,600 in 1990. A variety of factors were involved, including the naturalisation of foreigners and the development of the Italian economy, but the decline in job opportunities in France for unskilled workers also accounted for the collapse. In Germany, for instance, where there was no national minimum wage, the number of Italians declined much more moderately, by 11 percent, and the number of Greeks actually increased by 6 percent.[51]

## The stagnation of the freedom of establishment and of the recognition of qualifications

Skilled workers also came up against barriers limiting migratory opportunities within the Community. These barriers may have increased at the national level; yet they had also to do with the mere continuation of previous practices. Their protectionist impact appeared more strongly as the proportion of skilled workers in the Community was increasing.

In Belgium, which had the highest proportion of Community migrants, the professions opposed granting a right of establishment to foreigners. In 1974, the prospect of doctors from other member states operating in Belgium concerned Belgian doctors.[52] The average number of inhabitants per doctor was already low in the country. In December 1974, Professor Halter, secretary general of the Belgian Ministry of Public Health, expressed his concern within the Council, in the Committee of Permanent Representatives (COREPER). 'An intake of doctors from abroad risks [bringing about] a rapid deterioration . . . of' Belgium's 17,000 doctors, he said. Such intake was the result of both the large number 'of Community nationals in Belgium' and the large number of medical students. The latter came mostly from France, where a *numerus clausus* had been introduced in 1971. It limited the total number of students admitted in second-year and made medical studies highly selective in France. A number of French students therefore opted to study in Belgium, where it was easier to enter the profession. Following the *Reyners* judgment in June 1974, students from the Community who had studied in Belgium and were hence Belgian degree-holders, could not be denied the right of establishment in Belgium on the grounds of their nationality. Given the serious risk of an increase in the number of doctors in Belgium because of Community rules, Halter asked COREPER 'to draft a safeguarding clause to incorporate in the texts' on the right of establishment for doctors. German, Italian, and Dutch delegates, together with the Irish presidency, did not want to create a precedent likely to be used for other professions, and COREPER rejected Halter's request.

Yet to Halter's relief, meanwhile, the central negotiation on architects, which was to be used as a template for the right of establishment in other professions, was blocked over the question of the recognition of qualifications. In June 1976, the Belgian architect Dan Craet drafted a letter on behalf of the Liaison Committee of Architects of the Common Market to the Council of Ministers, calling for architectural training 'at the highest possible level' in the Community.[53] They opposed any equivalence between the training in universities and in Dutch and German technical schools. This could lead to an influx of architects from West Germany and the Netherlands in other countries. The risk was also that students could bypass university-training requirements, by going to West Germany or the Netherlands to study and by then claiming equivalence for their training in other countries. Ultimately, the increase in numbers and the reduction of entry requirements would lead to a drop in the status and income of architects. The Committee exploited the lack of knowledge of non-specialists regarding the correct regulation of this technical field: 'quality architecture,' they said, required training and 'insufficient training would be harmful.' The Committee called for 'university level' training, of 'a minimum of four years.'[54]

The member states of the Community were able to agree that the directive for the mutual recognition of degrees, certificates, and other qualifications in the domain of architecture should provide for a gradual increase in the length of study in German technical schools for architects, the *Fachhochschulen*, from three to four years. Yet disagreement persisted first on the additional requirements for those who had followed a three-year training course. In October 1975, Belgian delegates in the Council, inspired by the Liaison Committee of Architects, declared that the three-year training offered by the *Fachhochschulen* only entitled persons to the right to establishment in Belgium on condition that this was supplemented by ten years' professional experience or an additional six-year traineeship with a certified architect. Belgian delegates added that these measures should only apply during the four years after the directive came into force. After this period, only those holding a *Fachhochschule* degree in architecture after four years' study could benefit from the right of establishment in other member countries. Second, disagreement persisted on the equivalence between four-year training in *Fachhochschulen* and university training. The Belgians considered the former could confer the right of establishment in other countries only with an additional requirement of two years' professional experience.[55] German delegates made alternative proposals. Yet, in December 1977, British, Danish, French, and Irish representatives in COREPER still expressed reserve or opposition to these proposals, fearing, in the words of the British delegate, a 'downgrading of the level of architects' qualifications.'[56] With the opposition of France and Britain, negotiations on architects remained blocked fifteen years after they had begun.

As the *Reyners* judgment had recognised the abolition of discrimination based on nationality, the main way to the right of establishment in another country of the Community remained getting a degree there beforehand. Yet, accessing higher education in another country was still difficult.[57] In Belgium, many universities limited the proportion of foreign students to 2 or 3 percent, including Community students. In France, foreign students had almost no access to the *Grandes écoles* or the *Ecoles d'ingénieurs*, except under restricted quotas. Universities in the Paris area also applied a quota of 5 percent for foreign students in the first year of medical studies. In West Germany too, there were admission restrictions for undergraduates in some disciplines. The quota for foreigners, including those from the Community, was 6 percent in medicine, dentistry, veterinary medicine, and chemistry and 8 percent in other disciplines. In Britain, universities could limit the proportion of foreign students in each discipline.

The number of persons studying in another Community country remained low and grew only slowly. They were between 21,000[58] and 25,000[59] in 1976, that is only 0.5 percent of the total number of students in the Community. The two main countries of destination were West Germany, with around 6,750 Community students in 1975/1976, and France, with around 6,500 in 1974/1975.[60] The main countries of origin were Britain with around 4,200 students abroad in 1974/1975, and West Germany, with more than 3,600 students abroad in 1975/1976. In 1980/1981, the number of Community students had increased to more than 53,000.[61] Yet, Greek accession was responsible for much of this increase. Greek students then accounted for around half of Community students. Apart from Greek students, the number of Community students increased by less than 9 percent between 1976[62] and 1981,[63] that is an average annual increase of around 1.7 percent. The number of Greek students in other Community countries had not increased much between 1976 and 1981, remaining stable around 26,000. Once again the main countries of destination were West Germany and France, each with around 13,000 Community students in 1980/1981, Greek students included. Italy had become the first country of destination, with around 16,000 Community students in 1980/1981: most of them were Greek. Because of this low level of student migration, the recognition of academic qualifications remained a prerequisite for migration movements of qualified professionals. The impasse of negotiations had therefore serious consequences.

## Bypassing European rules

Besides the barriers affecting both unskilled and skilled migrants, the migration regime in the Community was also slightly affected in this period by the fact that member states did not always respect, in practice, the rules previously agreed in the Community.

The Commission took Belgium to the Court of Justice of the Community on the issue of jobs reserved for Belgian nationals in the railways. In May 1981, the director general of the *Société nationale des chemins de fer belges* (SNCB), Emmanuel Flachet, justified this practice in a letter to the Belgian Minister of Communications. All the reserved jobs, he wrote, were 'at the heart of network operations.'[64] According to Flachet these jobs interested 'not only the public administration . . . but also and above all, public security.' It was vital for the state, he explained, to enjoy total control on railways in times of war or, simply, in times of trouble. He pointed out that a specialised office of the SNCB was responsible for military affairs and that the SNCB had to provide the government with all the necessary means to transport troops or military material on any of the points served by railways if the government asked to do so. It was vital, he argued, that jobs that affected the heart of rail network operations were entrusted to nationals, because 'one cannot . . . expect as much obedience or loyalty from foreigners as from nationals.' He finally spoke of the 'enormous risks of spying or sabotage to the benefit of the enemy' if these jobs were opened up to foreigners. Behind such military arguments, quite at odds with the geopolitical environment of Belgium at the time, it was more likely that Flachet echoed staff concerns, anxious to avoid foreign competition: the letter, signed by the director general, indeed came directly from the human resources department of the SNCB.

The multiplication of exceptions to the free movement of labour did not involve only Belgium; it was general. In order to avoid a Court judgment with a strict interpretation of the exemptions to the free movement of labour, all the major immigration states, that is West Germany, France, and Britain, supported Belgium in the proceedings. An internal Commission note about that case stressed the 'sensitivity of member states on measures on free movement in the present situation of very high unemployment.'[65] In its report to the Court, on 28 October 1981, the Commission considered that Belgium's breach of the provisions of Article 48 of the Treaty of Rome and of Regulation 1612/68 was established. In a conciliatory move with all the governments involved on board, the Commission nevertheless proposed to recognise Belgium's right to implement restrictions in the cases of architects, managers, and some night watchmen in the railways sector.[66] In the judgement of 26 May 1982, the Court followed the Commission's approach.[67]

In the early 1980s, high unemployment, Greek enlargement, and the prospect of enlargement to Spain and Portugal drove member states to breaches of the free movement of employed workers. There were then two million Community migrant workers. The Commission discovered a campaign to recruit sixty technicians for the engineering offices of the *Société nationale des chemins de fer français* (SNCF) reserved for French nationals. The Radio télévision belge francophone asked for Belgian nationality when recruiting journalists. The Commission initiated proceedings against France for demanding French nationality in recruiting nurses for general care and dentists in public hospitals.[68] The Commission also sent Belgium a reasoned opinion, when university hospitals in Brussels demanded Belgian nationality when recruiting doctors.[69] More generally, in its report on the control of the application of Community law in 1985, the Commission denounced 'the tendency to [adopt a] systematically restrictive interpretation of Community law and jurisprudence in the domain of the free movement of workers, which had appeared in many member states.'[70]

Breaches of the freedom of establishment and the recognition of qualifications also multiplied. Between 1983 and 1984, the number of breaches found by the Commission of directives on the recognition of qualifications and the coordination of activities for professions doubled: doctors, nurses in general care, dentists, midwives, lawyers, hairdressers, and transport auxiliaries were concerned. The Commission found discrimination based on nationality for access to some professions particularly 'in France and Italy.'[71] In the case of lawyers, France, Italy, and West Germany incorrectly applied Directive 77/249 of 22 March 1977, tending to relax the exercise of the free provision of services by lawyers.[72] The exceptions and breaches made the right of establishment for the professions numerically insignificant.[73]

Finally, a last mark of defiance towards the open migration regime in the Community came with the revision of the Treaty of Rome through the Single European Act, signed in February 1986. The Act replaced majority voting on the free movement of workers in the Council by qualified majority voting.[74] This meant that a larger majority was required to pass new legislation on the free movement of workers. Majority voting had greatly facilitated decision-making in the previous decades in the sense that governments did not even bother to vote against a proposal when they could see a majority was in favour. The decision-making process was also working efficiently in the sense that most governments understood that an agreement without the support of major immigration countries, and first and foremost West Germany, might increase non-compliance and consequently weaken Community rules. West German delegates were outnumbered in Council final decisions in only few and marginal cases. This outcome had to do with the fact that there were few member states, which facilitated informal coordination, and, most importantly, with the fact that Italy was the only large emigration country, which guaranteed a majority dominated by immigration countries. The enlargements of the Community to three emigration countries between 1981 and 1986 made simple majority voting in the Council more dangerous. The requirement of a larger majority resulted from the Mediterranean enlargements, but also manifested more generally the growing reticence of some member states on the free movement of labour.

Inference

Alongside the closure to migration flows from outside the Community, serious barriers persisted in the migration regime within the Community, through increases of minimum wages or the non-recognition of qualifications. Governments responded to domestic pressure by interpreting the exceptions to Community law in a broad sense, or even sometimes by committing breaches.

## The absence of employment policies for migrants

Besides the ban of labour immigration from outside the Community and persisting barriers to migration within the Community, I will now turn to the asymmetric way in which governments treated national workers and migrant workers during the economic downturn of the 1970s and early 1980s. In the economic slump, governments invested to support their national workers through unemployment benefits and vocational training. Despite the fact that the unemployment rate was significantly higher for migrants than for nationals in most countries, I will show how little was done to support unemployed migrant workers or to promote their training.

### Limited financing for schooling with the prospect of return

The first training policy was education for children. Yet, the children of immigrants had low rates of educational enrolment in West Germany against the backdrop of a rapid increase in the number of school-age children of migrants. Between 1968 and 1972, the number of foreign children and adolescents, including nationals from outside the Community, doubled to 953,000 in West Germany. Their number continued to grow in the following years, due to a high birth rate among immigrants.[75] Only a minority of them attended school: in 1972/1973, only 149,100 were enrolled in primary schools and 111,500 in secondary schools in West Germany. Although France had 25 percent fewer migrant workers than West Germany, 1.77 million as against 2.35 million, the number of children of migrant workers educated in France was twice as high: 369,800 at the primary level and 156,000 at the secondary level for the year 1974/1975.[76] The great majority of these children did not possess the nationality of a member state of the Community: in France, this was the case of 90 percent of foreign children enrolled in primary school in 1974.[77]

In 1975, the Commission proposed a directive on the education of migrants' children to the Council. The Commission suggested including not only the children of Community workers, but also those of workers from outside the Community. Such a directive would have implied large transformations in West Germany, where the share of scolarised children among the children of migrant workers was low. As early as October 1975, German delegates in the Council argued that a directive, as proposed by the Commission, was not the appropriate way to deal with this problem. They favoured a simple recommendation[78] and wanted any measures adopted to apply exclusively to children of Community migrants, excluding the children of migrants from outside the Community.[79] Finally, Directive 77/486 of 25 July 1977 on the education of children of migrant workers only applied to the children of Community migrants.[80]

Another point of contention during the negotiations was whether states should teach immigrants' children the language and culture of their country of origin. At the time, the French education system carried out this sort of teaching in order to promote the return of immigrants to their country of origin. French support for this type of instruction was part of the shift in French immigration policy. The tensions on the French labour market had led from an immigration policy to repopulate France to the encouragement of the return of immigrants and their families to their country of origin, including Community immigrants. In October 1976, French delegates, supported by Italian delegates and the Commission, estimated that 'the humanisation of the free movement of workers' should include the return and reintegration in the country of origin, which teaching the language and culture of their country of origin to immigrants' children could greatly facilitate.[81]

British delegates pointed out that immigrants in Britain came from many different countries, languages, and cultures. They stressed the 'insuperable difficulties' that the British authorities would have to face if obliged to provide this sort of teaching.[82] Although the directive finally only applied to Community migrants, political relations with the Commonwealth meant that Britain could not limit its programmes to these migrants. German delegates also argued that encouraging return did not require such teaching.[83] In February and March 1976, they opposed any financial commitments in this domain.[84]

In the last instance, negotiators reached a limited agreement. The directive provided that member states would take appropriate measures to offer the children of immigrants covered by the directive, that is employed workers with member-state nationality, 'free tuition to facilitate initial reception . . . including, in particular, the teaching – adapted to the specific needs of such children – of the official language' of the host country.[85] When it came to teaching these children the language and culture of their country of origin, the directive mentioned the goal of 'facilitating their possible reintegration into the Member State of origin.' Yet the rest of the text boiled down to emphasising that member states should 'promote' this sort of instruction.[86] An interpretative declaration recorded in the Council minutes stated that the provisions of the directive did not grant 'subjective, individual rights' of entitlement to the children covered by it to instruction in the language and culture of their country of origin. Furthermore, a financial contribution from the country of origin was necessary for this instruction.[87] Britain and West Germany therefore managed to reduce their financial commitments in this respect.

Cultural differences between their country of origin and the country of residence meant that the children of migrant workers needed additional teaching programmes to follow the normal curriculum. The European Social Fund (ESF) – a body created by the Treaty of Rome to support social programmes in the Community – received several requests for specific actions to help them. In July 1977, the Fund's annual report mentioned requests for 'special courses organised for the children of migrant workers.'[88] The report stated that 'the volume of these applications far exceeded the budgetary resources allocated for interventions in favour of immigrants.' The Fund had helped around 125,000 children in the Community in 1976. Yet, the directive on the education of the children of migrant workers did not provide for an alternative source of financing for these needs. Immigration countries were already overwhelmed with the cost of supporting millions of unemployed and had little financing to support schooling, even for Community nationals.

## Limited exchange programmes for young workers

In a similar vein, immigration states, which were devoting considerable resources to support their unemployed national workers, did not set up migration programmes for young workers likely to reduce unemployment elsewhere. Youth employment collapsed in France by almost one-third, from 4.425 million jobs at the end of 1969 to 3.114 million at the end of 1984, despite the increase in the number of young people. This was largely the result of the parallel increase in the French minimum wage.[89] Under such conditions, the German government was unwilling to commit Community resources to exchange programmes of young workers meant to correct the dysfunctions in the French labour market.

The Treaty of Rome had provided for exchange programmes for young workers. In 1977, the first programme only involved young people who already held some qualification and were therefore less affected by unemployment. In 1979, during negotiations for a second programme, German delegates in the Council stated that 'it would not be appropriate to make a . . . programme for young jobseekers who [had] never had a job.'[90] On top of the condition of qualification, they added the second condition to have already been employed in order to benefit from the programme, which allowed excluding most young unemployed. French delegates requested that only one of the two conditions – training or occupational experience – be necessary.[91]

The Decision of 16 July 1979, which established the second programme for the exchange of young workers within the Community, provided for financial aid for the costs of the journeys between the place of residence and the place of stage within 75 percent of total costs and a fixed contribution per trainee and per week, 'within the limit of credits entered into the Community budget.'[92] The programme was limited to young people aged eighteen to twenty-eight years who had basic occupational training or practical occupational experience 'and' already 'in working life.' The start of active working life should also have taken place before the age of twenty.[93] This excluded most young unemployed and matched German preferences.

The number of beneficiaries of the first programme was tiny: 148 young people in 1977 and 198 in 1978, for total expenditure of respectively 68,000 and 140,000 European currency units (ECU).[94] In addition to long-term traineeships of between four and six months, the second programme introduced short-term traineeships lasting from three weeks to three months.[95] For 1979, the number of trainees was to be 460 and the expenditure in the order of 650,000 ECU.[96] As of 1981, the Commission envisaged expenses of 2 million ECU a year,[97] to triple the number of beneficiaries. Despite this increase, the programme only affected an insignificant number of young workers at the Community level.

## The failure of plans for unemployed workers

In the 1970s, faced with increasing unemployment among their unskilled national workers, member-state governments opted for large vocational training programmes to foster the employability of these workers. Yet, in a move similar to their lack of funding for immigrants' children education or for the mobility of young workers, they failed to enlarge those programmes to their immigrant workers, despite the fact that immigrant workers were mostly unskilled and were more affected by unemployment. In September 1975, unemployment in West Germany had increased overall by 154 percent, while it had increased by 338 percent among immigrant workers.[98]

Since Decision 74/57 of the Council of 27 June 1974, the European Social Fund could step in to finance occupational training for migrant workers. The volume of eligible applications to the Fund for assistance for migrant workers reached 61 million ECU in 1976, against 42 million ECU in 1975. In 1976, approved requests allowed governments to organise language and training courses for around 50,000 adult migrant workers. In addition, more than a million immigrants benefited from information services and orientation financed by the Fund in 1976.[99]

The Commission wanted to go further and proposed to the Council an Action Programme for migrant workers and their families. In such a programme, the Community would fund occupational training and language instruction for migrants. In September 1975, British and German delegates argued that 'the introduction of such measures specifically for migrant workers [risked] creating discrimination in relation to national workers.'[100] French delegates were more favourable and were ready to consider a 'training . . . adapted to [migrant workers'] specific needs and in particular the knowledge of the language and the integration in the milieu of the host country.' Yet they joined British and German delegates in recognising that migrant workers could only benefit from these measures on the same basis as national workers.

French and German points of view clashed when the French proposed to use the Action Programme to prepare immigrants for their return to their country of origin, which could, according to France, be outside the Community. On 30 October 1975, in the Economic and Social Committee, André Soulat, secretary general of the French union CFDT, proposed that the Action Programme provide 'migrant workers with practical training useful for a job in their country of origin after their return.'[101] He stressed the mismatch between the qualifications acquired by migrants in the country of immigration and the needs of their native country. He also stressed that the occupational training should be designed to contribute to the economic development of the country of origin when the migrant returned. Soulat wanted to include immigrant workers from outside the Community in these programmes. As the French labour market was ever less inclusive for immigrants, both the French government and French unions had a vested interest in facilitating the return of immigrants to their country of origin and they hoped to secure Community funding to achieve this.

Soulat's colleague in the Economic and Social Committee, Wolfgang Eichler, a representative of the Confederation of German Employers (*Bundesvereinigung der Deutschen Arbeitgeberverbände*), considered that 'Mr Soulat's proposal [was] not realistic.'[102] The easier departure of unemployed immigrant workers from West Germany made the type of programmes suggested by the French unnecessary there and German employers were not ready to finance them. In parallel, in October and November 1975, the German delegates in the Council intended to limit the scope of the Action Programme to nationals of member states.[103]

It was not until the second oil shock that the West German government had to adopt more stringent measures to reduce the size of the immigrant population. It was only in 1984 that the German government encouraged foreign workers who had been fully or partially unemployed for more than six months to return to their country of origin by offering them a return premium of DM 10,500. In contrast, France implemented a similar policy back in May 1977, offering unemployed immigrant workers a return premium of FFr 10,000. In both cases, the premium was only a compensation for the contributions paid by these workers, which they gave up when returning to their country in the absence of full transfers of social security benefits.[104]

As unemployment among migrant workers was increasing and as a number of them had to return to their countries of origin, the Community states of emigration tried to extend the duration of the exportation of unemployment benefits for their nationals. This was a way to reduce the burden these returns generated in emigration countries. The Italians and Dutch still represented the main contingents of Community migrant workers to West Germany. In October 1975, in the Economic and Social Committee, Italian trade unionist Bruno Fassina, from the Confederazione italiana sindacati lavoratori, and Dutch trade unionist P.J.G.M. van Rens, from the *Nederlands Katholiek Vakverbond*, estimated that 'in the current situation, the limitation to three months of unemployment benefits, which would be granted for a much longer period if the workers remained in the country of employment' was 'too short.'[105] They proposed a period of at least six months.

Regulation 1408/71 on the social security of migrant workers had limited the transfer of unemployment benefits to another country to just three months. Such a transfer also required that the unemployed worker had remained in the employment country for at least four weeks after being unemployed, available for the employers of that country. Wolfgang Eichler, from the *Bundesvereinigung der Deutschen Arbeitgeberverbände*, accepted to drop this requirement and supported a text proposed by Italian trade unionists:

> Keeping migrant workers available for four weeks for the job market of the country where they have worked, may not entirely meet the current economic and social situation in which it is not easy to reintegrate into productive activity. The member states can reduce the four-week period.[106]

The increase of unemployment among migrant workers meant that it was less useful to keep those unemployed on German territory.

This did not mean that immigration countries were ready to extend the duration of payment of unemployment benefits abroad. In October 1975, the British member of the Economic and Social Committee June Evans expressed concern about the 'cost of such measures.'[107] In September 1980, German delegates in the Council still opposed the attempt to extend the right to unemployment benefits in the case of a change of residence to six months, since 'it would lead to . . . an increase of financial charges of the competent state.'[108]

At the end of 1980, the Germans also clashed with the French in the Council on the export of early retirement benefits. The French wanted to use this export in order to 'encourage migrant workers to voluntarily give up their jobs in favour of nationals of the country where they [were working] and to stop looking for jobs in this country.' For the French it was important to reach a European deal, because a unilateral policy granting more rights to migrant workers in France than in other European countries would simply attract more migrants in France. Yet German delegates opposed the French proposal and pointed out that it was a 'matter reserved for social partners.'[109] Unemployed migrant workers in West Germany tended to leave more often than their counterparts in France. Consequently, the two states developed different policies to deal with them. The Germans did not need to increase their payments abroad to encourage unemployed foreigners to leave the country, whereas France needed such programmes and financial incentives to achieve it. On 18 March 1981, only France, Greece, and Italy in the Council defended the export of early retirement benefits. The seven other member states, particularly Britain and West Germany, expressed 'an unfavourable attitude.'[110] All attempts to extend the payment of unemployment benefits or early retirement benefits abroad thus failed.[111]

### Inference

The debate was thus articulated around the opposition between France on the one hand and Britain and West Germany on the other. The French labour market was no longer inclusive for most immigrant workers but France could not reduce the size of its immigrant population. France therefore supported a financial implication of Community member states in favour of the relocation of migrant workers, as a way to secure European funding and to avoid granting immigrants more rights than in other European countries. In addition, France was affected by mass youth unemployment and sought European opportunities for these workers. Britain and West Germany did not experience the problems faced by France and they were reluctant to commit additional spending for migrant workers. British-German preferences carried the day.

## A stalemate in social and political negotiations

The lesser interest of immigration states in foreign workers from the mid-1970s onwards to the early 1980s also led them to adopt more restrictive positions on their social and political rights and those of their family members. The West German government adopted a new policy on the export of family benefits. The states of North-West Europe tried also to avoid the intervention of public assistance for needy migrants. Immigration states in general were not ready to recognise political rights to Community migrants.

### The new German policy limiting exports of family benefits

After the halt to labour immigration, immigration states agreed to limit family reunification, which had become a key factor of increase of foreign populations on their territories. In 1975, British, French, and German delegates in the Council opposed the extension of the definition of family members for family reunification proposed by the Commission.[112] Regarding housing for migrant workers, which could be a condition for family reunification, the same delegates opposed the Commission proposal to create 'pilot programmes . . . to allow migrant workers and their families to find modernised housing at affordable prices.'[113] In September 1975, British delegates in the Council excluded favouring 'the category of migrant workers compared to other categories of people in a similar situation.'

To limit financial commitments abroad, the Germans eventually abandoned their previous line of conduct to discourage family reunification: the full export of family benefits, as calculated by the law of country of employment. While the Germans were more than ever willing to limit family reunification, their reversal had to do with the evolution of their demographic policy. The West German population was about to decline. From 1965 to 1973, the number of births had fallen by about 40 percent. In 1972, deaths outstripped births for the first time since 1946. To support births, the government made large increases to family allowances on 1 January 1975, which had been until then among the lowest in the Community.[114] From then onwards, German monthly family allowances for three children amounted to the equivalent of BFr 3,500, against BFr 4,500 in Belgium, BFr 2,600 in France, and only BFr 700 in Britain.[115] On 1 July 1979, these figures were BFr 6,970 for Belgium, BFr 5,501 for Germany, BFr 4,133 for France, BFr 3,429 for Britain, and BFr 1,055 for Italy.[116] From 1975 onwards, West Germany was therefore one of the member states offering the highest family allowances.

Due to the policies previously adopted, West Germany already accounted for the bulk of family benefits transfers in the Community. In 1979, 104,500 children in the Community benefited from the export of German allowances, among whom almost 80,000 were Italians. By comparison, there were about 15,000 children affected by the export of family benefits from Belgium and France under Community regulations.[117] The national increase of German family benefits thus had a large impact on the balance of payments. The enlargements to Greece, Spain, and Portugal, already anticipated in the second half of the 1970s, only worsened the problem. The solution based on the calculation of family benefits according to the law of the country of residence would allow West Germany to limit its payments abroad, given the low level of family allowances in the countries of emigration. In 1980, an Italian worker in West Germany whose family lived in Italy received BFr 8,644 a month for three children. With the country of residence system, he would only receive BFr 2,110 a month.[118]

In 1975, the Commission proposed a regulation to end the exception that had existed for France on this matter and to achieve the uniform solution required by Article 98 of Regulation 1408/71. The Commission suggested keeping only the solution that all other member states had been applying since 1971, based on the application of the law of the country of employment to calculate exported family allowances. The exception for France allowed it to calculate exported family allowances at the rate of the country of residence. On 15 July 1975, German and

French delegates in the Council, supported by Belgian delegates, did not join the Commission proposal based on the solution of the country of employment and in compliance with the intention of Article 98 of Regulation 1408/71.[119]

Member states with high family allowances opposed those with low family allowances. On 10 September 1975, the Commission proposal, based on the application of the law of the country of employment, received the support of Ireland, Italy, the Netherlands, and Britain.[120] All these countries paid low family allowances: on 15 September 1974, monthly allowances for three children were BFr 700 in Britain, BFr 1,450 in Italy, and BFr 2,300 in the Netherlands.[121] These delegates emphasised that a solution based on the law of the country of employment gave workers benefits that matched their paid contributions. They also stressed that this solution had

> already been accepted through a gentlemen's agreement reached in the Council during the adoption of Regulation (EEC) 1408/71; on this occasion the solution planned for France – based on the principle of the country of residence – had been considered an exception to the rule for the other member states, namely, the solution of the country of employment.[122]

On 6 April 1976, Belgian, French, and German delegates still opposed the Commission proposal.[123] These were not only the main countries of immigration, exporting the lion's share of the family allowances in the Community; these were also countries with the highest family allowances, because they enjoyed a high standard of living and operated pro-natal demographic policies. For this reason, whatever the flows, calculating exported family allowances in the Community on the basis of the law of the country of residence was always less costly for these countries. In January 1980, German delegates in the Council were still arguing in favour of the rate of the country of residence, by referring to the prospect of demographic decline that had hit a growing number of European countries. This had pushed them, German delegates continued, to increase their family benefits, and thus made them reluctant to export these benefits.[124] West Germany and the other states implementing demographic policies wanted to circumscribe the impact of such policies on their national territories.

As the Council was negotiating the extension of Regulation 1408/71 to the self-employed, COREPER agreed, on 29 April 1981, to exclude the articles of the Regulation on the export of family allowances. These articles continued to apply only to employed workers. In a declaration recorded in the minutes of the Council session, member states nevertheless committed themselves to conclude agreements, if necessary, in order to avoid the abolition of the right to family benefits for the self-employed.[125] The problem therefore still had to be dealt with through bilateral agreements, in which Germany would be in a better position to promote its preferred solution.

Regarding employed workers, under Article 149 of the Treaty of Rome, the modification of a Commission proposal required unanimity in the Council. For this reason, the continued opposition of Irish and Italian delegates to the modification of the Commission proposal blocked negotiation for several years.[126] Time was against the Germans. They managed to exclude the application of the rate of the country of employment to calculate exported family allowances in the case of the self-employed, but also, as previously noted, in the transition periods for the new Mediterranean members of the Community. Yet, without an agreement, the provisions of Regulation 1408/71 remained in force for other Community migrant workers. On 25 October 1983, Greek, Irish, and Italian delegates in the Council, along with the Commission representative, maintained their position, which was sufficient to block negotiations again.[127]

## Avoiding public assistance for needy migrants

In parallel, the states of immigration of North-West Europe were anxious to avoid paying public assistance for migrants with no income. In March 1974, the Council was negotiating on self-employed migrants in the Community. Dutch delegates shared the concerns of the Dutch Treasury. In many member countries, they argued, the self-employed did not enjoy the benefits of an insurance system as fully as employed workers. Accordingly, self-employed immigrants were more 'likely, in case of misfortune, to be completely reliant on the public funds to support the needy.'[128] Dutch delegates were particularly concerned by the risk that retired self-employed immigrants could be dependent on social assistance.[129] The delegates of Germany, France, Denmark, and other immigration countries expressed similar concern. On 17 December 1974, Directive 75/34 of the Council finally provided that member states should re-admit to their territories self-employed immigrants who had already worked there and who wished to return there when reaching retirement age, only if they had resided there permanently *for a long period of time*.[130] Instead of setting a precise time limit of residence beyond which member states should automatically grant readmission, this vague text left immigration states with a wide margin of evaluation to define what they meant by 'long period of time.'

The Council also negotiated the extension of Regulation 1408/71 to self-employed migrants and their family members. Several countries regulated the social security of self-employed workers within a broader category, including various assimilated persons. For practical reasons, a few states were ready to extend Regulation 1408/71 to 'persons assimilated' to self-employed workers under the different national forms of legislation. These persons often included economically inactive people. In spring 1979, for instance, the British representative in COREPER declared that 'the need to eliminate discrimination and injustice [called for] the inclusion of all non-working people.'[131] This British position resulted from the peculiarity of British social security law, which was based on universal coverage. This meant that Community immigrants legally resident in Britain already benefited from the social security rights provided for in Regulation 1408/71, even when they were not employed workers or their family members. In contrast, British migrants in the Community who were not employed workers or their family members did not benefit from such rights.[132]

Danish and German delegates opposed the British suggestion and wished to exclude inactive people from any entitlement in the field of social security. In spring 1979, Danish delegates reasoned that only economic objectives could be adopted on the basis of the Treaty of Rome. A regulation covering inactive persons would, they argued, constitute 'an undesirable precedent.'[133] Denmark and Germany were in a minority, but under both Article 51 of the Treaty, on the basis of which Regulation 1408/71 had been adopted, and Article 235 of the Treaty, on actions necessary to realise goals that had no legal basis elsewhere in the Treaty, any extension to the inactive required unanimity. In addition, Germany was the largest single Community provider of social security benefits to Community migrants: German opposition to the final agreement could jeopardise its actual implementation. On 27 November 1980, the Council therefore agreed to exclude 'assimilated persons,' in line with German and Danish preferences.[134]

On 9–10 December 1974, the heads of state and governments of the Community, meeting in Paris, had agreed to open negotiations on special rights for Community nationals. In July 1979, the Commission proposed to grant a general right of residence for Community migrants. In the European Parliament, British MP Alan R. Tyrrell stated that, in Britain, local authorities were legally bound to provide free housing, where necessary, to homeless persons, which meant 'a very heavy financial burden for the inhabitants of the main points of entry into the United Kingdom.'[135] He stressed that it would be 'insane for the United Kingdom . . . to assume this charge for an unlimited number of people' without minimum means of subsistence. On 27 May 1980, the delegates of all member states in the Council agreed that only those who could demonstrate that they had sufficient resources could benefit from this general right of residence.[136] The Commission proposed an exception for students, but was only supported by Greek delegates. Greek students accounted for half of Community migrant students.[137] Italy, hosting most of them, opposed this exception. German delegates also considered that there was no ground for such an exception.[138]

In 1980, the German Bundesrat argued, more broadly, that the Council had no competence for a directive on a generalised right of residence for Community migrants.[139] In May 1983, Danish delegates declared that the Commission proposal was 'unacceptable.' They stressed that, in Denmark, all residents enjoyed a range of social security benefits: the Commission proposal would create significant costs for Danish social security institutions, even if migrants were obliged to demonstrate a minimum of resources. Danish delegates also referred to the trend to reduce immigration, as part of 'current economic circumstances,' and to the prospect of Spanish and Portuguese enlargement.[140] No attempt to recognise a general right of residence or social security rights for inactive Community migrants succeeded in this period.

### The impasse of negotiations on participation in public life

The Paris Summit of December 1974 had also initiated negotiations on the participation of Community migrants in public life. The debate on the right to vote for Community migrants in local elections initially benefited from a favourable context. In 1977, Denmark granted such right to immigrants from Iceland, Finland, Norway, and Sweden; then, in 1981, to immigrants of all nationalities, on the condition of three years' residence in Denmark. The Dutch Parliament recognised voting and eligibility rights in local elections to all immigrants in 1985.[141] In Germany, the Social-Democratic government was ready to grant similar rights to Community immigrants, since the SPD (*Sozialdemokratische Partei Deutschlands*) was to be the main electoral beneficiary. In March 1976, German delegates in the Council accepted to attribute special rights to 'citizens of the Nine in their quality as members of the Community' with an act of 'a Community form' to facilitate 'its insertion in the national legal systems.' This was the best way to ensure reciprocity. This act was placed 'in the perspective of the creation of a European Union.'[142]

Yet, several immigration states opposed the project. In June 1980, Luxembourg delegates in the Council indicated that in some municipalities Community immigrants constituted a majority of the population. This was to be increasingly the case after 'the envisaged enlargements of European Communities.'[143] British delegates also pointed out the difficulty of granting voting rights in local elections only to Community immigrants, given Britain's relations with the Commonwealth. In Britain the Conservatives in power from 1979 opposed this plan. In France, the socialist government, which came to power in 1981, tried to grant voting rights in local elections to all migrants, but gave up after it failed to constitute a sufficient majority in Parliament. Finally, the Christian Democrats, which came to power in West Germany in 1982, withdrew German support for the plan. In July 1983, in a debate in the European Parliament, the German Christian Democrats opposed the Italian Christian Democrats on this issue.[144] British opposition, France's failure to carry out reforms at the national level, and the change of government in West Germany led to the failure of this negotiation.

### Inference

Unemployment and the prospect of demographic decline therefore had significantly changed the position of the German government regarding social rights for

Community migrants. The increase of German family allowances was decisive, as it led German delegates in the Council to challenge the application of the rate of the country of employment for exported family allowances. Voting rules in the Council allowed countries with low family allowances and the Commission to block negotiations and to maintain the status quo. The willingness of immigration states to limit their financial commitments to Community migrants also affected other negotiations on social security and on the right of residence. Moreover, negotiations on migrants' right to vote in local elections remained at a dead end, partly due to the prospect of Mediterranean enlargement. Economic interests in a context of unemployment prevailed over the political objectives proposed at the Paris Summit.[145]

## Coordinating closure to Southern migrants

During this period, the Europeans were able to find common positions and to conclude negotiations mainly to reduce migratory pressure from the Global South. In this section, I will show that, despite a widespread conviction,[146] European cooperation to stem immigration from the Global South did not start in the mid-1980s. As I will substantiate, the basic guidelines of such cooperation were already in place in the 1970s, when Western European states adopted the first measures of coordination. Their negotiations on a common policy for immigration from outside the Community failed, but otherwise they stepped up their common positions.

### Circumscribing cooperation

As European states were increasing barriers to legal immigration, clandestine immigration from outside the Community grew swiftly. In 1977, there were between 150,000 and 350,000 immigrant workers without a legal work permit in West Germany.[147] Many Turks and Pakistanis entered via Berlin, thanks to the interested laxity of the East German border control authorities.[148] In 1976, there were around 600,000 illegal immigrants employed in the Community.[149] Germany was determined to avoid 'a new influx of third-country workers in the Community.'[150] In January 1976, the member states agreed on a mutual consultation on their respective policies towards migrants from outside the Community. They underlined the 'current employment situation' and the 'zero or much reduced' prospect of admitting new immigrant workers.[151]

In December 1974, in an effort to foster political cooperation, the final communiqué of the Paris Summit had announced 'a stage-by-stage harmonisation of legislation affecting aliens' and 'the abolition of passport control within the Community.'[152] Yet, as soon as November 1975, most states in the Council stressed that immigration policies were 'closely dependent on their foreign policies.'[153] Immigration states' efforts to preserve their autonomy in foreign policy led to the failure of the attempts to harmonise visa policies. In June 1979, German delegates also declared in the Council that they preferred 'questions of repatriation and occupational training of workers from third countries and their recruitment not to be discussed among member states.'[154] The Germans wanted the problem to be dealt with nationally, in order to avoid spending on training, which France advocated, or constrained recruitment options, as Italy was promoting Community preference. In the project announced in the December 1974 Paris Summit, member states only agreed, in June 1981, to try to issue a standard passport by 1 January 1985.[155] A common immigration policy thus failed, but Western European states were ready to coordinate their positions against immigration.

## Closure to Arab and African countries

The member states of the Community increased their common positions in interregional forums. After the Yom Kippur War and the first oil shock, they launched the Euro-Arab Dialogue with the Arab League states. On migration, their common goal was to stem Arab immigration to Europe and encourage the return of Arab immigrants to their countries of origin. In the mid-1970s, there were 800,000 workers from Arab countries in the Community.[156] Unemployment affected them seriously: unskilled, often employed in public works and construction, they were the first victims of both the economic downturn and new labour market regulations, such as the increase of the French minimum wage. In 1979, 54 percent of unemployed immigrants in France were from the Maghreb, while workers from the Maghreb only accounted for 39 percent of the immigrant workforce.[157] In March 1977, the Council of the Community agreed that 'independently of cyclical reasons' it was important to stabilise 'the non-national labour force at a lower level than that reached on the eve of the worsening of the employment situation.'[158]

In contrast, Arab states promoted the vocational training of Arab migrants in Europe to help them to keep jobs abroad. In October 1976, within the Dialogue, they called for measures to allow migrant workers to access vocational orientation, apprenticeships, training, occupational specialisation, and occupational retraining.[159] The Europeans shifted the debate to training migrant workers for their return to their country of origin. At the end of 1974, France had started implementing such training. In cooperation with Algeria and Tunisia, French actions targeted unemployed Maghreb immigrants and the countries of origin had to contribute financially to this training.[160] In Tunis, in February 1977, the Arabs called for a colloquium on occupational training of Arab workers in Europe. The Europeans made a counter-proposal on occupational preparation of migrant workers to help them assimilate in their countries of origin.[161] Both parties only agreed, ambiguously, to 'promote cooperation on the issue of occupational training.'[162]

In March 1977, the Europeans declared that they wanted to promote 'a new international division of labour,'[163] in which Arab countries would specialise in labour-intensive activities so as to maintain as many workers as possible. In February 1979, shortly before the Dialogue came to an end, the Arabs questioned the Europeans on the guarantee of a right to occupational training for Arab workers in Europe, and on the number of Arab workers who had benefited from occupational training during their stay in the Community.[164]

Return programmes matched neither the hopes of migrant workers nor the needs of their countries of origin. In the best cases, on their return, migrants moved into the tertiary sector as artisans or traders, without making any contribution to industrialisation of their country of origin.[165] Most of the time, returns concerned workers who had fallen into unemployment: consequently, they had accumulated neither capital allowing them to set up a small business nor useful experience for industries in the country of origin. In any case, as stressed in an OECD report, 'the type of development in the country of immigration [was] too remote from the nature of development and manpower needs in countries of emigration to guarantee the appropriate use of skills and training acquired abroad.'[166] For these reasons, the Algerian government advised its nationals against returning.[167]

In addition, the Europeans granted only minimal training for migrants returning to their countries of origin. In February 1977, German delegates wanted to limit this to a 'preparation for the process of return,' in which 'appropriate information' would be the 'dominant element for the greatest number' of migrants.[168] While France wanted to encourage the return of Arab migrants, Germany was less interested, and less willing, to earmark expenditure to this end.

The same objective of returns meant that the Europeans remained inflexible on their freedom to expel Arab migrants. They emphasised the 'limitations [to Arab immigrants' stay in Europe] based on public order, public safety, and public health.' It was common practice in the Ministries of the Interior to treat the presence of jobless foreigners on the territory as a threat to public order and thus as grounds for expulsion. In October 1976, the Arabs tried to negotiate a right to 'appeal, before a competent court' before applying these limitations.[169] In December 1976, Italian delegates in the Council of the Community alerted their partners on the interest for the Europeans 'to have a clause providing for the opportunity to present a legal appeal against an act by a public authority taken by an Arab state.'[170] There were only a few Arab immigrants in Italy, but Italian companies were active in Libya and Tunisia. The Italian government wanted to protect them against arbitrary expropriation or expulsion. In January 1977, Italy proposed that migrant workers hit by an expulsion order could at least present their case before a legal authority. Britain, the Netherlands, and Denmark shared the Italian view: there were few Arab immigrants in those countries, but their companies were involved in Arab countries. Yet, France and Belgium, where most Arab immigrants in the Community resided, were hostile.[171] With the support of West Germany, which did not want to create a precedent for the Turks, this proposal was discarded.[172]

The Europeans thus managed to coordinate their positions in the Euro-Arab Dialogue in order to arrange restrictive immigration policies. The Dialogue came to an end in April 1979 in the context of difficulties within the Arab League in the wake of the Egypt-Israel peace treaty.

In parallel, the states of the Community also managed to coordinate their positions against immigration from the African, Caribbean, and Pacific (ACP) countries associated with the Community. Both parties continued the association under regular new association conventions every five years or so: the conventions of Yaoundé I (1963) and Yaoundé II (1969) were followed by the conventions of Lomé I (1975), Lomé II (1979), Lomé III (1985), and Lomé IV (1989). On 31 January 1979, in view of the negotiation of Lomé II, the Joint Committee of the Consultative Assembly of the Association called for an agreement to protect the rights and improve the living conditions of ACP migrant workers in the Community. The Organisation of African Trade Union Unity also repeatedly drew attention to the situation of migrants from these countries in the Community. Lomé II, signed on 31 October 1979, only provided for equal treatment for legal migrants regarding working conditions and pay, as well as employment-related social benefits in the country of employment.[173] The agreement did not recognise any entitlement to export social security benefits and the equal treatment regarding working conditions and pay was in any case a demand made by unions in destination countries likely to reduce employment opportunities for migrants.

In view of Lomé III, in February 1982, the same Joint Committee included the issue of ACP migrants and students in the Community on the agenda of the meeting to be held in Geneva in June between representatives of economic and social circles of both parties and a delegation of the Joint Committee.[174] During this meeting Community representatives focused the debate on the return of migrants to their countries of origin, considering that this policy would make 'an effective contribution to the development of the countries of origin.'[175] Thus Lomé III went no further than its predecessor. Western European states thus shared restrictive views on immigration and managed to translate them into common positions in the negotiations with other regional groups.

## Facing the protest of emigration countries in the United Nations

The Europeans managed to arrange restrictive provisions in bilateral agreements with other regional groups, but the resulting tensions with African and Arab countries re-emerged within the United Nations. Here again, the member states of the Community created a common front against immigration. On 17 December 1979, the U.N. General Assembly, where emigration countries were a majority, delegated a working group to study measures to 'improve the situation and to enforce human rights and dignity of all migrant workers.' The expression 'all migrant workers' could mean both legal and illegal migrants.[176] On 15 December 1980, the General Assembly went further and authorised the working group to draft a convention. This turn of events challenged the restrictive immigration policies the Europeans were carrying out. In the Council of the Community, West Germany, Belgium, the Netherlands, Denmark, Italy, and Greece asserted the need for the 'active participation of member states in all the stages of the drafting of the Convention'[177] in order to influence the direction taken.

In March 1981, the European Commission reacted to a first document prepared for the U.N. Convention and considered that 'the new international economic order should mean that labour migration – such as experienced in the last twenty-five years . . . – be not repeated.'[178] In the Council, in March 1981, delegates considered important that 'the term "family member" in the sense of the Convention [be] defined in a restrictive sense.'[179] Most delegates opposed including the mother and the father of the migrant.[180] In May 1985, a few delegates wanted to eliminate a paragraph, judged as futile, which mentioned 'the beneficial effects' of 'labour mobility at the international level.'[181] In April 1986, delegates agreed to accept, as family members, only children who were 'dependent, under eighteen, and single.'[182] German delegates also opposed a right for migrant workers and their families, then under discussion in the United Nations, to a refund of all or part of social contributions paid, in cases where there was no export of benefits and they risked losing any right to them.[183]

The text of the draft convention included persons without valid documents as early as 1981.[184] Immediately, in March 1981, in Council discussions, the majority of delegates argued that states should 'keep their entire freedom regarding the right to expel migrants illegally present on their territories.' French delegates agreed to tackle illegal migration in the Convention, but only 'in order to settle . . . the obligation of states of origin . . . to accept the return of their citizens illegally present in another state.'[185] German and British delegates shared French concern.[186] German delegates also refused to recognise access to schooling for children of undocumented migrants, as proposed by the U.N. working group.[187] They wanted to eliminate from the draft Convention a measure that provided that the state of employment would bear the cost of expulsion.

Finally, the U.N. General Assembly adopted the Convention on 18 December 1990. The Europeans failed to block it or to significantly influence its provisions. At the same time they maintained a common front against immigration and no Community state has ever ratified or even signed the Convention.[188]

### Inference

As far as immigration flows from less-developed countries outside the Community were concerned, the migration regime between Western European states favoured further restrictions. The regime guaranteed the autonomy of the migration policy of each state. Member states defended the power of each state to expel immigrants as a key principle and collectively promoted the return of Arab and African migrants to their countries of origin. Last but not least, they collectively promoted a restrictive global migration regime encouraging returns. These trends corresponded to the converging preferences of France, West Germany, and Britain.

## Synopsis

With the exception of the enlargements to three Mediterranean countries, the new form taken by the migration regime among European states from the closure of 1973–1974 to around 1984 was thus marked by an increase in barriers against external migration. Within the Community the status quo prevailed, even though the increase of minimum wages could reduce migration opportunities. Western European states did not achieve more cooperation on migration matters in the Community. The absence of recognition of qualifications in a context of increased demand for university degrees and qualifications meant persisting restrictions. France was desperate to reduce the size of its immigrant population, but was not able to obtain British and German support to finance programmes to promote returns, because turning away foreign workers who had lost their jobs was less difficult in West Germany. The new German pro-natal policy also questioned the direction taken by the regime, as the West German government promoted the export of family benefits at the rate of the country of residence. Western European states achieved more cooperation in their relations with the countries of the Global South, where they collectively promoted a restrictive global migration regime.

# 5

# A SELECTIVE AND REGIONALIST REGIME, 1984–1992

The new Western European migration regime assumed its final shape between 1984 and 1992, thanks to the renewed cooperation between Germany, Britain, and France. Albeit open, the regime developed a selective and regionalist character. To date, historians have not yet fully linked the negotiation of the European Single Market, enacted by the Single European Act in 1986, with the parallel Schengen Agreement on border controls.[1] Similarly, scholars have not yet fully linked the growth of flows of skilled workers within Europe and the parallel developments in the European migration regime.[2] In this chapter, I will show how plans to abolish border controls were integrated in the dynamic towards the Single Market, and I will also develop existing scholarship on the way member states formulated general common rules on migrants from outside the Community as a precondition for the abolition of controls on persons at internal borders. I will explain how the regime evolved to favour the movement of highly skilled workers, before presenting the development of European citizenship. Finally, I will explicate how, following these developments, the member states defined common action to limit migratory pressure on Europe.

## Abolishing internal border checks

In 1984, cooperation resumed with the German plan to abolish internal border checks for persons. In this section, I will show that France and Germany moved along this project not because of reciprocal fears of protectionist attitudes in those two countries, as is commonly believed to be the case.[3] I will instead explain the link between this issue and the threat of British exclusion, which determined British participation in the intergovernmental conference to prepare the Single European Act.[4]

### The calls for market opening in Europe

In the early 1980s, international trade and financial flows within the Community were declining. Intra-Community trade had shrunk from 54.5 percent of the total trade of member countries in 1979 to 50.7 percent in 1981. The general rate of investment as a percentage of gross domestic product (GDP) had declined from 23 percent in 1970 to 20 percent in 1982. The annual rate of growth of investment was still 3.4 percent in the period 1976–1980, but became negative in the early 1980s. In particular, the share of intra-Community investment flows in all foreign investment flows from member countries was declining. Investments in the United States leapt from 16 percent in the early 1960s to 47 percent in the early 1980s of total German investments abroad. At this later date, the share of German investments in other member countries had sunk to its 1964 level of 28 percent. In the early 1960s, the United States attracted 6 percent of French investments abroad, against 28 percent in the early 1980s. In the same period, the share of French investments to other countries of the Community fell sharply from 54 percent to 28 percent.[5]

For the German Commissioner for the Internal Market in the European Commission, Karl-Heinz Narjes, 'the accumulation of customs barriers' within Europe explained these trends. Those barriers 'often curbed the investments of economic actors, unable to ascertain whether the production that they wanted to undertake would find easy market access beyond their national borders.'[6] On 24 February 1983, Narjes pointed out, in front of the Economic and Social Committee, the competition of the 'large internal markets of the United States and Japan, then later, of Latin America.' He wanted to unify the 'ten partial markets of the Community' to 'reach a European dimension of investments.' It was necessary to innovate in 'advanced technology' or 'the latest manufacturing techniques,' in which the European economy should specialise in the new international division of labour.

Nevertheless, counter to what Narjes argued, the drop in the share of intra-Community trade was also due to an increase in the value of trade with oil-producing countries following the spike in oil prices. Furthermore, the drop in intra-Community investment did not only benefit the United States, but also low-wage countries, able to attract the relocation of a growing number of productive activities, given the higher and more rigid wages in Europe and the halt on the immigration of cheap labour in Europe.

Narjes' position matched that of large European companies. In February 1983, the Union of Industrial and Employer Confederations of Europe (UNICE) addressed the following declaration to the secretary general of the Council:

> A vast market of continental dimensions . . . [is a vital factor] in providing European managers with conditions of reliability and competitiveness of their products. Companies will thus benefit from the cost reductions generated by mass production.[7]

To achieve the unified European market, large companies criticised in particular the cost of border controls. In January 1983, the Executive Council of the Western

European Union of Chambers of Trade and Industry of the Rhine, Rhone, and Danube regions, bringing together eighty-four chambers in seven countries, called for the rapid and complete elimination of administrative, organisational, or infrastructural obstacles to cross-border traffic. Its president, Alsatian Roland Wagner, wrote on 15 February 1983 to the secretary general of the Council of the Community that these obstacles stood in the way of expanding international trade and had a negative effect on the economic development of regions on both sides of the internal borders.[8]

UNICE and other organisations representing industry, commerce, crafts, and public companies of the Community addressed on 18 May 1983 a joint resolution to German Minister for Economic Affairs Otto Graf Lambsdorff, then acting president of the Council. They stressed 'the urgent need to reinforce the internal market.' The resolution called for a simplification of controls at intra-Community borders 'in a near future.'[9] In a telex of 20 March 1984 to French minister Charles Fiterman, then acting president of the Council of Ministers of Transport, German Herbert Pattberg, president of the Permanent Conference of Chambers of Commerce and Industry of the Community, considered that 'the administrative obstacles at borders [meant] . . . a harmful waste of time and money that it [was advisable] to eliminate as soon as possible.'[10] The economic and monetary commission of the European Parliament also considered that the expenses incurred by the waiting time at internal borders amounted to 1 billion ECU a year and the total cost of passage of intra-Community borders would have been in the order of 12 billion ECU.[11]

## The abolition of controls on persons at borders

Relaxing checks on persons was the easiest way to make cross-border traffic more fluid swiftly, without addressing the question of the reciprocal recognition of standards on goods. From July 1982 the Commission proposed to the Council a 'resolution on relaxing conditions in which the control of member-state citizens is practiced when crossing intra-Community borders.'[12] In the Council, in March 1983, most delegates shared the goal proposed by the Commission for 'the reduction of the duration of control of member-state citizens when crossing intra-Community borders.'[13] Yet in November 1983 only the delegates of the Benelux states were in favour of the draft resolution.[14] These were small countries, dependent on international trade, and surrounded by land borders that were the main obstacles to the flow of transport.

Other delegates rejected the Commission's plan on the grounds of security and the need to control immigration from outside the Community. In March 1983, most delegates could accept proceeding by random checks, as proposed by the Commission, only 'as long as belonging [of travellers] to a member state [was] recognised.'[15] British, Greek, and Irish delegates refused to give up systematic control.[16] Britain, Greece, and Ireland had no intra-Community land borders. Their insularity with the rest of the Community meant that the relaxation of checks on persons would only contribute marginally to easing traffic of goods with the other member countries, what was the main incentive otherwise for abolishing border checks. On 7 June 1984, the Council on Labour and Social Affairs finally adopted a resolution that recalled the objective of a passport union, defined by the heads of state and governments at the Paris Summit in December 1974, arguing that this goal included 'the abolition of all controls of persons at internal borders.'[17] The resolution nevertheless stressed the need to first resolve specific problems: 'the transfer of controls of persons at internal borders to external borders, the admission of third-country nationals, including the harmonisation of measures on visas.'

From around 1984, West Germany became more anxious to respond to the concerns of its exporters in order to boost economic prospects, and negotiated agreements to abolish border controls with all its Western neighbours, from Denmark to Austria. Meanwhile, the British government, similarly eager to boost exports, was worried about non-tariff barriers in Europe and proposed a programme to abolish 'all' barriers to intra-Community trade.[18] In the face of British-German convergence, France risked being isolated and having to accept the Single Market without getting anything in return. To break the British-German front, France came closer to West Germany in a sensitive domain, which did not interest Britain, namely, the abolition of border controls for persons. On 29 May 1984, in Rambouillet, Chancellor Kohl and President Mitterrand agreed on the abolition of formalities at land borders between France and West Germany for Community citizens.[19]

Before the meeting of heads of state and governments of the Community in the European Council, on 25–26 June 1984, Helmut Kohl and François Mitterrand had three key issues to discuss: the liberalisation of the internal market, which interested West Germany and Britain; the abolition of border controls, on which France and West Germany had just started work on an agreement; and the extension of majority voting in the Council.[20] The last point was intended to facilitate the realisation of the internal market, and meant Treaty revisions. France championed these Treaty revisions in order to include the objective of economic and monetary union in the Treaty. France pressed for this in order to avoid massive capital outflows after the establishment of the single market for capital, and also to reinforce its currency and to attract foreign investment.[21] The June 1984 European Council in Fontainebleau requested the Council and member states to study measures to attain 'the abolition of all police and customs procedures at intra-Community borders for the movement of persons' by the end of June 1985, and simultaneously facilitate the movement of goods.[22] In parallel, the European Council created an ad hoc committee on 'a People's Europe,' responsible for, among other things, examining the suggestion of 'minting a European currency, ECU.' The abolition of border controls for persons was thus at the centre of a general agreement between West Germany, Britain, and France, as a result of a Franco-German rapprochement.

The agreement between Kohl and Mitterrand in Rambouillet in May 1984 only applied to Community nationals. On 13 July 1984, French Minister of European Affairs, Roland Dumas, and the Head of the German Chancellery, Waldemar Schreckenberger, signed the Saarbrücken Agreement on the gradual abolition of all controls at the Franco-German border.[23] The stated purpose was to 'facilitate the movement of goods.' Because the control of goods was more difficult to abolish, the agreement mainly dealt with the control of persons. As a result of the cutback of border controls on people, the two parties agreed to draft a harmonisation of rules on issuing visas required by both governments for nationals from outside the Community.

Underlying this cooperation with Germany was France's goal of a revision of the Treaty, in order to include the goal of economic and monetary union in the momentum towards the Single Market. To get this revision accepted by the British, Mitterrand strove to threaten them with a realisation of the Single Market without them, around the Franco-German cooperation in relaxing border controls outside Community institutions, if the British were to block Community negotiations. The Benelux states had already abolished controls on persons at their internal borders. From December 1984, Kohl and Mitterrand agreed to regroup the Franco-German agreement with that of Benelux.[24] Thus a progressive trend towards the Single Market was taking shape without the British.

In June 1985, the European Council in Milan was to be crucial for the French plan of Treaty revision. During a meeting at the Elysée on 11 June 1985, French Minister of European Affairs Roland Dumas envisaged the convocation by the European Council in Milan of an intergovernmental conference to revise the Treaty, but without the British.[25] The following day, Mitterrand asked French member of the European Parliament Jean-Pierre Cot, senator and former minister Maurice Faure, and his councillor Jacques Attali whether a veto would be possible in the European Council or, conversely, whether a majority vote was feasible. Mitterrand was ready to accept 'a Europe of variable geometry' for what he called a 'People's Europe,' a theme which included minting a European currency. To put pressure on the British government, he wanted to have 'made progress, in a smaller group,' on the relaxation of border controls.[26]

The French strategy to abolish border controls for persons became a reality with the Schengen Agreement, signed on 14 June 1985,[27] two weeks before the European Council in Milan. The agreement extended the Saarbrücken Agreement between France and West Germany to the Benelux countries.[28] From 15 June 1985, police and customs authorities should only exercise, as a general rule, a simple 'visual surveillance of tourist vehicles . . . without stopping the vehicles.'

To offset the reduction of controls at internal borders, the signatory states of the Schengen Agreement had to work to 'move closer their policies in the domain of visas as swiftly as possible.'

The relaxation of border controls for persons had become France's instrument to come closer to West Germany and to direct the move towards the Single Market. In addition, an implementation outside Community institutions was a way for France to maintain sensitive issues on security and immigration from outside the Community within an intergovernmental framework. The abolition of controls for persons at internal borders was an important French concession. On 21 June 1985, the services of the French Prime Minister, Laurent Fabius, considered it 'necessary, at least in the immediate [future], to keep national competences and to conclude intergovernmental agreements to conserve some degree of autonomy of action (especially if our partners do not keep their commitments) on rather sensitive issues.'[29] On 27 June 1985, Mitterrand's advisor for European affairs, Elisabeth Guigou, reminded him of the general constraint that weighed on French diplomacy: 'We would be very isolated if we were to show reluctance on the principle of the effective realisation of the internal market by 1992.' She then summarised the prevailing point of view in ministries vis-à-vis the relaxation of border controls on persons: 'We think that the method of intergovernmental agreements is essential on such sensitive issues (drugs, immigration).'[30]

The French strategy of rapprochement with West Germany to abolish controls of persons at borders favoured the success of the French plans for treaty revision at the European Council in Milan, despite British opposition. Under German-British influence, the Single European Act, signed in February 1986, completed the Treaty of Rome with Article 8a, providing that the Community would decide 'measures intended to progressively establish the internal market during a period expiring on 31 December 1992.'[31] The definition of the internal market corresponded to Germany's broadest perspective: the internal market meant 'an area without internal borders in which the free movement of goods, persons, services and capital [was] guaranteed,' even if the British government considered that this free movement of persons only applied to member-state nationals. In line with French preferences, the Single European Act finally evoked the objective of a progressive realisation of economic and monetary union, albeit rather vaguely.

## The postponement of decisions

Despite the indecisive evocation of the economic and monetary union in the Single European Act, the French strategy had not failed because the basic decisions on the abolition of border controls for persons were postponed. The Schengen Agreement did not need to be ratified by the French Parliament; Title I only covered practical measures relating to regulatory power and controls in airports remained unchanged.

Title II dealt with commitments to reinforce controls at external borders and harmonise visa policies.[32] As long as this was not achieved, controls at internal borders were maintained to prevent immigration from outside the Community.[33] The signatories of the Schengen Agreement also committed themselves to harmonising their policies on the residence of foreigners 'if possible by 1 January 1990.'[34] Confidential lists annexed to the Schengen Agreement prepared these negotiations specifying the countries requiring particular attention; Yugoslavia was one of them.[35]

In the Single European Act too, an annexed declaration stated that 'the date of 31 December 1992 [did] not create an automatic legal effect' as far as the free movement of persons as per the new Article 8a was concerned.[36] Another declaration when the Act was adopted also echoed British concerns: 'None of these provisions affects the right of member states to take the measures that they judge necessary to control immigration from third countries.'[37] The abolition of internal border controls for persons thus remained at the planning stage.

### Inference

The abolition of internal border controls was to bring about a deep change to the European migration regime; yet, it was not decided first on migratory grounds. Its aim was to reinforce market integration within the Community, while British and German companies tried to boost their exports in Europe. France ended up supporting it in a rapprochement with West Germany, so as to prevent progress towards the Single Market under the sole action of a German-British coalition. In compensation for the Single Market, France thus obtained, through a revision of the Treaty, a commitment to progress in parallel towards monetary integration. The negotiation of a common immigration policy was, however, a precondition for actual lifting of internal border controls.

## Building up external borders

In the following years, the rules applied by Western European states to immigration from outside the Community converged to realise the abolition of internal border controls for the Single Market. The first negotiations took place between the twelve member states within Community institutions on the basis of the Single European Act. I will show here how British reluctance to abolish controls led those discussions to failure. Negotiations continued within the intergovernmental Schengen framework. As has already well been shown, this framework was not only useful to bypass British obstruction, it also allowed the five participating states to put pressure on the Mediterranean member states of the Community to implement effective closure to trans-Mediterranean immigration.[38] In this section, I will further explain how France, West Germany, and the Benelux states negotiated the strong external border, with their results subsequently extended to Mediterranean member states.

## The first negotiations among the Twelve

The actual abolition of internal border controls came up against increased asylum-seeking and migration pressure on Western Europe. While asylum remained one of the rare channels open for migration to Western Europe, the flows of asylum seekers increased constantly from 16,000 a year in the early 1970s, to 67,000 in 1983 and 537,000 in 1991.[39] West Germany alone received 103,000 applications for asylum in 1988. Half the applicants were from Eastern Europe, Yugoslavs accounting for 20 percent of all asylum seekers.[40] Clandestine immigration was also widespread, although difficult to quantify. The trend was thus to step up controls and not to relax them. In France, the National Front experienced an electoral breakthrough with an anti-immigration platform, winning almost 11 percent of the vote in the 1984 European elections and over 14 percent in the 1988 presidential election.

Given Britain's concern about the development of an autonomous Schengen group, British Home Secretary Douglas Hurd, then acting president of the Council, initiated negotiations among the Twelve by setting up, in October 1986, a special working group[41] in charge of preparing the 'area without internal borders' planned in the Single European Act.[42] When negotiations started, French delegates declared that a precondition for the abolition of internal border controls was the obligation for 'nationals of countries posing a problem of security or of irregular immigration' to obtain a visa to enter the Community.[43] In 1989, French law required a visa for the nationals of 114 countries, against only 69 in British law.[44] The harmonisation of such different policies in the sense advocated by France risked undermining Britain's relations with a large number of states.

In addition, Britain was insensitive to the interests underlying the abolition of internal border controls. In Council discussions on 5 April 1989, British delegates, followed by Irish, Danish, and Greek delegates, refused to include port and airport borders among those where controls on persons should be abolished.[45] This meant that Britain, Ireland, and Greece would not abolish any control at all, since they did not have land borders with the rest of the Community. British Prime Minister Margaret Thatcher declared publicly that the control of persons and vehicles in British ports and airports was necessary to combat terrorism and to prevent clandestine immigration.[46]

The fact that Britain and Ireland are islands accounts for this position. The abolition of controls on persons at British borders would have no decisive effect in facilitating the cross-border traffic of persons and goods, whereas the borders between the five signatories of the Schengen Agreement – the Benelux countries, France, and West Germany – passed through open countryside and vehicles were only forced to stop because of controls. The traffic between Britain and other member countries was already subject to cargo handling delays and border controls on persons did not make a great difference. Moreover, because Britain was an island, British border controls were effective. In contrast, the great number of unguarded secondary routes at the borders between the Schengen Five made their controls ineffective.[47] The British proposal excluding port and airport borders appeared too restrictive for Belgium, France, and West Germany, and was rejected.

## The Schengen framework

In the face of British obstruction in Community institutions, the Germans backed the Schengen framework to speed up the abolition of border controls and clear the way for German exports of goods and services. In the first half of 1989, the German and Dutch governments called for a speeding-up of work to implement the Schengen Agreement among the Five, with the prospect of its coming fully into force on 1 January 1990.[48] For France, it was still a serious issue. Labour market tensions made it unlikely for immigrants from outside the Community to find a legal job in France. Clandestine immigration would then fuel the illegal labour market and the parallel economy, with serious consequences for internal security. On 13 December 1989, Chancellor Kohl's Minister for Schengen Affairs, Lutz Stavenhagen, announced to President Mitterrand's technical advisor for European Affairs, Elisabeth Guigou, that the Chancellery wanted the Convention of application of the Schengen Agreement to be signed by 15 December. To obtain French agreement, he pointed out that the Convention had already taken four years of negotiations, whereas it had taken 'very little time to reach an agreement on the principles of economic and monetary union.'[49] The trade-off with Germany between monetary integration and the abolition of border controls led Mitterrand to instruct his Minister of Foreign Affairs, Roland Dumas, to be ready to conclude the negotiation.[50]

French consent was not only the result of this trade-off. The Schengen Five framework was also favourable to define cooperation in compliance with French views on immigration controls. Among the Twelve, France's priority was to get all member states to agree on a visa obligation for the nationals of the Maghreb countries, Turkey, and Yugoslavia – then the main emigration countries to France. France's four partners in the Schengen group already enforced visas for nationals of these countries, with the exception of Yugoslavia.[51] France was therefore more likely to reach a satisfactory agreement in the Schengen group, to be extended later to the Twelve, than it would have been in a negotiation immediately among the Twelve. In addition, France's four Schengen partners agreed that nationals from outside the Community would have to report to an administrative authority on their arrival in the territory of any member state, even 'in a public office set up for this purpose' directly upon entry to the territory, which looked very much like a continued border control.[52]

However, French Minister of the Interior, Pierre Joxe, was still concerned about 'the gaps represented by the external borders of Federal Germany.'[53] While Joxe wanted a control of the dividing line with East Germany to combat clandestine immigration, the German Basic Law forbade considering it as a border.[54] Furthermore, with political developments in Central Europe during summer 1989, the West German government formulated an open policy. If Western European states, while negotiating the Schengen Area, set up closed borders to immigration from Eastern Europe, the pro-Western impetus in Communist countries risked petering out. The Schengen Five had accepted the principle of a hard core of countries subject to a visa by all partners, and the fact that this list could only be changed by a unanimity vote. At a meeting of the Five on 21 October 1989, German delegates wanted to exclude Eastern European countries from this hard core.[55] With the agreement of 13 November among the ministers of the Five, France won its bid for visas, which were maintained for 104 countries, including Eastern European countries. This French success was limited by the fact that the Germans still excluded Yugoslav nationals from any visa obligation.[56]

Yet while the convention implementing the Schengen Agreement had to be signed in December 1989, the disagreement on the permeable nature of Germany's Eastern borders persisted. Under the Convention, each member state committed to submit for approval by cosignatory states any agreement with another state relating to border crossing. The West German government wanted to exclude agreements with the German Democratic Republic from this measure, and wanted this reserve to be recorded in the text of the convention.[57] West Germany also wanted to declare that East Germany was not a foreign country.[58] Although the West Germans had always tried to speed up negotiations on the Schengen Convention, the irreconcilable nature of the positions and the strength of the interests at stake led them to postpone the signing of the Convention until German reunification was official and the text of the Convention could be duly updated.[59]

Another pending issue was France and West Germany's partners concern over their open asylum law. What would happen if asylum seekers were authorised to move freely within the Schengen Area?[60] The West German government expected 150,000 asylum applications for 1989, that is twice as many as two years earlier.[61] The Dutch Parliament voted a motion calling for the inclusion in the Schengen Convention of a commitment to harmonise the criteria of recognition of refugee status, with the intention to restrict those criteria. During the ministerial meeting among the Five in Bonn on 12–13 November 1989, French Minister for European Affairs Edith Cresson objected to the Dutch request[62] in order to avoid 'going towards a downgraded right to asylum' and nourishing 'the accusations on governments by non-governmental organisations and humanitarian associations.'[63]

The prospect of German reunification resolved the last difficulties shortly afterwards. In the first half of 1990, the German government asked the Dutch presidency of the Schengen group to restart negotiations. Under both Article 116 of the German Basic Law and the provisions of the Treaty of Rome, East German nationals were treated as West German nationals and enjoyed freedom of movement within the Community; nevertheless they had beforehand to hold documents issued by West Germany. Given the number of East German nationals then enjoying the opening of the border and likely to migrate within the Community, the West German government wanted to relieve its administrative services from the task of issuing these persons with the documents allowing them to assert their rights in the Community. The West German government therefore wanted East German nationals to be able to enter the territory of member states with their East German documents.[64] In that decisive year of 1990, the open migration regime in the Community was a key asset for the West German government to smooth East Germany's transition away from Communism.

Furthermore, the German government wanted to revise the list of countries subject to visa in the draft of the Schengen Convention and to remove the countries of Central and Eastern Europe. According to the president of the German delegation in the Schengen dialogue in March 1990, 'The recent development in the reforming states of Central and Eastern Europe allow us to relax visa obligations.' If its partners did not follow suit, Germany was ready to ask for the inclusion of special derogations in the convention: 'The delegation of the Federal Republic of Germany, he declared, reserves the right to propose an exception to Article 9(2) for specific states of the Conference for Security and Co-operation in Europe.'[65] Article 9(2) of the draft convention planned a common visa regime among the contracting parties in relation to third countries, and provided that the list of countries subject to visa requirement could only be changed by common agreement. German influence was sufficient to make France give in. The partners agreed to lift visas for Hungary and Czechoslovakia, but France managed to maintain them, for 'immigration control,' for Yugoslavia and the other countries of Central and Eastern Europe.[66] France agreed to authorise full access of East German nationals to the Schengen Area as of 1 June 1990. As regarded Schengen's external border, the partners agreed that, given the prospect of German reunification, the Convention would also extend to East Germany.[67]

France's agreement to German demands and its willingness to sign the Convention were facilitated by the partial satisfaction of the French demand to amend Article 2 of the draft convention. This article established the basic purpose of the Convention, that is the abolition of controls on persons at the Community's internal borders. French Minister of the Interior Pierre Joxe wanted this principle to be subject to the condition of 'declaration on entry' for nationals from outside the Community entering the territory of a member state from another member state, as per Article 22 of the draft convention.[68] On 31 May 1990 the Schengen central negotiating group adopted the French request for a reference to Article 22 in Article 2.[69] The Convention was then signed in Schengen on 19 June 1990. It provided for special exceptions to the abolition of internal border controls and to the common visa regime when public order or national security called for immediate action.[70] It also provided for sanctions against maritime or air carriers who transported a foreigner without the necessary documents to the territory of the contracting parties; they were legally bound to return any national from outside the Community to the country that had issued the travel documents.[71] These measures, together with the fact that the list of countries subject to visas still included 102 countries, reassured France.

## Negotiations among the Twelve and the enlargement of the Schengen Area

In parallel, negotiations between the Twelve continued in the Council. The most contentious point dealt with asylum seekers, with France's open asylum law being placed under scrutiny. In Brussels, in March 1989, French ambassador Emile Cazimajou stressed that the United Nations monitored asylum issues 'scrupulously.'[72] In September 1989, French delegate Jean-Marc Sauvé also stressed the pressure of 'associations in defence of foreigners' in the domain of asylum.[73] Consequently, member states could not agree about harmonising asylum law at the Community level, but only about avoiding 'the same asylum seeker [presenting] as many applications for asylum as there [were] states' to apply to.[74] To achieve this, the ministers of the Interior and Justice of the Twelve signed a convention in Dublin on 15 June 1990 within an intergovernmental framework, to determine 'the State responsible for examining applications for asylum lodged in one of the Member States of the European Communities.'[75]

The same provisions on asylum appeared in the Dublin Convention and in the Schengen Convention, signed four days later on 19 June 1990. The criteria to determine the state responsible for dealing with asylum applications were the following: a member state had already granted refugee status to a family member of the applicant;[76] a member state had issued the applicant with an entry visa or a residence permit;[77] or an applicant had reached the territory of the contracting parties by irregularly crossing the border of a member state.[78] In spite of these provisions, France wanted[79] and obtained[80] that each member state could still examine an application for asylum notwithstanding the normal criteria determining the state responsible. Shortly afterwards, the number of asylum seekers in Germany reached a significant magnitude. In a move to reduce the number of asylum requests, the immigration ministers of the Twelve met in London on 30 November and 1 December 1992 and adopted two resolutions on asylum applications in order to complete the Dublin

Convention. The London Resolutions excluded the asylum applications of persons coming from countries considered as safe or having passed through a country considered as safe.[81]

In 1991, the member states of the Community negotiated the Treaty of Maastricht to rearrange their relations within a European Union. On this occasion, the Twelve included in the Treaty of Maastricht, as the Justice and Home Affairs pillar, the common visa policy already defined in the Schengen Convention. The Council could decide with a qualified majority as of 1 January 1996 on the list of third countries whose nationals should hold a visa when crossing the external borders of the Union.[82] Yet, the negotiations among the Twelve on the abolition of internal border controls remained blocked, notwithstanding the deadline of 1 January 1993 stipulated by the Single European Act for the constitution of the area without internal borders. Britain and Denmark judged that Article 8a of the Treaty inserted by the Single European Act only applied to the nationals of member states and they maintained border controls to check the nationality of travellers.[83]

The failure to transfer all Schengen provisions into European Union law led instead to a gradual extension of the Schengen group to include other member states. France wanted to have the candidates for membership accept the Schengen Convention as it stood. As regarded Italy's application, at the meeting of the Schengen central negotiating group on 31 May 1990 in Brussels, French delegates emphasised 'the need to consider membership as a commitment without particular rules, since the text of the Convention formed an integral whole and the bloc of countries subject to common visa provisions could not be reduced.'[84] To reply to French demands, in November 1990, Italy drafted a law to 'control growing migratory flows.'[85] Italy accepted all Schengen provisions and signed the Schengen Agreement and the Schengen Convention in Paris on 27 November 1990.[86] In line with its obligations on the external border of the Schengen Area, in 1991 Italy announced a state of alert to reject Albanian 'boat people' and sent back almost 20,000 Albanians to Albania.[87] The Schengen group was then enlarged to take in other Mediterranean member states.

## Inference

The incompatibilities in the visa policies of France and Britain, and the divergence between Britain, as an island, and West Germany on the opportunity to abolish internal border controls for persons, resulted in Britain blocking the negotiations among the Twelve and letting the Schengen group develop on its own. West Germany, eager to promote its exports of goods and services in Europe, then called on France to bring about a rapid implementation of the Schengen Agreement, in return for a German commitment on economic and monetary union. France wielded significant power thanks to the strategic nature of its borders for the establishment of the border-free area envisaged by the Germans. While accepting the process, France dominated the implementation to deal with the security problem that the abolition of border controls created. With its Schengen partners, France defined restrictive rules before enlarging the Schengen group to Mediterranean member states.

## Helping the highly skilled

In parallel to the negotiations on border controls, the other elements of the Single Market gradually came in force. Britain and West Germany thus hoped to boost the opportunities for their companies in other member countries and lead to the constitution of companies of a European dimension, able to compete with North American and Asian companies. The prospect of letting such large companies emerge generated an incentive to go ahead with the mutual recognition of occupational and educational qualifications in the Community. This was a necessary precondition for the movement of managerial staff and business expansion in Europe. The geographer Russell King has emphasised the increase of the share of qualified migrants in intra-Community flows during those years.[88] In this section I shall complete the analysis by linking this trend with the developments of the European migration regime.

### Promoting the mobility of managerial staff

The formation of a single European market called for a greater degree of mobility for managerial staff, to promote the development of companies with a European dimension. In contrast with the impasse in negotiations during the previous decade, negotiations on the migration of employed workers were able to start again in the context of West German unemployment coming under control around 1984 and gradually declining thereafter.[89] Even though West Germany remained the main immigration country for Community migrants, Britain played a greater role in the Western European migration system in the 1980s. While the number of Community nationals residing in France increased by only 36,000 during the 1980s, it increased by 316,000 in Britain (171,000 excluding Ireland).[90] The two main actors in the Western European migration system – Britain and West Germany – were both interested in promoting the migration movements that mattered for the implementation of the Single Market, that is the migration of skilled professionals.

Under German influence, in June 1984, the European Council in Fontainebleau called for the study of 'measures which [could] permit to reach in a short time and in any case before the end of the first semester of 1985 . . . a general system of equivalence of university diplomas.'[91] In January 1985, German representative in COREPER Gisbert Poensgen called for the abolition of the obstacles of mutual recognition of diplomas, certificates, and other qualifications. In order to move more swiftly, he recommended giving up efforts to harmonise training. He looked for an easy way to achieve a 'breakthrough for a large number of professions.' The aim to gain entry for German firms in European markets, which required progress in the recognition of qualifications, drove the German position. As the recognition of qualifications had become firmly linked with the negotiation on the right of establishment, the German government was looking for ways to unblock the central negotiation on the right of establishment, that is for architects.[92]

Changes in the professional field of architects in Western Europe helped usher in an agreement. In June 1983 in West Germany, the Federal Chamber of Architects wrote to the German Minister of Foreign Affairs, Hans-Dietrich Genscher, on the importance of the architects directive, because 'German architects in the border areas with Belgium, France, etc. [were] prevented from practising their profession on the other side of the border.'[93] German architects pointed out how it was impossible to engage in 'export of design services' and the 'serious damage' that this created. Meanwhile, the national associations of architects reinforced their monopoly on activities in the domain of architecture. A French law of 3 January 1983 created a monopoly of architects for architectural projects. In Baden-Württemberg, a law of 28 November 1983 created a monopoly of architects for construction projects.[94] These trends allowed a convergence between West Germany and France.

In June 1985, the Council adopted a directive that liberalised opportunities to the benefit of a small category of practitioners of architecture.[95] The directive concerned both employed and self-employed architects, and both the right of establishment and the international provisions of services. While the West German government had blocked negotiations for several years on the question of engineers from *Fachhochschulen*, it gave up having the equivalence of training provided in these schools recognised. The directive covered only those certified to use the title of architect in member countries.[96] In some German *Länder* the *Fachhochschulen* still awarded degrees giving access to the profession of architect after three years' training. Under pressure from the German Chamber of Architects to make this negotiation succeed, the German government gave way and Article 4 of the directive stipulated that three years' training at a *Fachhochschule* had to be 'completed by four years' professional experience in West Germany, attested by a certificate issued by the German Association of Architects. The additional influence of the Association of Architects in West Germany thus facilitated the solution of the case that had blocked negotiations for several years. The Council created homogeneous opportunities for establishment and provision of services in the Community, but within a narrow definition of the profession of architect. The directive protected the claims of architects' associations and limited competition caused by this liberalisation.

In its communication to the media on the day the Council adopted the directive, the secretary general of the Council specified that this case was 'considered as a pilot project on how to realise free movement in the technical domain.'[97] Rapid progress on these matters corresponded to the demands of big companies. In December 1988, the Association of European Chambers of Commerce and

Industry, Eurochambers, considered that one of the goals of the internal market was 'the realisation of a true freedom of establishment and movement of persons within the Community,' which meant a 'correspondence of professional qualifications' for employed workers.[98] The Council adopted then a directive relative to a general system for the recognition of diplomas, applying to both self-employed and employed workers. The member states had to grant access on their territories to nationals of other member states practising a regulated profession, and holding a national diploma issued in another member state.[99]

The Council reached an agreement by limiting this recognition of diplomas to the highest university degrees, facilitating essentially the mobility of the most highly qualified. The Commission's initial proposal, on 22 July 1985, was for a general system for the recognition of higher education qualifications. Yet some governments wanted to keep the protection enjoyed by many categories of diploma-holders obtained after short-term training. Consequently, in May 1986, the Commission revised its proposal and limited it to diplomas 'awarded on completion of professional education and training of at least three years' duration.'[100] The system targeted highly qualified professionals and top managerial staff of large companies, likely to move from one country to another within the Single Market.

In addition, member states and the Commission wanted to stimulate student migration to promote the long-term mobility of highly qualified staff throughout Europe. In the academic year 1980/1981, only around 50,000 Community students were enrolled in another member country's university; more than half of them were Greek, with 16,000 studying in Italy.[101] The share of migrant Community students was only 1.1 percent in Britain and 2.25 percent in Italy.[102] In December 1985, the Commission justified its proposal of a Council decision to adopt an action programme for student mobility by pointing out that 'the degree of mobility [of] students [was] . . . inadequate in the face of the need . . . of Community countries for graduates with personal experience of other Community countries.'[103] Through the Erasmus programme, the Commission's goal was to expand 'the percentage of students spending a period of study in another member state during their university career to around 10 percent of the student population' by 1992.[104] The Commission targeted the 'future generations of decision-makers,' 'people in [future] positions of responsibility.'[105]

In March 1986, most national delegates in the Council's Education Committee recognised that the programme had to target 'highly qualified personnel.' Irish delegates summed up the dominant opinion whereby first-year university students were not eligible for the programme; to be eligible a student should have 'shown their capacity to remain in the system.'[106] The Commission proposal was to ensure that business 'alliances with companies of other countries of the European Community [would appear] as a natural and positive line of action' for those benefiting from the programme. They had to recognise 'the crucial need for growing cooperation with the partners of other member states.'[107] Most delegates in the Education Committee wanted that personnel to be 'able to work in a European spirit.'[108] On 15 June 1987, the Council adopted the Decision creating the Erasmus programme.[109] To prevent the programme from being dedicated to language students, on 28 July 1989 the Council adopted a separate programme, Lingua, dedicated to the latter. It was an 'essential complement to the Erasmus programme,'[110] insofar as it allowed the latter to focus on students in management, engineering, or science, who ended up occupying the top positions in large companies. Finally, the Erasmus programme provided for the mutual recognition of academic qualifications and periods of study, with a European system of transferable academic credits within the Community.[111]

As the main contributors to the Community budget, Britain, France, and West Germany only wanted to finance the programme for an initial period of three years[112] and to limit the budget to 85 million ECU. On 14 December 1989, the Council extended Erasmus for five years more and earmarked 192 million ECU for the first three years alone.[113] This increase took into account the demand that the programme had generated, three times as large in the first two years 1987/1988 and 1988/1989 as the sums that had been earmarked.[114]

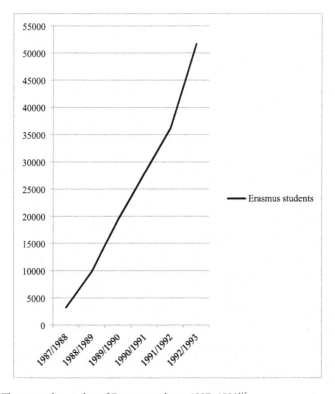

*Figure 5.1* The rise in the number of Erasmus students, 1987–1993[115]

In 1989 the Lingua programme also received a budget of 200 million ECU for a five-year period.[116] By recognising advanced academic qualifications and through programmes promoting student mobility, the migration regime between member states thus promoted the movement of qualified professionals, which mattered for the expansion of big companies within the Single Market.

The new pro-skill nature of the regime encouraged rich states in Western Europe to join in order to promote the mobility of their highly qualified workers. Austria and the Nordic states applied to join Erasmus through the intervention of Denmark and West Germany. In November 1989, German and Danish delegates in the Education Committee got their partners to open up Erasmus 'to the participation of EFTA [European Free Trade Association] countries.'[117] Shortly afterwards, the Porto Agreement, signed on 2 May 1992,[118] adopted in the framework of the European Economic Area, applied the provisions of the Treaty of Rome on the free movement of labour, social security of migrant workers, the right of establishment and the free provision of services between the Community and EFTA countries. The latter then included Iceland, Norway, Sweden, Finland, Austria, Liechtenstein, and Switzerland. Switzerland yet arranged to preserve its entry, residence, and work permits for foreigners and its quantitative restrictions for new residents and seasonal workers until 1 January 1998.[119]

### Protective measures

Many limitations remained. The directive introducing a general system for the recognition of qualifications included exceptions for legal professions. The directive underlined 'the differences between the legal systems of member states' and stated that the 'preparation attested by a university degree . . . in the law of the member state of origin as a general rule [did] not cover the legal knowledge required by the host member state.'[120] In such a profession, the destination member state was entitled to set a test for the migrant.

Furthermore, in France, the civil service enjoyed exceptional treatment. When adopting the directive on the general system for the recognition of higher education degrees, French delegates requested to be set down in the Council minutes that the directive in no way 'infringed the employer's right to insist on . . . recruitment by means of a public examination, irrespective of the nationality of the person concerned.'[121] The French Ministry for the Civil Service considered that the recognition of qualifications only meant that a person had satisfied the precondition of the university degree required to take a public examination. It did not give access to a position associated with the successful outcome of such an exam. In particular this affected the entire teaching profession.[122] The German government, albeit unsuccessfully, called on the French government to adapt this position: from the German point of view, German civil servants should be entitled to permanent appointment in the French civil service without having to pass a recruitment exam, often easier for French candidates. For access to internal exams within the Civil Service, which were less selective, the French Ministry for the Civil Service considered that the years spent working in the civil service of other member states could not be taken into account.[123]

As far as low-skilled or unskilled migrant workers were concerned, the regime did not become more open than in the late 1960s, despite the inclusion of the plan for European monetary integration in the Treaty of Maastricht, signed in February 1992. According to Robert Mundell's influential economic theory of optimal currency areas, developed in the early 1960s, monetary integration required indeed a high degree of labour mobility.[124] Yet, young workers with no professional qualifications still enjoyed few exchange opportunities. From 1979 to 1984, the second exchange programme for young workers within the Community only involved 5,366 young people, that is less than 900 a year on average. The budget had been cut to 2 million ECU in 1985, that is thirty-two times less than for the Erasmus programme at the time of its first renewal, although the latter only covered students and was supplemented by the Lingua programme. In the mid-1980s, there were around 52 million persons aged between 18 and 28 in the Community. Among them, only 6 million were students. The great majority were either employed workers or unemployed.[125] In France, by the end of 1984, 24.6 percent of active workers aged between 16 and 24 were unemployed. They amounted to half the total population of unemployed in France.[126]

France got its partners to use the third Community exchange programme for young workers to help the young unemployed.[127] Already from 1986 onwards, the young unemployed accounted for 40 percent of those taking part in the programme. Moreover the budget was boosted to 4.5 million ECU a year for 1986 and 1987. The number of participants grew to around 3,000 young people a year, also thanks to the reduction of the average duration of stay.[128] Compared to the number of young unemployed, which was over 1 million in France alone, the total of 3,000 young people involved in the programme each year throughout the Community was still minimal. Under the new form of the European migration regime, opportunities were proportional to the level of qualifications.

This evolution highlights the overrepresentation of skilled migrants in intra-Community migration flows from that time onwards. The geographer Russell King explained this pattern by the 'qualification of demand, Europe's growing need for scientists, technicians, administrators, and other persons with an international profile.'[129] The evolution of the European migration regime also favoured this trend. In parallel, the geography of flows also changed. Flows of less-qualified emigrants from Mediterranean Europe shrank. Beside the regime's selective bias, migration and trade flows with the rest of the Community had boosted the economic development of these countries and also accounted for this trend. New southbound flows appeared instead. During the second half of the 1980s, the countries of Mediterranean Europe attracted new immigrants from Northern Europe. These were often qualified or highly qualified employed or self-employed workers following the investments of big companies in Mediterranean Europe. In 1990 three-quarters of legal foreign residents in Italy, Spain, Greece, and Portugal were from developed countries.[130] Finally, cross-border migration flows in Northern Europe also increased. French frontier workers to West Germany accounted for around one third of all intra-Community flows, that is 110,000–120,000 persons.[131]

### Inference

In parallel to the construction of the European Single Market, the European migration regime thus came to favour the movement of qualified professionals. The recognition of qualifications facilitated the access of British and German companies to European markets. Not only could these companies move their managerial staff more easily, but also the movement of highly qualified self-employed workers (e.g. architects, doctors) could prepare the subsequent establishment of companies from the same countries. In addition, the Erasmus programme aimed at boosting the mobility of the future managerial staff of big European companies, moving from one country to another and working in a European spirit. Alongside this selective opening, unskilled migrants continued to come up against the same barriers as in the previous decade, including high minimum wages or the lack of financial support once unemployed. These features of the European migration regime went hand in hand with an evolution in the composition of flows, characterised by the overrepresentation of qualified migrants.

## Creating European citizens

Alongside the shift in the European migration regime to promote the movement of more skilled workers, the regime underwent an even more deep-rooted change with the development of European citizenship. This issue has already been interpreted in various ways, which put forward the impetus created by the Single European Act, the objective to improve the status of the highly skilled migrants within the Community, and the specific role of Mediterranean member states.[132] In this section, I will show why these explanations are unconvincing or inaccurate, and I will instead highlight the major role of geopolitical factors in this development.

## Momentum from Fontainebleau

The December 1974 Paris Summit of heads of state and governments had encouraged a reflexion on special rights to be recognised to the nationals of the Community member states. It did not succeed in the following decade, because member states could not agree on a general right of residence and voting and eligibility rights for Community migrants. The impetus allowing negotiations to restart came from the European Council in Fontainebleau on 25–26 June 1984. The Council considered it 'essential that the Community . . . adopts measures likely to reinforce and promote its identity and its image for its citizens and the rest of the world,' and created an Ad Hoc Committee on a People's Europe to 'prepare and coordinate these actions.'[133] The juxtaposition of its image for its citizens and the rest of the world highlighted the link between European citizenship and a common foreign policy. Such a step occurred against the backdrop of Europeans organising for their security. The deployment of SS20 missiles in Central Europe, with a range of only 5,000 km and sufficiently precise to hit military targets, rather than cities, raised fears of a decoupling of U.S. and Western European defence.[134] In Rome, on 26–27 October 1984, the Ministers of Foreign Affairs and Defence of the Western European Union reactivated this organisation created in 1954 and announced the definition of a European security identity with the progressive harmonisation of member-state defence policies.

On the basis of the Ad Hoc Committee's report, the Commission made proposals to the Council to introduce aspects of European citizenship: a general right of residence and electoral rights for Community migrants. It was in this context that the Council resolved the issue of family allowances when the family did not live in the country of employment. In the mid-1980s the Council had still not adopted the uniform solution provided for under Article 98 of Regulation 1408/71, despite the deadline of 1 January 1973. The exception for France, which allowed the export of family allowances at the rate of the country of residence (Article 73(2)), was only intended as a temporary measure. It therefore came as no surprise when, on 15 January 1986, the Court of Justice of the Community judged in *Pinna v. Caisse d'allocations familiales de la Savoie* that 'Article 73(2) of Regulation 1408/71 [was] invalid.'[135] In accordance with the text of the regulation, the Court invited the Council to find the uniform solution as per Article 98 so that all member states paid family allowances at the rate of the country of employment. A solution had to be achieved quickly following the Court's judgement, and West Germany gave up its position on applying the law of the country of residence. The stakes were high, since in 1985 1.2 million Community workers were resident in another member country.[136] In its Regulation 3427/89 of 3 October 1989 the Council agreed to extend the export of family benefits to all member states according to the rate of the country of employment.[137]

Beside this isolated German concession, negotiations between member states collapsed again after the momentum of the Fontainebleau Summit had petered out after the end of the missile crisis. As in previous decade, negotiations on a general right of residence and voting and eligibility rights for migrants failed. This issue divided Mediterranean member states and immigration states.

### The position of Mediterranean member states

By 1986, the Community included four major traditional countries of emigration, with important communities of emigrants in the rest of Western Europe: Italy, Spain, Portugal, and Greece. All favoured the creation of European citizenship granting a general right of residence, voting and eligibility rights to their emigrants. In its presidency of the Council in the first half of 1989, the Spanish government wanted to realise the Commission's proposal for a directive on the right for Community citizens to vote in local elections.[138] In May 1990, the Greek government drafted a memorandum calling for European citizenship and the right for Community migrants to vote in local and European elections.[139] In late September 1990, the Spanish government sent its partners a note titled 'Towards European Citizenship,'[140] in which it argued that the core of citizenship had to be the 'full freedom of movement, the free choice of the place of residence, and the free participation in the political life of the place of residence.' The latter should include the participation 'in electoral consultations organised in the country of residence.'[141] At the end of November 1990, the Portuguese government adopted a similar position.[142]

Mediterranean member states tried to improve the situation of their sizeable communities of nationals in other member countries. Yet not all emigration countries promoted voting rights for their nationals abroad: Morocco, for example, was hostile to the idea.[143] For Mediterranean member states, the right to vote in local elections would grant their citizens abroad nationality-based rights, thus reducing their interest in acquiring the nationality of the destination country. As a result, it could promote their return and keep them within the national community, which could use emigrants as a lever of international influence. Returns were less important for Morocco. In these conditions, European citizenship corresponded to a status for their nationals abroad that maximised the interests of Mediterranean member states.

These member states were also ready to enhance the status of foreign residents from the Community on their territories through European citizenship. Spain and Portugal were becoming 'the well-known destinations for retired people from Community member states.'[144] The main host regions were the Algarve in Portugal and the southern and south-eastern coasts of Spain. The number of European nationals living in Spain grew by 48 percent during the 1980s, reaching 174,000 in 1990. In Italy, that number rose by 68 percent and reached 267,000. These new immigrants were to a large extent professionals and pensioners.[145] It was beneficial to attract this type of immigrants. An extended right of residence for retirees and political rights allowing them to take part in the political life of their place of residence would encourage such movements. This upgrading of the status of foreign residents from Europe might have been possible unilaterally, but this would not have guaranteed reciprocity and it would have been diplomatically difficult to justify discrimination against foreign residents from the Maghreb, who were more and more numerous in the Iberian Peninsula. The creation of European citizenship integrated this upgrading of the status of foreign residents in the framework of the measures taken by a regional organisation, which justified an unequal treatment of Maghreb immigrants.

## The position of immigration states in North-West Europe

The member states with the largest foreign population on their territories nevertheless had the greatest power over these questions, since it was on their territories that the rights associated with European citizenship would or would not be applied. Moreover they were those likely to experience costs with this upgrading of status, whereas for Mediterranean member states it was mostly a beneficial operation. The proportion of foreigners in the total population, irrespective of nationality, was below 1 percent for Spain, Greece, Italy, and Portugal.[146] In the three member states that had already introduced the right to vote in local elections for foreigners – Denmark, Ireland, and the Netherlands – the number of foreigners was also low. In Britain, the stock of Community migrants, with the exception of the Irish, still accounted for a small share of the population. Around 85 percent of Community migrants lived in Belgium, France, or West Germany. In Belgium, foreigners accounted for 9 percent of the total population, two-thirds of whom were Community nationals, frequently Italian, French, or Spanish. Generally these foreigners were more francophone than Dutch-speaking, which meant that they could alter the political balance among linguistic communities in Belgium if they received the right to vote. Belgian worries were stronger in the Brussels conglomeration, where Community nationals were numerous: in the municipality of Saint-Josse for instance, foreigners accounted for 51 percent of the population. In Luxembourg, foreigners accounted for 26.3 percent of the population: 92.7 percent were Community nationals, mostly from Portugal.

The presence of a large foreign population from outside the Community could also shape a state's position on European citizenship, since it might prove difficult to grant political rights to Community residents without doing the same, sooner or later, for all foreign residents. In the mid-1980s West Germany had around 4.5 million foreign residents, amounting to 7.3 percent of the population: 12.9 percent were Italian, 6.4 percent Greek, 3.7 percent Spanish, and 2.3 percent Portuguese.

The 3.7 million foreigners in France in 1982 accounted for 6.8 percent of the population. Community nationals were 42 percent of all foreigners, and were mainly Portuguese, Italian, and Spanish. The natural position of immigration states was to oppose European citizenship.

## The end of the Cold War

With the upheavals associated with the end of the Cold War, Germany's security concern helped relaunch plans for European citizenship. After the fall of the Berlin Wall, West Germany was determined to achieve German reunification and to roll back Russian influence in the East. In Western Europe the projected losses for Russia in this period raised the spectre of Russia using force to maintain a territorial status quo. The risk of armed conflicts in Europe was increasing.

It mattered to have Russia accept change by demonstrating that any aggressive behaviour on its part would only speed up the construction of a European defence policy. European citizenship was a key element of a common foreign and security policy, because ensuring political rights to migrants from the European Union was a way to create the civic basis necessary to make this common foreign policy

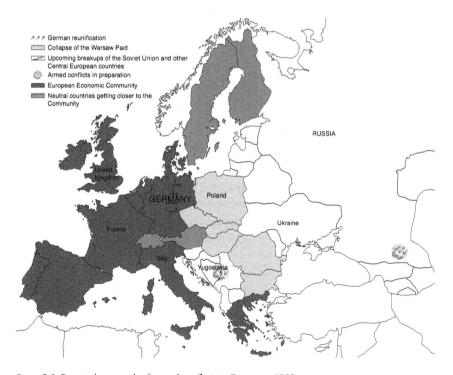

*Figure 5.2* Russian losses, risk of armed conflicts in Europe in 1990

credible. On 18 April 1990, Chancellor Kohl and President Mitterrand sent a joint message to the president of the Council, in which they called on the upcoming European Council of 28 April to launch 'preparatory work for an intergovernmental conference on political union.'[147] Two objectives were 'to reinforce the democratic legitimacy of the Union,' from which could emerge European citizenship; and 'to define and implement a common foreign and defence policy' (Common Foreign and Security Policy, CFSP).

It was in this context that the negotiation on a general right to reside was unblocked in the Council, on the basis of the earlier Commission proposals. The main problem was related to the risk of having to involve public assistance in immigration countries. For students, expanding the right to reside was linked to the new forms of mobility promoted in the European Single Market. In order to avoid migrant students becoming a burden on welfare systems, in November 1989, Belgian, British, and French delegates in the Council Group on Citizens' Special Rights demanded that if a student was supported by the social assistance of the immigration member state, then that member state would be reimbursed by the student's member state of origin. German delegates, supported by most other delegates, warned against the administrative complications 'of such a system' and preferred that a student's right to reside be subject to proof of being in possession of sufficient resources.[148] On 28 June 1990, the Council reached an agreement in a directive on the right to reside for students. They had to guarantee the national authority involved that they held sufficient resources and would not become 'a burden on social assistance of the host member state during their stay.'[149] They also had to be enrolled 'in an approved educational institution to follow, as their main objective, professional training' and hold 'health insurance to cover all the risks in the host member state.' The right to reside was limited to the duration of the period of study.

On the same day, 28 June 1990, the Council adopted two other directives. Under the directive on the right of residence for retired employed and self-employed workers, such right was acquired on the condition of having a pension or annuity guaranteeing revenue higher than the resource threshold for receiving social assistance in the destination country. Beneficiaries also had to demonstrate health insurance covering all risks in the destination country.[150] The extension of the right to reside to retired people cannot be explained by the drive to promote new forms of mobility for skilled workers. Indeed, it was not a question of the right to remain in a country after having worked there, which had already been recognised for several years in the Community, but to allow retired people to settle in a country where they had never worked. The third directive granted a general right to reside throughout the Community to all the nationals of member states and their family members, whatever the latter's nationality, on the sole condition of holding sufficient resources to avoid becoming dependent on social assistance and on condition of having the necessary health insurance coverage.[151] Despite these precautions, this general right of residence created a large risk that migrants of other member states would become net recipients of the system of social protection in the country of destination.

Meanwhile negotiations on Political Union continued. In his speech to the European Council in Dublin, on 26 June 1990, Mitterrand stated that, for France and Germany, Political Union meant defining common positions 'especially on the future of Europe and its security,' in the context of the upheavals taking place in Central and Eastern Europe.[152] The European Council in Dublin listed four chapters of Political Union, two of which the representatives of the ministers of Foreign Affairs reviewed immediately: on the one hand, the unity and consistency of Community action on the international scene; on the other hand, the general objective of political union, and hence the question of European citizenship. The connection between European citizenship and common foreign policy led the representatives of the ministers, 'starting from the experience gained due to the Gulf crisis,' to consider that 'Community citizens, whatever their member state of origin, should be able to benefit from the protection of diplomatic missions of all member states outside the Community.'[153]

On 2 October 1990, the president of the Council of Ministers of Foreign Affairs, Italian Foreign Minister Gianni De Michelis, considered that it would be 'the policy of external relations and of security as well as Community citizenship that [would] probably constitute the basic components of Political Union.'[154] Until then Community citizenship had only included rights. In relation to defence concerns, the only possible duty that could be added to European citizenship – as per the note of the Spanish delegation, 'Towards European Citizenship,' prepared for the Council of General Affairs of 22 October 1990 – was 'military service or . . . its equivalent,' which could be 'performed in any country of the Union.'[155] On 4 December 1990, several representatives of the Ministries of Foreign Affairs declared in the Council that 'European citizenship [was] one of the basic elements of the credibility of Political Union.'[156]

By 1990 thus, a growing number of member states recognised the link between the CFSP and European citizenship. Yet, Germany and France had not officially accepted the integration of European citizenship into the Treaty on European Union. In their letter of 18 April 1990, Kohl and Mitterrand had only expressed a desire to 'reinforce the democratic legitimacy of the Union,' in relation to the development of the CFSP. On 6 December 1990, as the Soviet Union became more and more unstable, Kohl and Mitterrand sent a joint letter to the president of the Council, Giulio Andreotti. For the first time officially, they defined their proposals on democratic legitimacy and accepted 'the institution of proper European citizenship,' to be formulated in the Treaty on European Union on the basis of the 'proposals made by the Spanish government,' which had referred to the possibility of a European 'military service.'

The same letter detailed the trade-off: an enlargement of the objectives linked to the CFSP. The 'priority domains' defined in the letters interested German security: 'the relations with the USSR and with the countries of Central and Eastern Europe, the implementation of the conclusions of the Summit of the Thirty-four and the development of the CSCE process, disarmament negotiations'; or French security: 'the relations with the countries on the Southern shores of the Mediterranean.' The Summit of the Thirty-Four referred to the Conference on Security and Cooperation in Europe, which brought together thirty-four heads of state in Paris to reflect on the recent upheavals in Europe and the future architecture of the continent. The CFSP, Kohl and Mitterrand added, might lead to 'a common defence.'[157]

France and Germany therefore accepted at the highest decision level the costs associated with European citizenship in a framework that related it to a European foreign and security policy, in the context of uncertainty of the end of the Cold War. These political lines were written down in the Treaty on European Union, signed in Maastricht on 7 February 1992. Article J of the Treaty established the CFSP. The member states were to support it 'actively and unreservedly in a spirit of loyalty and mutual solidarity.' They should 'refrain from any action ... contrary to the interests of the Union or likely to impair its effectiveness as a cohesive force in international relations.'[158] Mention was also made of 'the eventual framing of a common defence policy, which might in time lead to a common defence.'[159] As a statute unifying member states' nationals by granting them rights, European citizenship was the vital factor of cohesion for the success of the CFSP; it could also become an element of a European defence, if a compulsory military service was established.

The second part of the treaty establishing the European Community, as defined by the Treaty of Maastricht, detailed citizenship rights in Article 8: the general right of residence, as previously defined, voting and eligibility rights in local and European elections in the country of residence, together with diplomatic protection. Union citizenship could not be acquired outside the nationality of member states. Article 8 stated: 'Every person holding the nationality of a Member State shall be a citizen of the Union.' A declaration on the nationality of a member state annexed to the Treaty of Maastricht stated: 'The question whether an individual possesses the nationality of a member state shall be settled solely by reference to the national law of the member state concerned.' Article 8e mentioned 'provisions to strengthen or to add to the rights' attached to the citizenship of the Union that had to be adopted not only by the Council unanimously, but also by the member states 'in accordance with their respective constitutional requirements.'

## Inference

The conditions under which European citizenship could emerge reveal the important links with the development of a European foreign and defence policy in the context of Germany's security problems at the end of the Cold War. Foreign policy and military defence rest on the strength of civic cohesion, which can only be strong when the authority that conducts foreign policy and military defence guarantees rights to improve the condition of those who are asked to support such foreign policy and, sometimes, to be mobilised for such military defence. Immigration countries at the centre of the Union agreed to guarantee political rights to the populations of other member states because they were expecting not only their diplomatic support but potentially also military support.

## Dealing with poor migrants

After the upheavals in Central and Eastern Europe, the developments in the Mediterranean brought its final form to the European migration regime. Between the late 1980s and the early 1990s, migratory pressure from the South was on the rise. It proved to be a long-lasting problem. The abolition of controls at the internal borders of the Schengen Area convinced European governments to develop a common response to the growing migratory pressure from poor countries.

### Migratory pressure from poor countries

Britain, France, and West Germany hosted 85 percent of the immigrants from outside the Community. In West Germany, in 1987, the largest groups were the roughly 1.5 million Turks and around 600,000 Yugoslavs. In 1982, France hosted over 1.4 million immigrants from the Maghreb. In Britain, the main groups of immigrants came from India, Pakistan, Bangladesh, and the Caribbean.[160] Thus the great majority of immigrants from outside Western Europe came from poor countries. On the whole, Turkey and the Maghreb were the two main regions of origin of immigrants in the Community.[161]

In the countries of immigration, unemployment affected these populations. In Belgium, unemployment fell by nearly 16 percent for Belgians between 1982 and 1987, but increased by 17 percent for Moroccan and Turkish immigrants. In Britain, in 1987, the unemployment rate among Indians, Pakistanis, and Bangladeshis was double the general unemployment rate of the active population. The same year, in Denmark, the unemployment rate for Danish nationals was 6.7 percent whereas for Turkish nationals it reached 34.6 percent.[162] Marginality in trade union activity accompanied labour-market exclusion. In France and Belgium, migrants from the Maghreb had little contact with local trade unions, which in turn displayed a degree of distrust towards these workers, who were less responsive to union action.[163]

Despite these integration problems, migratory pressure from these regions was set to intensify. The fertility rate in the North African countries was 5.1 children per woman between 1985 and 1990, against 1.6 in Western Europe. The population of North Africa was projected to increase by fifty million in the 1990s.[164] Each year the labour force grew by 2.17 million in the countries on the southern banks of the Mediterranean, compared to 460,000 in the entire Community. Turkey and Egypt would have to create 880,000 new jobs a year to match the growth of the labour force.[165] Starting in 1991, the conflict in Yugoslavia intensified another major source of emigration to Western Europe. In September 1992 already, 532,000 persons had emigrated from the former Yugoslavia as a result of the conflict and there were over two million displaced persons within the former Yugoslavia.[166]

Economic growth in Mediterranean Europe added economic differences to demographic differences between Mediterranean countries. The richer countries of Mediterranean Europe became countries of immigration. In the late 1980s, Italy had nearly 620,000 regular foreigners, plus 300,000–450,000 clandestine migrants. Spain had almost 360,000 regular foreigners and 300,000 clandestine migrants. The figures for Portugal were respectively 100,000 and 40,000–50,000. The number of foreigners holding a residence permit in Greece was 140,000; the number of irregular foreigners rose to around 40,000. In Spain, the inflow of Africans matched the inflow of Europeans between 1980 and 1990; in Italy the former was twice as high as the latter.[167] In Italy, migrants originated from neighbouring countries, such as Yugoslavia and Tunisia, with Tunisian agricultural labourers in Tuscany, and Egyptian or Tunisian sailors in Sicily. Then there were migrants from former colonies: Eritreans, Ethiopians, Somalis, and some Sudanese. In Spain the new migrants came from Morocco, Algeria, Latin America, Guinea, and the Philippines. The new immigrants to Portugal included Cape Verdeans, many of whom were employed as agricultural labourers in the Algarve.[168] Some categories of migrants – Senegalese street sellers, domestic helpers from the Philippines and Cape Verde – were present in several Mediterranean European countries.[169]

During the 1980s, the number of Africans legally resident multiplied sevenfold in Italy – from 30,000 in 1980 to 209,000 ten years later – and twelvefold in Spain – from 5,000 to 62,000.[170] States in Mediterranean Europe lost control of this immigration. The length of coastline, the large number of islands, and tourism all led to lax border controls. In addition, there was a sizeable informal sector in Mediterranean countries, which offered work opportunities for clandestine migrants. In 1985 this sector accounted for around 5 percent of Spanish gross national product (GNP) and between 20 and 30 percent of Italian GNP. It provided work in construction, mining, textiles, and domestic service.[171]

For poor countries of origin, migration was a lever of development. In 1988 migrant remittances to their country of origin accounted for 35.6 percent of export revenue in Morocco and 22.5 percent in Tunisia.[172] In May 1992 the European Parliament adopted a resolution stressing the importance of migration for the development of particular countries. It emphasised how migration helped regulate demographic pressure in relation to the local demand for employment, how it provided occupational training, and how it guaranteed important money transfers to poor countries.[173]

## Breaking down chain migration from Turkey

Nevertheless, the European migration regime evolved so as to reduce these flows. The member states first tried to interrupt chain migration from Turkey to Europe. After the Community had violated its agreement on free movement with Turkey, the European Commission proposed to, at least, relax migratory relations with Turkey by means of a Council decision. In 1986, the Commission suggested allowing Turkish workers to be joined by their spouses and any children under the age of fifteen. After the West German government had stopped immigration in 1973, the Turkish population had continued to grow by almost 500,000, as a result of family reunification.[174] Consequently, German delegates in the Council opposed family reunification for children over the age of six years,[175] which matched the provisions in German law. They insisted on 'the need to break the immigration chain of successive generations.'[176] As West Germany was the main country of Turkish immigration, the Council's final position, on 24 November 1986, was in line with German views. National legislation exclusively would continue to define rights of family reunification.[177]

The rivalry between emigration countries in the Community and Turkey also limited the opening up of migratory opportunities for Turks. Greek delegates in the Council backed German delegates in considering that there were no grounds for Turkish family reunification.[178] The Community position adopted on 24 November 1986 also considered that the Association Agreement with Turkey should not violate the priority that Community migrants should enjoy, as per Regulation 1612/68. In addition, at the request of the new Mediterranean member states, Turkish workers could not be treated more favourably than Community nationals, including taking into account the 'Treaties of accession of Greece, Spain, and Portugal.' This meant that the limitations in these treaties, in the form of transitional periods for implementing the free movement of workers, had to apply to Turkish migrants.[179]

Greece also opposed the settlement of Turkish populations in areas that could be subject to territorial claims, such as Thrace and the Aegean Islands. Article 10 of the decision proposed by the Commission specified that each member state could 'resort to suitable measures,' in cases of 'serious problems' brought about by the application of the decision, but also stipulated that these measures would be 'communicated to the EEC-Turkey Association Council.' Greece then expressed a general reserve on the entire decision, and requested 'for reasons of national security, . . . a general exemption that would not be subject to review by the Association authorities.'[180] The Community position, approved by the Council on 24 November 1986, took up the Commission's proposed Article 10, but a declaration recorded in the Council minutes specified that Greece intended, for reasons of 'national security' to indeed resort to such 'suitable measures.' A confidential exchange of letters also stipulated that the adoption of those measures would not be subject to review by the Association authorities.[181]

The Commission proposed granting Turkish workers who had reached retirement age a right to remain on the condition that they had held a job for two years and resided in the country of immigration for five years. German delegates called for at least five years' work and eight years' residence, in line with German legislation.[182] Once again, the Community position coincided with German demands, since West Germany wielded the most important negotiating power in this domain. The right to remain would only be granted after having 'held a job [in the country of immigration] during the last five years at least and [having] resided [there] continuously for more than eight years.' Yet the right of residence could be withdrawn if the worker was unable to meet their own needs and those of their family dependents and had to resort 'to public funding that [was] not financed by employees wage contributions.'[183]

Finally, in comparison with Decision 1/80, the Community's proposal to Turkey in November 1986 reduced the necessary requirement to be entitled to take up any job offer in the destination country from four to three years of professional activity. There was also a reduction from three to two years' residence of the duration after which free access to employment was to be granted to workers' family members.[184] Given the disagreement over the meaning of Article 12 of the Ankara Agreement and Article 36 of the Additional Protocol, Turkey furiously rejected such a meager offer. In its judgement of 30 September 1987 on *Meryem Demirel v. Stadt Schwäbisch Gmünd*, the Court of Justice of the Community denied direct effect to the provisions of the Ankara Agreement and the Additional Protocol on the free movement of persons between Turkey and the Community.[185] The migration of Turks towards the Community remained regulated by Decision 1/80.[186]

## Reducing pressure for emigration in countries of origin

In addition to barriers to migration flows, the European migration regime evolved towards reducing pressure to emigrate in the countries of origin. In the late 1980s, Western European states exerted more influence in the global governance of migration by reactivating the Intergovernmental Committee for European Migration (ICEM). They had set up that body with the United States in 1951 to manage European emigration. They renamed it the Intergovernmental Committee for Migration (ICM) in 1980. Member states started overhauling the constitution of the organisation in 1985, which was completed by May 1987, when it became the International Organisation for Migration (IOM).[187] The constitution of the IOM came into effect in November 1989. Like the ICEM, it remained a service provider:

its purpose was not to draft international rules on migration but only to organise specific migration movements, for which it received funding. In this sense, IOM goals remained aligned to those of its fund providers. In contrast to the ICEM, the IOM mandate had no geographical limits, and it could organise migration movements outside continental Europe. According to the Preamble of its new constitution, the four types of migration services that the organisation could implement were temporary migration, return migration, intraregional migration, and refugee migration.[188] None of these types of migration included the most frequent type, that is long-term economic migration from poor countries to rich ones. This provision matched the preferences of the Europeans, keen to reduce poor immigration in Europe.

The ICM undertook in the first place return programmes for skilled migrants.[189] The Association between the Community and African, Caribbean, and Pacific countries (ACP) funded these programmes. The ICM implemented the first between 1980 and 1985 on the basis of the Convention of Lomé II. With a budget of 3.75 million ECU, it allowed a little more than 300 skilled African migrants working in the Community to return to their countries of origin. One-third of these migrants were health professionals; the rest were architects, economists, accountants, lawyers, engineers, or scientists. The countries of origin involved were Kenya, Somalia, and Zimbabwe. In November 1987, the Association granted the ICM 7.3 million ECU for a second programme on the basis of the Convention of Lomé III. Six African countries took part: Ghana, Uganda, and Zambia in addition to Kenya, Somalia, and Zimbabwe. Between 1984 and 1987, the European Commission granted the ICM 1.4 million ECU to implement a similar programme for the return of around seventy skilled Latin American migrants from Europe to their countries of origin: Costa Rica, the Dominican Republic, Honduras, Nicaragua, and Panama. The Western Europeans expected these programmes to trigger local development, less emigration, but also other returns.

In addition, the Western Europeans expected the states that benefited from these programmes, and from the Association in general, to implement measures to help reduce migratory pressure on Europe. In December 1984, Article 103 of Lomé III provided for 'the maximal use of ACP human resources' in ACP countries – an objective repeated in Article 158 of Lomé IV, signed on 15 December 1989. Article 155 of Lomé IV, titled 'Population and Demography,' provided for the preparation and implementation of demographic programmes to stem demographic growth, including family planning policies. Furthermore, under Annex V to the final act of Lomé IV, associated ACP states agreed in exchange for European aid to 'take the necessary measures to discourage irregular immigration of their nationals in the Community.'[190] Finally, in La Baule, on 20 June 1990, President Mitterrand declared in the Conference of Heads of State of Africa and France that development aid would be linked to democratic consolidation and the rule of law in Africa.[191] In Amsterdam, in September 1991, the Joint Parliamentary Assembly of the Association between the Community and ACP countries adopted a resolution on democracy and development, which stressed that 'respect for human, civil, and political rights [was] fundamental for . . . long-term economic and social development' and hence for reduced emigration.[192] Strengthening the rule of law in Africa would also make possible to treat such countries as safe, and refuse asylum applications to their emigrants, as allowed by the 1992 Resolutions in London.

The states of Mediterranean Europe called for other European measures to reduce migratory pressure from countries on the southern shore of the Mediterranean. In September 1990, the Spanish and Italian Ministers of Foreign Affairs, Francisco Fernandez Ordóñez and Gianni De Michelis, made a joint proposal to allocate 0.25 percent of Community GDP to development aid for countries on the southern shore of the Mediterranean in exchange for a reduced influx of migrants.[193] On the basis of a report drafted by the Portuguese José Mendes Bota,[194] in May 1992 the European Parliament adopted a resolution to encourage 'labour-intensive' projects to 'reduce migratory tensions' from these countries.[195] The Parliament called for a 'revamped Mediterranean policy' of the Community, with more funding, to 'promote local employment.' In 1991, the member states allocated 1 million ECU to a migration observatory in the Mediterranean basin, with a remit to examine the extent to which development programmes had helped create employment *in loco* and reduce migration to Europe. But Britain and the other states of Northern Europe opposed larger financial commitments in the Mediterranean, as this area was not a priority for them.[196]

After the outbreak of the Algerian civil war in January 1992, the danger of political instability in the countries of the Southern Mediterranean made the member states of the European Union consider new measures. They projected more thorough cooperation to promote stability and development in the Mediterranean, and thus reduce migratory pressure on Europe, along with the terrorist risk. These concerns culminated with the Barcelona Conference in November 1995 and the creation of the Euro-Mediterranean Partnership. Britain and Germany thus agreed on greater investment in favour of the Mediterranean, but the Northern states reduced the Partnership funding by 20 percent, from 5.5 billion to 4.7 billion ECU in comparison to the proposal of Spanish Commissioner Manuel Marín.[197] This investment remained six times lower than funding for the countries of Central Europe in proportion of the number of inhabitants in the two regions.[198] Northern Europe's greatest concern was Central Europe, which explains the slow progress the Euromed cooperation achieved after the Barcelona Conference.[199]

## Inference

The poorest immigration came from the Mediterranean, with its marked demographic and economic imbalances. West Germany was anxious to stem Turkish immigration. The Mediterranean member states of the Community, including France, were more exposed and promoted European programmes to favour the political stability, economic growth, and demographic decline of countries of origin. The European member states used the IOM to divert migration flows and implement return programmes. Trans-Mediterranean cooperation also started, but had little success due to a lack of interest from the rich states of Northern Europe.

## Synopsis

The European migration regime assumed its final shape in 1984–1992 thanks to a series of developments that were largely the result of German preferences. The decision to abolish controls on persons at Europe's internal borders was to promote market integration and support British and German exports in Europe. France played a key role in drawing up a restrictive visa regime and external border controls for migrants from outside the Community, in line with the general thrust of French migration policy. The European migration regime came to favour skilled migrants, to accompany the European expansion of big firms, often German or British. The Community encouraged the mobility of their managerial staffs, but also of self-employed professionals likely to provide services to those firms. In parallel, the status of European migrants was redefined with European citizenship, which materialised in the context of the development of a common foreign and security policy at the end of the Cold War. In spite of the commitment by Northern European member states to reduce migratory pressure from the Mediterranean, this goal remained less important, coming second to the political and economic integration of the Central European countries.

# CONCLUSION

After 1992, the European migration regime remained relatively stable for about twenty-five years. Post-1992 developments were the consequence of earlier achievements. Following the Treaty of Maastricht, the European Union gradually implemented European citizenship. In December 1993, the Council arranged for the exercise of the right to vote and stand as a candidate in elections to the European Parliament for European migrants.[1] The Council defined the right to vote and stand in municipal elections for these migrants in December 1994.[2] By the end of the 1990s, voting and eligibility rights in municipal and European elections had fully entered into force.[3] Even the contentious debate about the posting of workers did not lead to serious modifications of the regime. On 16 December 1996, the Council maintained, with Directive 96/71, the application of the labour law of the country of destination intact in those cases, which was the main point of controversy.[4] On 29 April 2004, the Council brought together the provisions of various previous directives to clarify European citizens' rights in a single text, Directive 2004/38.[5]

Similarly, regarding immigrants from outside the Community, the member states slowly implemented the Schengen Convention. After France's request for postponement, it entered into force in March 1995, included Italy in 1997, and became part of the law of the European Union in the same year with the Treaty of Amsterdam, which was effective as of 1 May 1999. Like before, Britain could continue to exercise any border controls it deemed necessary.[6] The member states then furthered, within the framework of the European Union, cooperation on visas, asylum, and immigration from outside the Union, in continuity with the Schengen Convention.[7]

In the wake of the end of the Cold War, the regime expanded to the countries of Central Europe, with the enlargements of 2004, 2007, and 2013 of the European Union. The number of European migrants rose fast between 1999 and 2012, from 5.9 million to 13.6 million people.[8] Germany used the maximum restrictions provided for in the transition periods of those enlargements, to cope with high unemployment after the Reunification until the mid-2000s. In contrast, Britain opened up swiftly. As a result, the annual flow of immigrant workers from new member states of Central Europe in Britain leapt from 25,000 in 2003 to 337,000 in 2007. Until 2008, Italy and Spain also played an important role as destination countries, even though a significant proportion of European immigrants there were still skilled professionals or pensioners, unlikely to generate increases in public spending or tensions in labour markets. With the Great Recession of 2008 and 2009, resentment against European immigration in Britain favoured the return to power of the Conservative Party in 2010 with a platform against immigration and the European Union. It eventually led to the Brexit referendum of June 2016, whose result may affect the European migration regime. Yet, meanwhile, Germany's unemployment rate dropped sharply, from more than 12 percent in early 2006 to around 4.5 percent in 2015. Germany's immigration balance reached 437,000 in 2013, 550,000 in 2014, and continued to increase in 2015, alleviating tensions in other immigration countries.

This book has therefore traced the path along which Europe's migration regime was formed, between 1947 and 1992. This regime became more open and more homogenous. There was virtually no openness at the Western European level in the period between 1947 and 1954. The European Economic Community then emerged as the dominant framework for a regime change. The free movement of workers was enshrined in the Treaty of Rome in 1957 and had almost completely entered into force by the mid-1960s. There was no closure between 1973 and the mid-1980s as far as Community migrants were concerned. From the 1970s onwards, a European regime of closure towards immigration from outside the Community gradually developed. After 1984, the regime took on its final shape, by favouring skilled migrants and strengthening its regionalist character.

I have shown that states, and not supranational institutions, held the central position in all the important steps of the formation of the European migration regime. They coordinated a multitude of interests: those of their employers, the domestic labour force, professions fearing foreign competition, and local populations sensitive to demographic pressure and to increased demand in the housing market. They upheld the interests of social security institutions, insofar as migratory movements affected their accounts. They developed security interests and considered migration questions as central in defining the European order. As a result, the role of the Council of the Community was preponderant. All political issues were discussed within the Council and solved there between states representatives. Ministers solved the most important issues.

The European Commission only played a minor role in the formation of the European migration regime. Even as a possible consensus builder, the Commission was hardly important, because government representatives often assumed the role of conducting negotiations and looking for a consensus themselves. The European Court of Justice played a role by recalling the content of agreements states had previously reached. The role of law in the formation of the regime should not be overestimated. Law played a practical role in stabilising and homogenising the regime, yet when interests changed, states disregarded previous agreements. For instance, the agreement with Turkey was not respected, although it had been recorded in a treaty.

Migration was a highly contentious issue and only a superior political interest overcame the various conflicts it generated. My analysis has highlighted the leading role constantly and consistently played not by Italy, but by Germany. Italian pressures were never the driving force in the evolution of the European migration regime. The Italian case, far from being a mainspring in the reconfiguration of the postwar European migration regime, was in the late 1940s and the 1950s an obstacle. Italian migratory pressure worried France, Britain, and Belgium, and hindered a loosening of the migration regime within the Organisation for European Economic Cooperation. The Italian government undoubtedly played a role in the following decades in constantly reminding North-Western European governments of the importance of the emigration problem in Italy. Italian delegates usefully underlined in several occasions the factor of international instability that mass unemployment created in Italy. Nevertheless, my analysis has shown that Germany, rather than Italy, was the country that shaped the European migration regime.

This regime corresponded to a German project whose broad guidelines were already defined in 1949 and 1950, without a reference to the specific Italian case. The new Federal Republic of Germany defined its strategy as early as 1949. It consisted in opening outlets in the West to the surplus workforce that migratory inflows from the East created. This mattered in order to maintain openness for those flows and destabilise Popular Democracies. The open migration regime stemmed from the concern of German authorities in the early 1950s to be in position to absorb waves of refugees from East Germany irrespectively of the economic conditions in West Germany. The support of other countries might be critical in exceptional circumstances and such absorption was a key instrument to weaken Communist governments in Eastern Europe. The second German interest in an open migration regime in Western Europe was to prevent the defection of strategic allies. In hard times, the open migration regime would offer opportunities, diminish social tensions, and reduce support for Communism in peripheral but geographically strategic countries of Western Europe, including Italy. By doing so, it was meant to reinforce the cohesion of Western Europe, which was vital to increase the bargaining power of Germany towards the Soviet Union and achieve the Reunification. Last but not least, already at that time, German policy-makers also anticipated an open migration regime would also facilitate the expansion of German companies in Europe.

In the first post-war decade, Germany's economy was too weak to allow the West German government to challenge the prevailing migration regime. The Germans could only use their assets in the coal and steel sectors in the early 1950s to promote there the principle of the free movement of workers. A break took place in the mid-1950s. First, it was linked to the new trust between West Germany and its Western neighbours thanks to German military concessions in the Paris Agreements, in October 1954, and Germany's participation in the European Coal and Steel Community. German immigration in other Western European countries became a less sensitive matter, which could have otherwise prevented migration liberalisation in a multilateral regime. More importantly, economic growth in West Germany absorbed unemployment and placed the government in a superior position of power to define the European migration regime. The size of the West German labour market could stabilise an open regime, which brought about the agreement of other immigration states.

A redefinition of the Western European migration regime ensued within the new European Economic Community, created by the Treaty of Rome in 1957. French support certainly promoted German plans. The increase in labour demand in France in the late 1950s and early 1960s was helpful. Yet, the German concessions in the field of the Common Agricultural Policy played also a role to secure French participation. Similarly, Community priority was linked to the French concern that the German economy absorbed most of the flows created by the more open migration arrangements in the Community, so as to avoid social tensions in France. This was not the result of Italian demands. By the early 1960s, the German economy had come to absorb a disproportionate share of almost 80 percent of migrants within the Community.

Given the role of Germany in this evolution, the new regime matched German interests. The geographical framework was centred on Europe and corresponded to German preferences. It excluded overseas territories and included precisely those countries whose stability was crucial to contain the Soviet Union. In addition to Italy, which was a member of the Community, the Germans promoted looser migratory arrangements between the Community and Greece, as well as Turkey. Far from being a secondary concession to the governments of emigration countries, the openness of the European migration regime was a central aspect of German geopolitical and geo-economic strategy in Europe during the Cold War.

Furthermore, in line with German preferences, the regime favoured the movement of the economically active and encouraged their families to remain in the country of origin. As West Germany experienced a serious housing shortage, it mattered to reduce population pressure. The social security of migrant workers was a major instrument to shape migration flows. German social security institutions transferred abroad a disproportionate share of total benefits transferred between the countries of the Community (unemployment benefits, pensions, family allowances). Those enormous amounts encouraged Community migrant workers and their families to remain abroad as much as they wished. Despite French opposition, the Germans convinced their partners to implement similar policies at the Community level, avoiding an asymmetry that would have oriented even more migrants towards Germany. Yet, France secured a temporary exception.

Whereas France had been a major country of immigration in Europe over the previous century, the transformation of the French labour market in the 1970s rendered the country unable to absorb any large-scale labour immigration for decades. This development did not jeopardise the open migration regime in the Community. In the short run, it led to a renewed interest of the French in Community migrant workers, who threatened fewer French workers' wages. France put its weight to make the occupational status of those migrants subject to the interests of the local workforce. Yet, French reluctance to take on poor immigrant workers did threaten the capacity of the Germans to support, after the early 1970s, the originally planned migratory openness towards Turkey. France also wielded a high blocking capacity regarding self-employed migrant workers, since it would have had to support most adjustments, as the German economy was less developed in those sectors.

In the mid-1970s, the drop in labour demand in West Germany reduced the resources with which it had supported the expansion of an open migration regime during the previous years. German trade unions tried to limit the increase in labour supply, which meant the definitive failure of negotiations with Turkey, despite previous commitments. In parallel to the slow enlargements to Greece, Spain, and Portugal, the regime developed from that time onwards its regionalist character by preventing immigration from outside the Community. Within the Community, the regime remained formally open, but without any further opening. West Germany strove to reduce spending for migrants. In the wake of the oil shocks and the increases in the minimum wage, France struggled with immigrant unemployment, but the French government could not obtain a financial contribution from the Community to promote the return of immigrants. For the same reason, France also struggled with youth unemployment and similarly failed to secure Germany's support to give a broader dimension to exchange programmes for unemployed young workers between the member states. There were even a few breaches of the Community law in various countries receiving immigrants. Professional associations blocked negotiations on the right of establishment for self-employed workers. Finally, the prospect of demographic decline led West German authorities to increase family benefits in 1975. Accordingly, they redefined their position on the export of family allowances at the higher rate of the employment country, thus questioning a central aspect of the Community migration regime.

Around 1984, West Germany curbed unemployment, which slowly fell in the following years. By the mid-1980s, the British and West German governments were both trying hard to boost economic growth through an increase in exports. The Germans contemplated in particular the abolition of internal border controls in the Community, as a way to ease cross-border traffic. Given the importance of its geographical location for the achievement of such a project, France was able to use this political leverage to obtain compensations, namely European monetary integration to increase foreign investment in France and the definition of a restrictive European visa policy, along with stringent controls at Europe's external borders. To also favour the expansion of their firms in Europe, Britain and Germany supported a broader recognition of qualifications, as a way to ensure the movement of managerial staff and skilled professionals. The tendency of the regime to promote the movement of the highly skilled, who were less likely to compete with local workers, thus increased in the 1980s. Member states recognised diplomas only after three years' higher education and the Erasmus programme was intended only for university students.

Shortly afterwards, instability and upheavals in Eastern Europe reinforced the security problem of West Germany. Favouring a common foreign and security policy between the member states of the Community, the West German government was ready to recognise political rights for Community migrants. The definition of European citizenship had little to do with the pressure of Mediterranean countries. European citizenship went hand in hand with the prospect of a common foreign and security policy and a common defence. As in the mid-1950s, German security concerns in a favourable economic context fostered the openness of the European migration regime. The pace of change was linked to the development of Germany's resources and to the international events that affected that country. The interest of France and the other Mediterranean member states in a European policy to reduce migratory pressure in the Mediterranean did not produce significant results, due to reduced interest on the part of Northern European states.

Overall, Germany did assume the leading role and the regime favoured German interests. The formation of the European migration regime was the result of the hegemonic strategy of the Federal Republic of Germany, which controlled an important share of the means of production in the Western European migration system. German hegemony was the capacity of that single actor to support, given its economic resources, the open migration regime. In other words, the 'German hegemon' maintained support for the regime even when other actors defected and did not apply the rules. Hegemony did not mean a monopoly of scarce resources. Germany did not have such a monopoly and multilateralism remained necessary to involve a variety of actors in supporting the regime. French support in the 1950s and 1960s and British support in the 1990s and 2000s were thus important, but overall secondary. German hegemonic management was less a question of imposing costs than of granting advantages, amounting to a form of benevolent hegemony. Germany's hegemony entailed neither the use of military force nor military preponderance.[9] It has been the argument of this book that the open European migration regime could occur only because it was the key instrument to create a

European order maximising German interests over the long run. German policymakers, such as Konrad Adenauer, Walter Hallstein, or Helmut Kohl, pursued such logic. But overall it involved hundreds of politicians and civil servants, making thousands of choices over several decades.

The case of the European migration regime thus does not invite to consider that European Integration was a series of agreements driven by the prospect of mutual economic advantages, still less an attempt of other European states to control Germany.[10] European Integration appears, instead, as the outcome of the specific international strategy of Germany towards surrounding countries, whose support was vital, given Germany's relations with Russia. The driving force of European Integration resided in the multiple advantages – migratory, trade, financial, monetary – that Germany granted to neighbouring countries in order to integrate them into a framework that ensured German economic and political interests. This case leads to a different assessment of the respective roles of economic and geopolitical factors in European Integration.[11] It shows how geopolitical factors determined the German strategy to support an open migration regime in Europe. Economic interests cannot explain alone the openness of the European migration regime. It remains true, nevertheless, that the European migration regime could only develop because the German economy was, most of the time, strong enough to support this regime. It is also true that Germany did pursue certain economic interests through the regime.

Consequently, the history of the European migration regime also highlights the dynamics of the Cold War in Europe. An insufficient examination of the role of West Germany stands in the way of a full understanding of the end of the Cold War and of the new European order that followed. The cohesion of the Western camp in Europe was not self-evident; West German policies decisively contributed to it by curbing, through a liberal international order, the social discontent that could have otherwise promoted Communism. The economic benefits Italy, Greece, and Turkey enjoyed in their relations with the Community deeply aligned their foreign policies to West German interests. The history of the European migration regime highlights the instruments that revisionist West Germany used to guarantee the containment of Soviet influence in Europe, the German Reunification, and finally the rollback of Russian influence from Central Europe. By the end of the Cold War, the open migration regime in Western Europe epitomised the liberal international order and acted as a magnet for the populations of Eastern Europe. The prospect of accessing the open migration regime of the European Union was key to pull Eastern European countries out of Soviet influence and to secure their realignment in the Western European order. The end of the Cold War did certainly affect German concessions in a number of fields. Yet, the open European migration regime remained in force in an effort to consolidate the new European order reached at the end of the Cold War.

# ACKNOWLEDGEMENTS

The Ecole normale supérieure financed the main part of this research; the Université Paris-Sorbonne provided the final financing needed. This research has received the PhD Prize awarded by the French Ministry of Social Affairs, through its Committee for the History of Social Security. I have used the Max Weber Fellowship of the European University Institute to turn my research into a book.

This research has benefited from an in-depth collaboration with Eric Bussière, Gérard Bossuat, Kiran Klaus Patel, Catherine Wihtol de Wenden, and Lorenzo Mechi. I also thank the other members of my PhD defence committee: Barbara Curli, Rainer Hudemann, and, especially, N. Piers Ludlow. Numerous researchers helped me in my research in the various institutions in which I worked: the Ecole normale supérieure, the Université Paris-Sorbonne, the European University Institute, and the University of California, Berkeley. I would like to thank in particular Guia Migani, Laurent Warlouzet, Youssef Cassis, Dirk Moses, and Stefan-Ludwig Hoffmann. The teams of archivists of the Council and of the Commission of the European Union, in Brussels and Florence, of the Organisation for Economic Cooperation and Development, of the Archives nationales in Paris, and of the Auswärtiges Amt in Berlin also were of invaluable assistance.

I thank Eugenia Vella, who corrected several pieces for the manuscript and did much more.

# NOTES

## INTRODUCTION

1 Ernst B. Haas, "Words Can Hurt You; or, Who Said What to Whom about Regimes," *International Organization* 36, no. 2, 207–43 (1982); Donald J. Puchala and Raymond F. Hopkins, "International Regimes: Lessons from Inductive Analysis," *International Organization* 36, no. 2, 245–75 (1982); Oran R. Young, "Regime Dynamics: The Rise and Fall of International Regimes," *International Organization* 36, no. 2, 277–97 (1982); Yasemin Nuhoglu Soysal, *Limits of Citizenship: Migrants and Postnational Membership in Europe* (Chicago: University of Chicago Press, 1994), p. 32; Rafaela M. Dancygier, *Immigration and Conflict in Europe* (Cambridge: Cambridge University Press, 2010), p. 25.
2 IOM Press Release, "Migrant Deaths Worldwide Top 7,100 – Over Half in the Mediterranean," 16/12/2016.
3 Klaus J. Bade, *Migration in European History* (Oxford: Blackwell, 2003), p. 217.
4 Simone Alberdina Wilhelmina Goedings, *Labor Migration in an Integrating Europe: National Migration Policies and the Free Movement of Workers, 1950–1968* (The Hague: Sdu Uitgevers, 2005), p. 368.
5 H. Rieben, "Intra-European Migration of Labour and Migration of High-Level Manpower from Europe to North America," in *North American and Western Economic Policies*, ed. C. P. Kindleberger and A. Shonfield (London: Macmillan, 1971), p. 458.
6 AHUE, CM2 1967 1113, V/2997/66 rév., Commission note, September 1966.
7 Ville Kaitila, "Convergence of Real GDP Per Capita in the EU 15: How Do the Accession Countries Fit In?," in *European Network of Economic Policy Research Institute Working Papers* (Brussels, 2004), p. 7.
8 Ettore Recchi, *Mobile Europe: The Theory and Practice of Free Movement in the EU* (London: Palgrave Macmillan, 2015), pp. 52, 56, 58.
9 Christina Boswell and Andrew Geddes, *Migration and Mobility in the European Union* (Basingstoke: Palgrave Macmillan, 2011), pp. 91, 185.
10 Chris Prosser, Jon Mellon, and Jane Green, "What Mattered Most to You When Deciding How to Vote in the EU Referendum?," *British Election Study*, 11 July 2016. www.britishelectionstudy.com/bes-findings/what-mattered-most-to-you-when-deciding-how-to-vote-in-the-eu-referendum/#.WJ9OgxjMxE4. Access date: 15/03/2017.
11 Frontex, "710,000 migrants entered EU in first nine months of 2015," 13 October 2015. http://frontex.europa.eu/news/710-000-migrants-entered-eu-in-first-nine-months-of-2015-NUiBkk. Access date: 15/03/2017.
12 EU-Turkey statement, 18 March 2016, www.consilium.europa.eu/en/press/press-releases/2016/03/18-eu-turkey-statement/. Access date: 15/03/2017.
13 Federico Romero, *Emigrazione e Integrazione europea, 1945–1973*, Studi di storia (Roma: Edizioni lavoro, 1991); Federico Romero, "Migration as an Issue in European Interdependence and Integration: The Case of Italy," in *The Frontier of National Sovereignty: History and Theory, 1945–1992*, ed. Alan Steele Milward (London: Routledge, 1993); Goedings, *Labor Migration in an Integrating Europe*.

14 Eytan Meyers, *Multilateral Cooperation, Integration and Regimes: The Case of International Labor Mobility* (Center for Comparative Immigration Studies, University of California, San Diego, Working Paper 61, 2002), p. 31.
15 Alan S. Milward, *The Frontier of National Sovereignty: History and Theory, 1945–1992* (London; New York: Routledge, 1993), p. 21; Andrew Moravcsik, *The Choice for Europe: Social Purpose and State Power from Messina to Maastricht*, Cornell Studies in Political Economy (Ithaca, NY: Cornell University Press, 1998), pp. 90, 491.
16 Alan S. Milward, George Brennan, and Federico Romero, *The European Rescue of the Nation-State* (Berkeley: University of California Press, 1992).
17 Alan S. Milward, *The Frontier of National Sovereignty: History and Theory, 1945–1992*, p. 29; Fernando Guirao, Frances M. B. Lynch, and Sigfrido M. Ramírez Pérez, *Alan S. Milward and a Century of European Change*, Routledge Studies in Modern European History (New York: Routledge, 2012), p. 93.
18 For an idea of how the role of Western European actors in the stabilisation of the Cold War in Europe has been downplayed, see Marc Trachtenberg, *A Constructed Peace: The Making of the European Settlement, 1945–1963*, Princeton Studies in International History and Politics (Princeton, NJ: Princeton University Press, 1999).
19 Charles Poor Kindleberger, *The World in Depression, 1929–1939*, History of the World Economy in the Twentieth Century (Berkeley: University of California Press, 1973); Robert Gilpin, *War and Change in World Politics* (Cambridge; New York: Cambridge University Press, 1981); Ernst B. Haas, "Words Can Hurt You; or, Who Said What to Whom about Regimes," p. 213; Robert O. Keohane, *After Hegemony: Cooperation and Discord in the World Political Economy*, 1st Princeton classic ed., A Princeton Classic ed. (Princeton, NJ: Princeton University Press, 2005), chap. 3.
20 Sandra Destradi, "Regional Powers and Their Strategies: Empire, Hegemony, and Leadership," *Review of International Studies* 36, no. 4 (2010), pp. 908, 912–13.
21 Keohane, *After Hegemony*.
22 N. Piers Ludlow, *The European Community and the Crises of the 1960s: Negotiating the Gaullist Challenge*, Cass Series-Cold War History (London; New York: Routledge, 2006), pp. 8–9.
23 Milward, *The Frontier of National Sovereignty*, p. 31.

## 1 AN UNSTABLE REGIME, 1947–1954

1 Gary S. Cross, *Immigrant Workers in Industrial France: The Making of a New Laboring Class* (Philadelphia: Temple University Press, 1983), pp. 22–3.
2 Ewa Morawska, "Labor Migrations of Poles in the Atlantic World Economy, 1880–1914," *Comparative Studies in Society and History* 31, no. 2 (1989), pp. 246–66.
3 Klaus J. Bade, "'Preussenganger' und 'Abwehrpolitik': Ausländerbeschäftigung, Ausländerpolitik und Ausländerkontrolle auf dem Arbeitsmarkt in Preussen vor dem ersten Weltkrieg," *Archiv für Sozialgeschichte* 24 (1984), pp. 91–162.
4 AAPA (Auswärtiges Amt, Politisches Archiv, Berlin), B15, 121 (5), FRG, 10/1950.
5 Ordonnance n° 45–2658 du 2 novembre 1945, *Journal officiel de la République française* (JORF), n° 259, 4/11/1945.
6 AHUE (Archives historiques de l'Union européenne, Florence), MAEI, PS20, Uff. II, D b.28, France, 6/10/1950.
7 Ordonnance n° 45–2658, article 82 a) du livre 1$^{er}$ du Code du Travail modifié, JORF, n° 259.
8 AN (Archives nationales, Paris), F7 16115, 25/06/1948.
9 AN, F7 16066, 24/03/1948.
10 AHUE, MAEF, 501, Belgium, 10/1950.
11 Ibid.
12 AHUE MAEI, PS20, France, 6/10/1950, pp. 14–15.
13 Paul-André Rosental, "Migrations, souveraineté, droits sociaux. Protéger et expulser les étrangers en Europe du XIX$^e$ siècle à nos jours," *Annales. Histoire, sciences sociales* 2, no. 6 (2011), p. 344.

## NOTES

14 Christoph Rass, *Institutionalisierunsprozesse auf einem internationalen Arbeitsmarkt: Bilaterale Wanderungsverträge in Europa zwischen 1919 und 1974*, Studien zur historischen Migrationsforschung (Shm) (Paderborn: Schöningh, 2010), p. 354.
15 AAPA, B10, 412–00, 2365, 01/1949, pp. 18–19; AOECD (OECD Archives, Paris), CEEC, 366, 9, CEEC(2)14, 16/03/1948.
16 AAPA, B10, 412–00, 2365, 01/1950.
17 AAPA, B10, 412–00, 2365, 01/1949, pp. 3, 28.
18 AAPA, B10, 412–00, 2365, 01/1949.
19 AN, F7 16115, 21/02/1949.
20 AAPA, B10, 412–00, 2365, 01/1949, pp. 15, 19–21.
21 AN, F7 16115, 1/06/1949.
22 Ibid.
23 ACE (Archives centrales du Conseil de l'Europe, Strasbourg), Congrès de l'Europe, La Haye, Rapport Verbatim des sessions de la Commission économique et sociale, 8/05/1948 (21:30), pp. 52–3.
24 JORF, 19/03/1946, p. 2264.
25 AN, F7 16100, Lettre Direction des Mines à MAE, around 9/08/1947.
26 ACE, Doc. 331, 10/02/1955.
27 AOECD, Film 125, MO(54)49, 10/1954.
28 Federico Romero, *Emigrazione e Integrazione europea, 1945–1973*, Studi di storia (Roma: Edizioni lavoro, 1991), pp. 31–2.
29 My translation of Romero, *Emigrazione e Integrazione europea, 1945–1973*, pp. 29–30.
30 ACE, Verbatim, 8/05/1948 (21:30), pp. 57–8.
31 My translation of a quote by: Federico Romero, *Emigrazione e Integrazione europea, 1945–1973*, p. 30.
32 Federico Romero, "Migration as an Issue in European Interdependence and Integration: The Case of Italy," in *The Frontier of National Sovereignty: History and Theory, 1945–1992*, ed. Alan Steele Milward (London: Routledge, 1993), pp. 39–40.
33 AN, F7 16115, 8/01/1948 Meeting.
34 AN, F7 16100, Lettre au préfet des Alpes-Maritimes, around 06/1948.
35 AN, F7 16100, Lettres du préfet des Alpes-Maritimes, 13/11/1946 and 30/04/1947.
36 AN, F7 16100, 18/01/1949.
37 AN, F7 16100, Note pour le ministre de l'Intérieur, around 06–11/1948.
38 Louis Henry, "Evolution démographique de L'Europe, 1938–1947, d'après un article de Grzegorz Frumkin dans le Bulletin économique pour L'Europe," *Population* 4, no. 4 (1949), p. 745.
39 Michel Hubert, "La population allemande: ruptures et continuités," in *L'Allemagne, 1945–1961: De la catastrophe à la construction Du Mur*, ed. Jean-Paul Cahn and Ulrich Pfeil, Histoire et civilisations (Villeneuve-d'Ascq: Presses universitaires du Septentrion, 2008), p. 76.
40 Charles de Gaulle, *Discours et messages*, 5 vols., vol. 1. Pendant la guerre, juin 1940–janvier 1946 (Paris: Plon, 1970), p. 530.
41 Georges Photios Tapinos, *L'Immigration étrangère en France: 1946–1973*, Travaux et documents—Institut national d'études demographiques (Paris: Presses universitaires de France, 1975), p. 16.
42 "La Société des nations en 1930 et la fédération européenne," *L'Europe nouvelle*, no. 659 (1930).
43 Tapinos, *L'Immigration étrangère en France: 1946–1973*, p. 16.
44 AOECD, Film 124, MO(49)14, 8/02/1949, Annex.
45 AOECD, CEEC, 366, 4, Executive Committee Minutes, 31/07/1947.
46 AOECD, CEEC, 366, 1, Cooperation Committee Minutes, 1/08/1947.
47 AOECD, CEEC, 366, 2, CCEE/59, 4/09/1947.
48 Lorenzo Mechi, *L'Organizzazione internazionale del lavoro e la ricostruzione europea: Le basi sociali dell'integrazione economica (1931–1957)*, Storia e memoria (Roma: Ediesse, 2012), pp. 122–3.
49 J. E. Meade, *Negotiations for Benelux: An Annotated Chronicle, 1943–1956*, Princeton Studies in International Finance (Princeton, NJ: International Finance Section, Dept. of Economics and Sociology, Princeton University, 1957), pp. 6–7.

50 AOECD, CEEC, 366, 9, CCEE(2)14, 16/03/1948.
51 AOECD, CEEC Boîte 366, 3, CCEE/63.
52 AOECD, CEEC, 366, 9, CCEE(2)5.
53 AOECD, CEEC, 366, 15, 3rd session.
54 AOECD, CEEC, 366, 5.
55 AOECD, CEEC, 366, 5, 23/03/1948.
56 AOECD, CEEC, 366, 15, 8/04/1948.
57 AOECD, CEEC, 366, 10, 9/04/1948.
58 AOECD, CEEC, 366, 9, CCEE(2)44 (revised), 15/04/1948.
59 ACE, Doc. 1, 10/08/1950. Annex II.
60 AHUE, MAEF, 501, Belgium, 10/1950.
61 AOECD, Film 48, CE(50)23, 13/03/1950.
62 AOECD, Film 124, MO(49)38, 8/06/1949.
63 AOECD, Film 125, MO(54)49.
64 Pierre Guillen, "Le projet d'union économique entre la France, l'Italie et le Benelux," in *Histoire des débuts de la Construction européenne, mars 1948-mai 1950: Actes du colloque de Strasbourg, 28–30 novembre 1984*, ed. Raymond Poidevin and European Liaison Committee of Historians (Bruxelles: Bruylant, 1986), p. 149.
65 Pierre Guillen, "L'immigration italienne en France après 1945, enjeu dans les relations franco-italiennes," in *Mouvements et politiques migratoires en Europe depuis 1945: Le cas italien*, ed. Michel Dumoulin (Bruxelles: Éditions Ciaco, 1989), p. 41.
66 Guillen, "Le projet d'union économique entre la France, l'Italie et le Benelux," p. 149.
67 Vincent Auriol and Pierre Nora, *Journal du septennat, 1947–1954*, vol. 1. 1947 (Paris: A. Colin, 1970), p. 391.
68 Guillen, "Le projet d'union économique entre la France, l'Italie et le Benelux," p. 151.
69 Albert Martens, *Les immigres: Flux et reflux d'une main-d'œuvre d'appoint. La politique belge de l'immigration de 1945 à 1970*, Sociologische Verkenningen (Leuven, Krakenstr, 3: Universitaire Pers, 1976), pp. 74–6, 78.
70 AOECD, Film 124, MO(49)38, 8/06/1949.
71 Simone Alberdina Wilhelmina Goedings, *Labor Migration in an Integrating Europe: National Migration Policies and the Free Movement of Workers, 1950–1968*, pp. 56–7.
72 Pier Luigi Ballini and Antonio Varsori, *L'Italia e l'Europa: 1947–1979*, 2 vols. (Soveria Mannelli: Rubbettino, 2004), pp. 67–72.
73 Marie-Claude Blanc-Chaléard, *Les immigrés et la France: XIX$^e$-XX$^e$ siècles* (Paris: La Documentation française, 2003), p. 51.
74 Ordonnance n° 45–2250 du 4 octobre 1945, JORF, 6/10/1945, p. 6280.
75 AOECD, Film 125, MO(54)49.
76 Marina Maccari Clayton, " 'Communists of the Stomach': Italian Migration and International Relations in the Cold War Era," *Studi Emigrazione*, no. 155 (2004).
77 AHUE, CM2 1958 946, 1/02/1958, p. 11.
78 AAPA, B10, 412–00, 2365, 01/1950, p. 59.
79 Hubert, "La population allemande: ruptures et continuités," p. 84.
80 Klaus J. Bade, *L'Europe en mouvement. La migration de la fin du XVIII$^e$ siècle à nos jours*, trans. Olivier Mannoni and Faire L'Europe (Paris: Éd. du Seuil, 2002), p. 461.
81 Alan S. Milward, *The Reconstruction of Western Europe, 1945–51* (Berkeley: University of California Press, 1984), pp. 337, 339, 346.
82 AAPA, B10, 412–00, 2365, 01/1950.
83 Ibid.
84 AAPA, B10, 221–35–12, 703, CM(51)69, 8/10/1951.
85 AOECD, Film 125, MO(54)49.
86 AOECD, Film 124, MO(50)5, 1/02/1950.
87 AAPA, B10, 412–00, 1877, Grundsätzliche Fragen einer Auswanderung.
88 Ibid.

## NOTES

89  AAPA, B10, 412–00, 1877, Vorschlag der deutschen Delegation zur Frage der Auswanderung.
90  AAPA, B10, 412–00, 1877, 28/07/1950.
91  AOECD, Film 71, C(51)175, Annex B.
92  AAPA, B10, 412–00, 1877, Grundsätzliche Fragen einer Auswanderung.
93  ACE, Doc. 51, 17/09/1952.
94  ACE, Doc. 331, 10/02/1955.
95  AOECD, Film 124, MO(53)2, 11/1952.
96  AAPA, B10, 221–35–21, 704, CM(53)148.
97  AOECD, Film 124, MO(50)4, 1/02/1950.
98  Ibid.
99  AOECD, Film 84, C(52)127, 9/05/1952.
100  AOECD, Film 85, CE/M(52)014, 23/05/1952.
101  AOECD, Film 124, MO(51)15.
102  ACE, Res(53)20, 7/05/1953.
103  E. M. Thompson, "Emigration from Europe," *Editorial Research Reports*, 2 (1951). http://library.cqpress.com/cqresearcher/cqresrre1951112700. Access date: 15/03/2017.
104  Quoted by: Marina Maccari Clayton, " 'Communists of the Stomach': Italian Migration and International Relations in the Cold War Era," p. 590.
105  Ibid., pp. 587–8.
106  25/06/1952: www.presidency.ucsb.edu/ws/?pid=14175. Access date: 15/03/2017.
107  Refugee Relief Act of 1953, in *U.S. Statutes at Large*, Public Law 203, Ch. 336, pp. 400–7.
108  AOECD, Film 124, MO(50)28, 19/07/1950.
109  AOECD, Film 48, CE(50)003.
110  AOECD, Film 49, C(50)045, 13/02/1950.
111  ACE, Doc. 1, Annex IX.
112  AOECD, Film 46, C/M(50)011, 21/04/1950.
113  Mechi, *L'Organizzazione internazionale del lavoro e la ricostruzione europea*, p. 112.
114  AOECD, Film 46, C/M(50)016, 9/06/1950.
115  AOECD, Film 124, MO(51)13, 16/04/1951.
116  AOECD, Film 84, C(52)002, 16/01/1952; Mechi, *L'Organizzazione internazionale del lavoro e la ricostruzione europea*, p. 143.
117  ACE, Doc. 176, 02/09/1953.
118  AOECD, Film 84, C(52)002, Appendices III and IV.
119  Convention Relating to the Status of Refugees. www.ohchr.org/EN/ProfessionalInterest/Pages/StatusOfRefugees.aspx. Access date: 15/03/2017.
120  AOECD, Film 71, C(51)173, 17 mai 1951, Annex C; AOECD Film 125, MO(54)49; AOECD Film 126, MO(56)20, 27/06/1956; ACE Doc. 331.
121  ACE, CM(51)28, 18/04/1951 and CM(51)54, 30/05/1951.
122  ACE, Doc. 201, 22/09/1953.
123  AOECD, Film 49, C(50)060, Annex 4, 5/01/1950.
124  CEE, *Textes. Sécurité sociale des travailleurs migrants. État au 1ᵉʳ janvier 1965. Liste des instruments intervenus entre les États membres en matière de sécurité sociale* (Services des publications, 1965), pp. 147–67.
125  AOECD, Film 126, MO(56)20, 27/06/1956.
126  AOECD, Film 49, C(50)060, 6/03/1950, Annex.
127  AHUE, MAEI, PS20, France.
128  AN, F7 16100.
129  Romero, *Emigrazione e Integrazione europea, 1945–1973*, p. 156.
130  For this paragraph: Francesca Fauri, "Free but Protected? Italy and Liberalization of Foreign Trade in the 1950s," in *Explorations in OEEC History*, ed. Richard Griffiths (Paris: OECD, 1997), pp. 140–2.
131  Romero, "Migration as an Issue in European Interdependence and Integration," pp. 41, 45.
132  ACE, Doc. 1, 05/05/1951.

133 AOECD, Film 85, CE/M(52)029, 5/12/1952.
134 ACCUE, CM1 1953 61, Suppression des visas à compter du 1ᵉʳ juillet 1953.
135 AOECD, Film 110, C(54)318, 4/12/1954.
136 ACE, Res(52)39F, 11/07/1952.
137 John Torpey, *L'Invention du passeport: États, citoyenneté et surveillance*, trans. Elisabeth Lamothe (Paris: Belin, 2005), p. 184.
138 ACE, CM(54)188, 1/12/1954.
139 AOECD, Film 125, MO(54)4, 20/01/1954.
140 AHUE, MAEF, 501, Belgium, p. 3.
141 AOECD, Film 124, MO(51)47, Appendix VIII.
142 AOECD, Film 125, MO(54)35, 21/06/1954.
143 AOECD, Film 52, CE(51)043, 17/04/1951.
144 AOECD, Film 52, CE/M(51)029.
145 AOECD, Film 124, MO(52)3.
146 NATO documents online: www.nato.int/cps/fr/natolive/official_texts_17303.htm?selectedLocale=fr. Access date: 15/03/2017.
147 Romero, *Emigrazione e Integrazione europea, 1945–1973*, p. 51.
148 AOECD, OEEC, 9, 6, SG/MO 1/1/02, 7/01/1953.
149 AOECD, Film 124, MO(53)25, 26/06/1953.
150 AOECD, Film 107, C/M(53)030, 29–30/10/1953 Meeting.
151 AOECD, Film 124, MO(53)25, 26/06/1953.
152 AOECD, Film 107, C(53)251, 14/10/1953.
153 ACCUE, CM2 1958 946, 31/01/1958.
154 AOECD, Film 107, C(53)251(Final).
155 AOECD, Film 125, MO(54)2, Annex I, 14/01/1954.
156 AOECD, Film 125, MO(54)21 and MO(54)22.
157 AOECD, Film 125, MO(54)4, 20/01/1954.
158 Communiqué final de la Conférence des Six Puissances chargée d'établir l'Autorité internationale de la Ruhr (London, 28 December 1948). Source: Ministère d'Etat du Luxembourg, *Bulletin d'information*, 31/12/1948.
159 Milward, *The Reconstruction of Western Europe, 1945–51*, p. 165.
160 AHUE, MAEI, PS 20, France, p. 21.
161 AHUE, MAEF, 501, Belgium, p. 14.
162 AOECD, Film 125, MO(54)49.
163 AAPA, B15, 120 (4), p. 2, 19/09/1950 Meeting.
164 AAPA, B15, 120 (4), 28/09/1950 Meeting.
165 AHUE MAEI, PS20, French Proposal, 28/09/1950.
166 Jean Monnet, *Mémoires*, New ed., Le Livre De Poche (Paris: Librairie générale française, 2007), pp. 487–500.
167 AHUE MAEF, 501, Proposition française, 11/10/1950.
168 *Treaty Establishing the European Coal and Steel Community* (Paris, 18 April 1951). www.cvce.eu/en/obj/treaty_establishing_the_european_coal_and_steel_community_paris_18_april_1951-en-11a21305-941e-49d7-a171-ed5be548cd58.html. Access date: 15/03/2017.
169 ACCUE, CM1 1954 197, 17/11/1954.
170 For this paragraph: (1) AHUE, CM1 1954 196, 27/10/1954 Meeting; (2) AHUE, CM1 1954 194, 27–28/07/1954 Meeting.
171 Jean Charles Asselain, *Histoire économique du XXᵉ siècle. La réouverture des économies nationales (1939 aux années 1980)*, Collection "Amphithéâtre" (Paris: Presses la Fondation nationale des sciences politiques, Dalloz, 1995), p. 120.
172 ACCUE, CM1 1959 359, 22/09/1959 Meeting.
173 Quoted by: Lorenzo Mechi, *La politica sociale de la CECA*. Tesi di Laurea: Storia delle Relazioni internazionali, Università di Firenze (1995), pp. 124–5.
174 ACCUE, CM1 1954 200, 26/05/1954.

175 ACCUE, CM1 1954 197, 17/11/1954.
176 AHUE, CM1 1954 194, 27–28/07/1954.
177 ACCUE, CM1 1956 336, Part II, ch. 2.
178 ACCUE, CM1 1954 200, 22/05/1954 Meeting.
179 ACCUE, CM1 1954 197, 17/11/1954, Art. 18, 19, 20, 26.
180 AHUE, CM1 1954 194, 14/07/1954.
181 AHUE, CM1 1954 194, 27–28/07/1954 Meeting.
182 AHUE, CM1 1954 194, 14/07/1954.
183 ACCUE, CM1 1954 197, 17/11/1954.
184 AN, F7 16100, 6/03/1951.
185 AN, F7 16100, 10 and 25/08/1953.
186 AOECD, Film 125, MO(54)49.
187 AN, F7 16115, Letter to Pierre Bideberry.
188 AN, F7 16115, 21/10/1952.
189 Pascaline Winand, "The U.S. And European Integration from the Second World War to the Mid-1950s: Opportunities, Challenges and Control," in *America, Europe, Africa, 1945–1973*, ed. Éric Remacle and Pascaline Winand (Bruxelles, Bern, Berlin, Frankfurt am Main, New York, Oxford, Wien: Peter Lang, 2009), pp. 91–2.
190 Friedrich Naumann Stiftung Archiv. www.freiheit.org/2907-liberale-stichtage-50-todestag-von-max-becker. Access date: 15/03/2017.
191 AOECD, Film 85, CE(52)005, Annex.
192 AHUE, AH 124, 21/11/1952 Meeting.
193 AHUE, AH 116, 7/02/1953.
194 AHUE, AH 9, 10/03/1953 Meeting.
195 AAPA, B10, 224–44–30, 890.
196 AAPA, B10, 224–23–00, 871, 12/02/1954.
197 AHUE, CM3 NEGO1 44.
198 AAPA, B10, 224–23–41, 884, 13/02/1954.
199 AAPA, B10, 224–23–00, 871, 13/01/1954.
200 AAPA, B10, 224–44–30, 890, 24/10/1953.
201 Goedings, *Labor Migration in an Integrating Europe*, p. 370.
202 AAPA, B10, 224–23–00, 871, 24/02/1954.
203 AAPA, B10, 224–23–00, 871, 24/02/1954; R.T. Griffiths and A. S. Milwards, "The Beyen Plan and the European Political Community," in *Noi Si Mura*, ed. Werner Maihofer, Selected Working Papers of the European University Institute (1986), pp. 614–5.
204 AAPA, B10, 224–23–00, 871, 24/02/1954; AHUE, CM3 NEGO1 44, Title VII.
205 AAPA, B10, 224–44–30, 890, 24/10/1953; AAPA, B10, 224–23–00, 871, Doc. 2; AHUE CM3 NEGO1 44.

## 2 A NEW REGIME TAKING SHAPE, 1955–1964

1 Alan S. Milward, George Brennan, and Federico Romero, *The European Rescue of the Nation-State* (Berkeley: University of California Press, 1992), p. 201; Andrew Moravcsik, *The Choice for Europe: Social Purpose and State Power from Messina to Maastricht*, Cornell Studies in Political Economy (Ithaca, NY: Cornell University Press, 1998), pp. 91, 95.
2 Marc Trachtenberg, *A Constructed Peace: The Making of the European Settlement, 1945–1963*, Princeton Studies in International History and Politics (Princeton, NJ: Princeton University Press, 1999), p. 129.
3 JORF, 27/12/1957, p. 11765.
4 AN, F7 16100, 18/03/1957.
5 Ulrich Herbert, *Geschichte der Ausländerpolitik in Deutschland: Saisonarbeiter, Zwangsarbeiter, Gastarbeiter, Flüchtlinge* (Munich: CH Beck, 2001), p. 202.
6 AHUE, CM1 1955 282, 3/01/1955.

## NOTES

7 Michel Hubert, "La population allemande: ruptures et continuités," in *L'Allemagne, 1945–1961: De la catastrophe à la construction Du Mur*, ed. Jean-Paul Cahn and Ulrich Pfeil, Histoire et civilisations (Villeneuve-d'Ascq: Presses universitaires du Septentrion, 2008), p. 84.
8 AN, F7 16115, 6/12/1955.
9 Haute Autorité, *Obstacles à la mobilité*, 1956, 2nd Part, ch. 2; AN, F7 16115, 31/05/1955.
10 Quoted by: Herbert, *Geschichte der Ausländerpolitik in Deutschland: Saisonarbeiter, Zwangsarbeiter, Gastarbeiter, Flüchtlinge* (Munich: CH Beck, 2001), p. 203.
11 AN, F7 16115, 31/05/1955.
12 AN, F7 16115, 18/06/1955.
13 AOECD, Film 125, MO(56)3.
14 Quoted by: Roberto Sala, "Il controllo statale sull'immigrazione di manodopera italiana nella Germania federale," *Annali dell'Istituto storico italo-germanico in Trento/Jahrbuch des italienisch-deutschen historischen Instituts in Trient* (2004), p. 126.
15 AOECD, Film 125, MO(56)3.
16 AN, F7 16115, 23/12/1955.
17 Kenneth A. Dahlberg, "The EEC Commission and the Politics of the Free Movement of Labour," *JCMS: Journal of Common Market Studies* 6, no. 4 (1967), p. 311; Ronald Stanley Klein, *The Free Movement of Workers: A Study of Transnational Politics and Policy-Making in the European Community* (University Microfilms, 1983), p. 56; Federico Romero, *Emigrazione e Integrazione europea, 1945–1973*, Studi di storia (Roma: Edizioni lavoro, 1991), p. 69; Luciano Tosi, "Un obiettivo italiano a lungo perseguito: La libera circolazione della manodopera," in *L'Italia e la dimensione sociale nell'integrazione europea*, ed. Luciano Tosi (Padova: Cedam, 2008), p. 196.
18 Klein, *The Free Movement of Workers*, pp. 58, 73. Giuseppe Bertola and Pietro Garibaldi, *The Structure and History of Italian Unemployment* (CESIFO Working Paper, 2003), pp. 3, 21.
19 AAPA, B10 225–10–01, 900, 1, *Zur Sitzung vom 3. Mai 1955*.
20 ACCUE, CM3 NEGO 6, 01–03/06/1955 Meeting.
21 www.cvce.eu/viewer/-/content/e9a3ab7a-442a-47ab-8e8f-3947d565a5f2/b763087b-2c4c-407e-99d9-9baf7de1f904/fr. Access date: 15/03/2017.
22 AAPA, B2 221–09, 104, 16/05/1955.
23 Konrad Adenauer, *Memoirs, 1945–1953* (London: Weidenfeld, 1966), p. 387.
24 Trachtenberg, *A Constructed Peace*, pp. 173, 195.
25 Source: https://it.wikipedia.org/wiki/Partito_Comunista_Italiano#Risultati_elettorali. Access date: 15/03/2017. The April 1948 election does not appear, because the Communist Party then campaigned with the Socialist Party, within the Popular Democratic Front.
26 ACCUE, CM3 NEGO 6, 01–03/06/1955 Meeting.
27 www.cvce.eu/viewer/-/content/e9a3ab7a-442a-47ab-8e8f-3947d565a5f2/b763087b-2c4c-407e-99d9-9baf7de1f904/fr. Access date: 15/03/2017.
28 ACCUE, CM1 1959 359, 22/09/1959 Debate.
29 ACE, Doc. 331, 10/02/1955.
30 ACE, Doc. 932, 19/01/1959.
31 ACE, Doc. 331, 10/02/1955.
32 John Lewis Gaddis, *We Now Know: Rethinking Cold War History* (Oxford; New York: Clarendon Press; Oxford University Press, 1997), pp. 139, 143; Emma Haddad, *The Refugee in International Society: Between Sovereigns* (Cambridge: Cambridge University Press, 2008), pp. 144–5.
33 ACCUE, CM3 NEGO 6, 01–03/06/1955 Meeting.
34 Benelux Memorandum, in: Roberto Ducci and Bino Olivi, *L'Europa incompiuta*, vol. 22 (Padova: Cedam, 1970), pp. 273–6.
35 Italian Memorandum, in: Pier Luigi Ballini and Antonio Varsori, *L'Italia e l'Europa: 1947–1979*, 2 vols. (Soveria Mannelli: Rubbettino, 2004).
36 AAPA, B2 221–09, 104, 16/05/1955; AAPA, B10 225–10–01, 900, 26/05/1955; Milward et al., *The European Rescue of the Nation-State*, p. 201.
37 AAPA, B10 225–10–01, 900, 24/05/1955.

# NOTES

38 'Mémorandum du gouvernement fédéral allemand sur la poursuite de l'intégration,' In: Ducci and Olivi, *L'Europa incompiuta*, pp. 276–9.
39 ACCUE, CM3 NEGO 6, Doc. 8.
40 ACCUE, CM3 NEGO 6, Messina Resolution.
41 ACCUE, CM3 NEGO1 45: (1) 01/09/1955, MAE/CIG Doc. n° 193; (2) 30/08/1955, MAE/CIG Doc. n° 176.
42 ACCUE, CM3 NEGO1 45, 01/09/1955, MAE/CIG Doc. n° 193.
43 AHUE, CM3 NEGO 230, 20/07/1956.
44 ACE, Doc. 351, 10/06/1955.
45 ACCUE, CM3 NEGO1 45, 30/08/1955, MAE/CIG Doc. n° 176.
46 AHUE, CM3 NEGO 229, 21/12/1956.
47 AHUE, CM2 1964 1144: (1) 11298/V/63; (2) 30/10/1963, 1399/63 (SOC 122).
48 Simone Alberdina Wilhelmina Goedings, *Labor Migration in an Integrating Europe: National Migration Policies and the Free Movement of Workers, 1950–1968*, pp. 132–4.
49 AAPA, B10 225–10–01, 900, 27/05/1955.
50 AAPA, B10 022–48, 140, 4/10/1954.
51 ACCUE, CM3 NEGO 254, 7/03/1957.
52 AOECD, Film 125, 3/03/1955, MO(55)5, Annex II; Andrée Michel, *Les Travailleurs algériens en France* (Paris: CNRS, 1956), p. 51.
53 ACCUE, CM3 NEGO 254, 19/02/1957.
54 AAPA, B10, Abteilung II, Politische Abteilung, Bd. 917, 20/02/1957.
55 ACCUE, CM3 NEGO 255, 28/02/1957.
56 ACCUE, CM2 1959 856, 19/12/1958, COM(58)267 rev.
57 Goedings, *Labor Migration in an Integrating Europe*, p. 173.
58 OJEC, 13/12/61, pp. 1513–6.
59 AHUE, CM2 1964 1189, Council Meeting, 25/03/1964.
60 ACCUE, CM3 NEGO 253, Article 132.
61 ACCUE, CM2 1959 858, Council Meeting, 23–24/11/1959.
62 OJEC, 147/60, 10/02/1960.
63 OJEC, 06/10/1958, n° 17.
64 ACCUE, CM2 1959 857, 8/04/1959, CES 38 f/59.
65 OJEC, 147/60, 10/02/1960.
66 See earlier in this section. ACCUE, CM2 1959 858, Council Meeting, 23–24/11/1959.
67 ACCUE, CM2 1959 856, 19/12/1958, COM(58)267 rev.
68 AHUE, CM2 1961 321, 30/05/1961, T/238/61.
69 OJEC, 11/06/1964, 1439/64–1441/64.
70 OJEC, 11/06/1964, 1439/64–1441/64.
71 Archives historiques de la Commission européenne, Bruxelles (AHCE), BAC 42 1991 323, 21/04/1964.
72 ACCUE, CM2 1964 1131, II/V/COM(63) 299 final, 29/07/1963.
73 Georges Photios Tapinos, *L'Immigration étrangère en France: 1946–1973*, Travaux et documents—Institut national d'études demographiques (Paris: Presses universitaires de France, 1975), pp. 60, 63–4.
74 AHCE, BAC 23 1967 62, V/4539/63.
75 Tapinos, *L'Immigration étrangère en France*, pp. 63–4.
76 Heinz Werner, "Migration and Free Movement of Workers in Western Europe," in *Les Travailleurs étrangers en Europe occidentale*, ed. P. J. Bernard (Paris: Mouton, 1976), p. 71.
77 ACCUE, CM5 ADH1 115, 10/04/1962.
78 ACCUE, CM5 ADH1 197, British Note, Annex, 7/05/1962.
79 Klein, *The Free Movement of Workers*, pp. 107–9; Romero, *Emigrazione e Integrazione europea, 1945–1973*, p. 106; Goedings, *Labor Migration in an Integrating Europe*, pp. 210–6.
80 AHUE, CM3 NEGO 44, 2/08/1955, Doc. n° 104.

## NOTES

81 ACCUE, CM2 1961 375, COM(61)100 final, 12/07/1961.
82 AHUE, CM2 1961 379, GSQ Meetings, 2–3/02/1961, Annex I.
83 AHUE, CM2 1961 383, Council Meeting, 29–30/05/1961, 652/61 (MC/PV 5) rév.
84 AHUE, CM2 1961 383, Council Meeting, 12/06/1961.
85 OJEC, 26/08/1961, 1073–84.
86 AHUE, CM2 1961 383, Council Meeting, 12/06/1961.
87 Goedings, *Labor Migration in an Integrating Europe*, p. 370.
88 Michele Salvati, *Occasioni mancate. Economia e politica in Italia dagli anni '60 a oggi* (Roma-Bari: Laterza, 2000), p. 9.
89 AHCE, BAC 23 1967 62 (1963), V/4539/63.
90 AHUE, CM2 1964 1169, 1081/63 (SOC 96), GSQ Meetings, 8–10/07/1963.
91 AHUE, CM2 1964 1196, 16/07/1962, CES 199/62.
92 OJEC, 17/04/1964, 965/64–980/64, Art. 29, 30.
93 AHCE, BAC 7 1986 1626 (1963–1964), V/8106/63-F.
94 Ibid.
95 Ettore Recchi, *Mobile Europe: The Theory and Practice of Free Movement in the EU* (London: Palgrave Macmillan, 2015), p. 50.
96 AOECD, Film 301, 18/03/1957, TOU(57)5.
97 AOECD, Film 177, C/M(56)43, 7/12/1956.
98 AHUE, CM2 1961 220, 2/01/1962.
99 OJEC, 17/04/1964, 981/64.
100 AHUE, CM3 NEGO 44, 2/08/1955, Doc. n° 104.
101 OJEC, 26/08/1961, 1073–84.
102 OJEC, 17/04/1964, 965/64–980/64.
103 Recchi, *Mobile Europe*, p. 50.
104 OJEC, 17/04/1964, 965/64–980/64.
105 AHUE, CM2 1964 1140, 16/02/1962, V/COM(62)25.
106 AHUE, CM2 1958 946, p. 24.
107 AHCE, BAC 6 1977 465, V/5664/1/60.
108 AHUE, CM2 1964 1184, Council Meeting, 6–7/02/1964, Doc. 165/64.
109 AHCE, BAC 6 1977 465, 23/07/1962, V/COM(62)162 final.
110 AHUE, CM2 1961 383, 29–30/05/1961.
111 Dahlberg, "The EEC Commission and the Politics of the Free Movement of Labour," p. 318.
112 AHUE, CM2 1964 1168, 943 (SOC 88), GSQ Meeting, 18–20/06/1963.
113 AHUE, CM2 1964 1184, 6–7/02/1964, doc. 165/64; OJEC, 17/04/1964, 965/64–980/64, art. 9, par. 2.
114 AHUE, CM3 NEGO 229, 9/10/1956.
115 AHUE, CM3 NEGO 229, Article 48, Deutscher Bundestag, 1953, Doc. n° 3660, p. 25.
116 Arnold Zelle, *Das Handwerk in Deutschland* (Bonn: Presse- und Informationsamt der Bundesregierung, 1963), pp. 5, 11, 19.
117 AHUE, CM2 1961 339, 2/02/1960, CES 20/61; AHUE, CM2 1961 318, 22/03/1960. III/C/573/60.
118 AHUE, CM2 1961 332, 6/10/1960, R/CES 191/60 rév.
119 ACE, Doc. 1738, 10/04/1964.
120 AHUE, CM2 1961 338, 10/02/1961, CES 21/61.
121 AHUE, CM2 1963 626, ESC Meeting, 16–17/07/1962, CES 211/62.
122 Laurent Warlouzet, "The Deadlock: The Choice of the Cap by De Gaulle and Its Impact on French EEC Policy (1958–69)," in *Fertile Ground for Europe? The History of European Integration and the Common Agricultural Policy since 1945*, ed. Kiran Klaus Patel (Baden-Baden: Nomos, 2009).
123 AHUE, CM2 1961 338, CES 21/61, 01–02/02/1961.
124 OJEC, 20/04/1963, 1326/63–1328/63.
125 OJEC, 20/04/1963, 1323/63–1325/63.
126 Moravcsik, *The Choice for Europe*, p. 63.

## NOTES

127  Werner, "Migration and Free Movement of Workers in Western Europe," p. 70.
128  ACCUE, CM1 1956 343, Doc. N° 2999/56 f., 5/04/1956, Annexes II.B. and II.C.
129  Ibid.
130  ACCUE, CM1 1957 362, 592 f/57, 26/07/1957.
131  ACCUE, CM3 NEGO1 44, 22/07/1955, MAE/CIG Doc. n° 47.
132  ACCUE, CM1 1956 346, Doc. N° 8337/56 f., 22/10/1956.
133  ACCUE, CM1 1957 368, 16/01/1957, 41 f/57.
134  ACCUE, CM1 1957 365, CME/D.213/1957; ACCUE, CM1 1957 362, 592 f/57, 26/07/1957.
135  ACCUE, CM1 1957 365, CME/D.213/1957.
136  ACCUE, CM1 1957 362, 592 f/57, 26/07/1957.
137  OJEC, 561–96/58, 16/12/1958, Art. 20, par. 1 and art. 40, par. 5.
138  ACCUE, CM1 1957 362, 592 f/57, 26/07/1957.
139  OJEC, 561–96/58, 16/12/1958, Art. 20, par. 1.
140  OJEC, 597–664/58, 16/12/1958, Art. 88, par. 1.
141  ACCUE, CM1 1957 362, 592 f/57, 26/07/1957.
142  ACCUE, CM1 1957 360, 24/01/1957, 107 f/57.
143  AHUE, CM2 1958 932, 641/58.
144  OJEC, 561–96/58, 16/12/1958, Art. 37, Annex C.
145  AHUE, CM2 1958 931, COREPER Meeting, 28/06/1958, 688 f/58.
146  Commission administrative pour la sécurité sociale des travailleurs migrants. *Premier rapport annuel sur la mise en œuvre des règlements concernant la sécurité sociale des travailleurs migrants. Année 1959.* Luxembourg: Office des publications officielles des Communautés européennes, March 1961.
147  AHUE, CM2 1958 932, 700 f/58.
148  For all statistical information in this paragraph and the next: *Rapport annuel sur la mise en œuvre des règlements concernant la sécurité sociale des travailleurs migrants*, Years 1961, 1962, 1963, and 1964–1965. All published by: Commission administrative pour la sécurité sociale des travailleurs migrants. Luxembourg: Office des publications officielles des Communautés européennes.
149  *Rapport annuel, 1962.* Annex 2.
150  Recchi, *Mobile Europe*, p. 50.
151  OJEC, 1649/61, 31/12/1961, 4th Considérant.
152  Warlouzet, "The Deadlock," p. 106.
153  AHUE, CM2 1961 390, 492/62 (MC/PV 1) rév.
154  OJEC, 1649/61, 31/12/1961.
155  AHUE, CM2 1963 719, 21/02/1963, Doc. 333/63; AHUE, CM2 1963 727, 2/05/1963, 653/63 (SOC 63).
156  AHUE, CM2 1963 719, Doc. 333/63.
157  AHUE, CM2 1963 716, T/466/62 (SOC).
158  OJEC, 20/04/1963, 1314/63–1322/63, Art. 19.
159  AHUE, CM2 1963 727, COREPER Meeting, 21/05/1963, Doc. 839/63.
160  OJEC, 7/08/1964, 2138/64–2139/64. Regulation 108/64 of 30 July 1964.
161  OJEC, 4/04/1964, 845/64–847/64, Art. 3.
162  AHUE, CM2 1964 998, 18/10/1963, 1382/63 (E.S. 52).
163  OJEC, 4/04/1964, 845/64–847/64, Art. 4.
164  OJEC, 17/04/1964, 965/64–980/64, Art. 17 (1).
165  OJEC, 17/04/1964, 965/64–980/64, Art. 17 (3).
166  AHUE, CM2 1964 1189, Council Meeting, 25/03/1964, Doc. 593/64.
167  AOECD, Film 125, 23/05/1955, MO(55)2/13.
168  AOECD, Film 160, C/M(55)36, Council Meeting, 20/12/1955.
169  AOECD, Film 125, 11/08/1955, MO(55)29/16.
170  Goedings, *Labor Migration in an Integrating Europe*, pp. 75, 123.
171  AOECD, Film 159, C(55)149, 6/07/1955.
172  AOECD, Film 129, 19/12/1959, MO/WP7(59)10.

NOTES

173 AOECD, Film 178, 20/06/1956, C(56)131.
174 ACE, Doc. 1068, 22/12/1959.
175 AOECD, Film 192, 8/08/1960, MO(60)17.
176 AOECD, Film 177, C/M(56)43, Council Meeting, 7/12/1956.
177 AOECD, Film 177, C/M(56)43.
178 AOECD, Film 548: (1) OECD/P(61)34, 7/07/1961; (2) Corr. OECD/P(61)34, 27/09/1961.
179 Christoph Rass, *Institutionalisierunsprozesse auf einem internationalen Arbeitsmarkt: Bilaterale Wanderungsverträge in Europa zwischen 1919 und 1974*, Studien zur historischen Migrationsforschung (Shm) (Paderborn: Schöningh, 2010), p. 356.
180 AHUE, CM2 1967 1113, V/2997/66 rév.
181 ACCUE, CM7 ASS1 261, 27/09/1966, CEE-TR 17/66.
182 AHUE, CM2 1967 1113, V/2997/66 rév; AHUE, CM2 1967 1112, 20/03/1967, I/III/2914/67.
183 ACCUE, CM2 1966 1044, 29/10/1965, S/802/65 (NT 18), Annex.
184 ACCUE, CM7 ASS1 261, CEE-TR 17/66.
185 ACE, Doc. 699, 23/09/1957.
186 Ibid.
187 ACE, Doc. 1034, 12/09/1959.
188 ACE, CM(55)PV2F, Committee of Ministers Meeting, 13/12/1955.
189 ACE, Res(56)9F, 16/04/1956.
190 ACE: (1) Doc. 1107, 01/04/1960; (2) Doc. 1363, 22/09/1961.
191 ACE, Doc. 1059, 24/11/1959.
192 ACE, Doc. 1630, 19/08/1963.
193 ACE, Doc. 1059, 24/11/1959.
194 AOECD, Film 129, 4–9/11/1959, MO/M(59)4.
195 AOECD, Film 192, C/M(60)12, 6/05/1960.
196 OJEC, 22/05/1964, 1225/64.
197 ACCUE, CM2 1962 908, Response of the FRG.
198 ACCUE, CM2 1962 909, 1458/61 (SOC 126), 17/11/1961.
199 ACCUE, CM2 1962 910, 8/06/1962, CSS/PV2.
200 ACCUE, CM2 1962 910, N° 41, Art. 6 and 7.
201 Ibid.
202 ACCUE, CM2 1962 910, 22/06/1962, CSS/PV14.

## 3 A SHRINKING DYNAMIC, 1965–1973

1 Alan S. Milward, George Brennan, and Federico Romero, *The European Rescue of the Nation-State* (Berkeley: University of California Press, 1992), pp. 212–17.
2 Willem Molle and Aad Mourik, "International Movements of Labour under Conditions of Economic Integration: The Case of Western Europe," *JCMS: Journal of Common Market Studies* 26, no. 3 (1988), pp. 317–22.
3 ACCUE, CM2 1975 2174, SEC(75) 37 final, 17/01/1975.
4 Federico Romero, *Emigrazione e Integrazione europea, 1945–1973*, Studi di storia (Roma: Edizioni lavoro, 1991), p. 111.
5 AHUE, CM2 1967 1113, V/2997/66 rév.
6 Wolf Rüdiger Böhning, *The Migration of Workers in the United Kingdom and the European Community* (London: Oxford University Press, 1972), p. 60.
7 AHUE, CM2 1967 1113, V/2997/66 rév.
8 Böhning, *The Migration of Workers in the United Kingdom and the European Community*, p. 79.
9 Georges Photios Tapinos, *L'Immigration étrangère en France: 1946–1973*, Travaux et documents—Institut national d'études demographiques (Paris: Presses universitaires de France, 1975), p. 99.
10 World Bank, GDP per capita (current US$) per country, since 1960. Online: http://data.worldbank.org. Access date: 30/06/2017.

## NOTES

11 Tapinos, *L'Immigration étrangère en France: 1946–1973*, p. 99.
12 World Bank, GDP per capita (current US$) per country, since 1960. Online: http://data.worldbank.org. Access date: 30/06/2017.
13 Francesco Petrini, "Il '68 e la crisi dell'età dell'oro," *Annali dell'Istituto Ugo La Malfa* 22 (2007), p. 65.
14 AHUE, CM2 1968 982, SEC (67) 4625 final, 1/12/1967.
15 AHUE, CM2 1969 1058, 502/69 (PV/CONS 6) Extr. 1, Council Meeting, 13/03/1969.
16 Böhning, *The Migration of Workers in the United Kingdom and the European Community*, p. 60.
17 Christian Baudelot and Anne Lebeaupin, "Les salaires de 1950 à 1975," *Economie et statistique* 113, no. 1 (1979), p. 22.
18 Ibid., p. 20.
19 AHUE, CM2 1968 1018, 19/05/1969.
20 Böhning, *The Migration of Workers in the United Kingdom and the European Community*, p. 67.
21 Ibid., pp. 69–70.
22 AHCE, BAC 6 1977 470 (1967), 15157/V/67.
23 ACCUE, CM2 1975 2174, SEC(75) 37 final.
24 Luigi Fascetti, "Le restrizioni all'emigrazione: 'Alt' in Svizzera ai 'falsi turisti'," *La Stampa*, 15–16/02/1965; Helen S. Feldstein, "A Study of Transaction and Political Integration Transnational Labour Flow within the European Economic Community," *JCMS: Journal of Common Market Studies* 6, no. 1 (1967), p. 52.
25 Domenico Bartoli, "Restrizioni all'immigrazione. Perchè la Svizzera ha chiuso la porta," *Corriere della sera*, 18/02/1965.
26 Fascetti, "Le restrizioni all'emigrazione: 'Alt' in Svizzera ai 'falsi turisti'."
27 Enzo Ferraiuolo, "La polizia elvetica ferma al confine e rimanda in Italia 1300 lavoratori," *Gazzetta del Popolo*, 16/02/1965.
28 Arnaldo Marchetti, "Trentamila lavoratori italiani dovranno lasciare la Svizzera," *La Nazione*, 17/02/1965.
29 For this paragraph: AHCE, BAC 144 1992 250 (1964–1965), SEC (65) 2483, 30/07/1965; Cesare Maestripieri, *La Libre circulation des personnes et des services dans la CEE* (Heule, Belgium: Uga, 1971), p. 30; Simone Alberdina Wilhelmina Goedings, *Labor Migration in an Integrating Europe: National Migration Policies and the Free Movement of Workers, 1950–1968* (The Hague: Sdu Uitgevers, 2005), pp. 187–8.
30 Accords de Grenelle (27/05/1968). http://travail-emploi.gouv.fr/IMG/pdf/Constat_de_Grenelle.pdf. Access date: 15/03/2017.
31 Décret n° 67–508 du 29 juin 1967 portant majoration du salaire minimum national interprofessionnel garanti et réduction du nombre de zones. JORF, 30/06/1967, p. 6492.
32 INSEE, Euro-Franc Converter: Purchasing Power of the Euro and the Franc. www.insee.fr/fr/themes/calcul-pouvoir-achat.asp. Access date: 15/03/2017.
33 Décret n° 50–1029 du 23 août 1950 portant fixation du salaire national minimum interprofessionnel garanti. JORF, 24/08/1950, pp. 9061–2.
34 Loi n° 70–7 du 2 janvier 1970 portant réforme du salaire minimum garanti et création d'un salaire minimum de croissance. JORF, 4/01/1970, pp. 141–2.
35 Décret n° 69–243 du 18 mars 1969, portant publication de l'accord franco-algérien. JORF, 22/03/1969.
36 Tapinos, *L'Immigration étrangère en France: 1946–1973*, pp. 98–9.
37 JORF, 1972–1973, n° 113, 14/12/1972, pp. 6105–8; JORF, 1973–1974, n° 75, 20/12/1973, pp. 6105–8.
38 François Grosrichard, "Le gouvernement retire son projet de loi sur le nouveau statut des marins," *Le Monde*, 22/12/1972, p. 41.
39 JORF, 1973–1974, n° 75, 20/12/1973, pp. 6105–8.
40 Circulaire du 29 avril 1975 relative aux conditions d'embarquement sur les navires battant pavillon français. JORF, 2/05/1975, p. 4471.
41 Source: Goedings, *Labor Migration in an Integrating Europe*, p. 369.

42 AHUE, CM2 1968 1006, 554/68 (SOC 68), Annex I.
43 Roberto Sala, "Il controllo statale sull'immigrazione di manodopera italiana nella Germania federale," *Annali dell'Istituto storico italo-germanico in Trento/Jahrbuch des italienisch-deutschen historischen Instituts in Trient* (2004), p. 147.
44 *Daily Telegraph*, 28/01/1971; *The Sun*, 19/05/1971.
45 Décret n° 71–880 du 29 octobre 1971 portant application du protocole franco-portugais. JORF, 31/10/1971.
46 AHUE, CM2 1971 1227, 1605/70 (PV/CONS 26) extr. 1, Council Meeting, 27/07/1970.
47 AHUE, CM2 1968 1006, 554/68 (SOC 68), Annex I.
48 OJEC, L 257, 19/10/1968, pp. 2–12, Art. 4.
49 AHUE, CM2 1968 1011, Doc. 1297/68.
50 AHUE, CM2 1968 1019, 350/68 (SOC 48).
51 AHUE, CM2 1968 1013, Council Meeting, 14–15/10/1968, Doc. 1836/68.
52 AHUE, CM2 1968 1011, Doc. 1297/68.
53 AHUE, CM2 1968 1013, Doc. 1836/68.
54 Tapinos, *L'Immigration étrangère en France: 1946–1973*, p. 108.
55 AHUE, CM2 1971 1270, 1764/69 (SOC 193), GSQ Meeting, 30/10/1969.
56 Article 35 of Regulation 3.
57 AHUE, CM2 1971 1259, 1722/68 (SOC 237), GSQ meeting.
58 ACCUE, CM2 1971 1291, 19/05/1971, 552/1/71 (SOC 60 rév. 1).
59 Article 35 of Regulation 3.
60 AHUE, CM2 1971 1259, 85/69 (SOC 5), GSQ Meeting, 7–8/01/1969.
61 AHUE, CM2 1971 1262, 647/69 (SOC 57), GSQ Meeting, 28–29/04/1969.
62 ACCUE, CM2 1971 1274, Council Meeting, 24–25/11/1969, Doc n° 2008/69 (PV/CONS 27).
63 AHUE, CM2 1971 1262, Council Meeting, 13/03/1969, Doc. N° 502/69.
64 ACCUE, CM2 1972 1411, 2101/71 (SOC 203), GSQ Meeting, 20–21/10/1971.
65 ACCUE, CM2 1972 1417, 28/02/1972, R/355/72 (SOC 51), Annex.
66 AHUE, CM2 1968 1020, 717/68 (SOC 94), GSQ Meeting, 22/04/1968.
67 AHUE, CM2 1968 1013, Doc. 1836/68, Council Meeting, 14–15/10/1968.
68 AHUE, CM2 1968 1005, 190/68 (SOC 28), GSQ Meeting.
69 AHUE, CM2 1968 1018, 19/05/1969.
70 AHUE, CM2 1968 1011, Doc. 1297/68, 29/07/1968.
71 Comité permanent pour l'étude des problèmes posés par le Marché commun européen dans l'industrie de la construction.
72 Syndicat professionnel des entrepreneurs de travaux publics de France et de l'Outre-Mer.
73 ACCUE, CM2 1971 1298, 24/07/1969.
74 AHUE, CM2 1971 1257, 1524/68 (SOC 206), GSQ Meeting, 22–23/09/1968.
75 AHUE, CM2 1971 1265, 1170/69 (SOC 118), GSQ Meeting, 9–10/07/1969.
76 OJEC, L 149, 5/07/1971, pp. 2–50, Art. 14.
77 JORF, 1972–1973, n° 113.
78 JORF, 1973–1974, n° 75.
79 AHUE, CM2 1968 1006, 655/68 (SOC 87), GSQ Meeting, 4–5/04/1968.
80 AHUE, CM2 1968 1013, Doc. 1836/68.
81 JORF, 1972–1973, n° 113.
82 ACCUE, CM2 1971 1295, 30/12/1967, Doc. 158.
83 Albert Martens, *Les Immigres: Flux et reflux d'une main-d'œuvre d'appoint. La politique belge de l'immigration de 1945 à 1970*, Sociologische Verkenningen (Leuven, Krakenstr, 3: Universitaire Pers, 1976), p. 122.
84 AHUE, CM2 1968 1011, Doc. 1297/68.
85 ACCUE, CM2 1971 1295, Doc. 158.
86 AHUE, CM2 1971 1262, 629/69 (SOC 56), GSQ Meeting, 21–22/04/1969.
87 AHUE, CM2 1971 1264, 1072/69 (SOC 98), GSQ Meeting, 1/07/1969.

88 Source: EEC Commission administrative pour la sécurité sociale des travailleurs migrants, *Sixième et septième rapports annuels sur la mise en œuvre des règlements concernant la sécurité sociale des travailleurs migrants. Années 1964–1965. Annexe relative aux résultats d'application des règlements* (Luxembourg: Office des publications officielles des Communautés européennes), p. 27.
89 Ettore Recchi, *Mobile Europe: The Theory and Practice of Free Movement in the EU* (London: Palgrave Macmillan, 2015), p. 50.
90 AHUE, CM2 1971 1259, 85/69 (SOC 5), GSQ Meeting, 7–8/01/1969.
91 AHUE, CM2 1971 1265, 939/69 (SOC 86), GSQ Meeting, 9/07/1969.
92 AHUE, CM2 1971 1262, 629/69 (SOC 56).
93 OJEC, L 149, 5/07/1971, pp. 2–50, Article 36.
94 ACCUE, CM2 1971 1291, 552/1/71 (SOC 60 rév. 1).
95 AHUE, CM2 1971 1262: 1) Doc. N° 502/69; 2) Doc. R/540/69 (SOC 44).
96 N. Piers Ludlow, *The European Community and the Crises of the 1960s: Negotiating the Gaullist Challenge*, Cass Series-Cold War History (London; New York: Routledge, 2006).
97 AHUE, CM2 1971 1262, R/540/69 (SOC 44); AHUE, CM2 1971 1264, 917/69 (SOC 84), GSQ Meeting, 30/05/1969.
98 AHUE, CM2 1971 1264, 917/69 (SOC 84).
99 AHUE, CM2 1971 1269, 1759/69 (SOC 190), GSQ Meeting, 30/10/1969.
100 ACCUE, CM2 1971 1274, Doc n° 2008/69 (PV/CONS 27).
101 AHUE, CM2 1968 1005, 190/68 (SOC 28).
102 OJEC, L 149, 5/07/1971, pp. 2–50.
103 ACCUE, CM2 1973 1670, 1277/72 (SOC 150), GSQ Meeting, 4/07/1972, Annex.
104 It became Directive 68/360.
105 AHUE, CM2 1968 1020, 479/68 (SOC 61). GSQ Meeting, 7/03/1968, Annex.
106 AHUE, CM2 1968 1021, Doc. 1297/68, Council Meeting.
107 AHUE, CM2 1968 1005, 354/68 (SOC 49), GSQ Meeting, 23/02/1968.
108 AHUE, CM2 1968 1005, 354/68 (SOC 49), GSQ Meeting, 23/02/1968; AHUE, CM2 1968 1011, Doc. 1297/68.
109 OJEC, L 257, 19/10/1968, pp. 2–12, Art. 10.
110 Ibid.
111 Article 48(3)d.
112 AHUE, CM2 1968 1009, 8/07/1968, 1084/1/68 (SOC 139 rév. 1), German proposal, 8/07/1968.
113 AHCE, BAC 38 1984 344, COM(69) 1203, 4/12/1969.
114 OJEC, L 142, 30/06/1970, pp. 24–6, Art. 2.
115 My investigations did not allow me to find out how this unusual responsibility of the Commission had been accepted at the time of the Treaty's negotiation.
116 Serge Berstein, Jean-Claude Casanova, and Jean-François Sirinelli, *Les années Giscard: La politique économique 1974–1981* (Paris: Armand Colin, 2009), p. 114; John Lewis Gaddis, *The Cold War: A New History* (New York: Penguin Press, 2005), pp. 153–4.
117 Communiqué final de la réunion des chefs de gouvernement de la Communauté à Paris, les 9 et 10 décembre 1974, *Bulletin des Communautés européennes*, December 1974, n° 12, pp. 7–13.
118 Emmanuel Comte, "Les origines de la citoyenneté européenne, de 1974 à 1992," in *L'Europe des citoyens et la citoyenneté européenne. Évolutions, limites et perspectives*, ed. Michel Catala, Stanislas Jeannesson, and Anne-Sophie Lamblin-Gourdin (Bern: Peter Lang, 2016).
119 AHUE, CM2 1967 994, 18/01/1966, Doc. 117.
120 EEC Commission, SEC(71)2850 final, 23/07/1971.
121 AHUE, CM2 1970 1021, 6/10/1969, Doc. 110, Annex.
122 AHUE, CM2 1968 925, Doc. 23.
123 ACCUE, CM2 1974 1543, 30/07/1970, 1423/70 (E.S. 121), Annex.
124 AHUE, CM2 1968 925, Doc. 23.
125 ACCUE, CM2 1974 1543, 1423/70 (E.S. 121), Annex.

126 AHUE, CM2 1967 1000, 715/67 (E.S. 41), Group on Economic Questions (GEQ) Meeting, 20–21/04/1967.
127 AHUE, CM2 1968 875, 510/68 (E.S. 23), COREPER Meeting, 19/03/1968.
128 AHUE, CM2 1968 875, 179/68 (ES 7), COREPER Meetings of 12–13/07 and 13–15/12/1967.
129 *Code rural*, Articles 550 and 552; Décret n° 59–286 du 4 février 1959 relatif au statut juridique de la coopération agricole, Art. 20, modified by Décret n° 61–867 du 5 août 1961, Art. 28.
130 Décret n° 65–576 du 15 juillet 1965 relatif aux prêts à long terme consentis par le Crédit agricole mutuel, Art. 11.
131 AHUE, CM2 1970 1023, CES 591/69, ESC Meeting, 29/10/1969.
132 John T. S. Keeler, "De Gaulle et la Politique agricole commune de L'Europe: Logique et héritages de l'intégration nationaliste," in *De Gaulle en son Siècle, Tome V, L'Europe*, ed. Institut Charles de Gaulle (Paris: Plon, 1992), p. 163.
133 AHUE, CM2 1968 878, 4/03/1966, 206/66 (E.S. 3).
134 OJEC, 22/10/1968, L 260/1–5, Art. 2.
135 They were not included in Directive 68/363. OJEC, 22/10/1968, L 260/1–5.
136 ACCUE, CM2 1974 1487, 1502/72 (E.S. 101), GEQ Meetings, 18/05–23/06/1972.
137 ACE, Doc. 2629, 18/09/1969, Annex 1.
138 OJEC, 22/10/1968, L 260/1–5.
139 AHUE, CM2 1968 882, 5/01/1967, 1457/66 (E.S. 46).
140 OJEC, 22/10/1968, L 260/6–9.
141 AHUE, CM2 1968 882, 1457/66 (E.S. 46).
142 AN, F7 16046, Incidences pratiques de la libération du droit d'établissement.
143 AN F7 16046, Étrangers exerçant en France, 1965.
144 AHUE, CM2 1968 884: (1) 1041/68 (E.S. 50), COREPER Meeting, 26/06/1968; (2) Council Meeting, 30/07/1968, doc. 1298/68 PV/CONS 22.
145 AHCE, BAC 201 1989 309 (1939–1973), 313/2/III/68-F Rév, 25/03/1968.
146 ACCUE, CM2 1974 1481, 23/06/1967, CES 252/67.
147 ACCUE, CM2 1974 1477, 2/03/1970, 375/70 (E.S. 35), Annex.
148 AHUE, CM2 1968 927, 22/03/1967.
149 ACCUE, CM2 1974 1440, 6/07/1970, Doc. 80.
150 ACCUE, CM2 1974 1481, CES 252/67.
151 ACCUE, Liste Rouge 40844, 24/01/1968, CES 45/68 bp.
152 ACCUE, CM2 1974 1476, 1964/69 (E.S. 115), Annex, GEQ Meetings, 20–21/11/1969.
153 ACCUE, CM2 1974 1480, 1/04/1974, 649/74 (E.S. 65), Annex.
154 Roger Millot, "Le Secteur Des Professions Libérales," in *Les Aspects économiques de la liberté d'établissement et de prestation de services dans la Communauté économique européenne*, ed. Commission des Communautés européennes (Pont-à-Mousson, France: Services des publications des communautés européennes, 1967). Declarations of Mr de Crayencour.
155 ACCUE, CM2 1974 1481, 7/11/1967, CES 302/67 fin.
156 ACCUE, Liste Rouge 40844, CES 45/68 bp.
157 Ibid.
158 ACCUE, Liste Rouge 40844, Directive 85/384/CEE 3/3, 23 juin 1967, CES 252/67 jp.
159 AHCE, BAC 38 1984 344 (1969), 11/10/1969.
160 ACCUE, CM2 1974 1482, 9/05/1972.
161 Louis Tart, "Les avocats de nationalité étrangère," *La Belgique judiciaire*, 77th year, No. 7, 16 February 1919, column 231.
162 AHCE, BAC 371 1991 1729 1974, Case 2/74.
163 "Reyners v Belgium (2/74)," *Common Market Law Reports*, 2 (1974), pp. 305–30.
164 AHUE, CM2 1968 927, Opinion of the German government, 22/03/1967.
165 AHCE, BAC 371 1991 1728 1971–1974, Case 2/74, Vol. 1, Rapport d'audience.
166 AHCE, BAC 371 1991 1729, Court Ruling, En droit.
167 See first section of Chapter 2.
168 ACCUE, CM2 1974 1544, SEC(74)4024 final, 30/10/1974.

NOTES

169 Alberto Trabucchi, "L'esercizio dell'avvocatura non subordinato in Europa alla cittadinanza nazionale," *Rivista di diritto civile* 2 (1974), pp. 317–21.
170 AHUE, CM2 1968 1017, 1483/67 (CES 139) (SOC 170), ESC Session, 26/10/1967.
171 AHUE, CM2 1968 1005, 186/68 (SOC 25), GSQ Meetings, 24–29/01/1968, Annex; AHUE, CM2 1968 1008, 918/68 (SOC 118), GSQ Meeting, 5/06/1968.
172 AHUE, CM2 1968 1006, 554/68 (SOC 68), Annex I.
173 Ibid., Annex II.
174 OJEC, L 257, 19/10/1968, pp. 2–12, Art. 16, par. 3.
175 Federico Romero, *Emigrazione e Integrazione europea, 1945–1973*, pp. 121–2.
176 ACCUE, CM2 b. 30542, 2/02/1972, in: Pier Luigi Ballini and Antonio Varsori, *L'Italia e l'Europa: 1947–1979*, 2 vols. (Soveria Mannelli: Rubbettino, 2004).
177 AHUE, CM2 1971 1227, 1605/70 (PV/CONS 26) extr. 1.
178 AHUE, CM2 1967 1113, V/2997/66 rév.
179 Ibid., Annex II.
180 ACCUE, CM7 ASS1 261, 27/07/1965, Doc. CEE-TR 11/65.
181 ACCUE, CM2 1966 1044, S/802/65 (NT 18), Annex.
182 ACCUE, CM7 ASS1 261, Déc. 1965, Annex VII.
183 ACCUE, CM2 1966 1037, Rec. 431 (1965).
184 ACCUE, CM2 1966 1044, 8291/3/V/65-F, Fev. 1966.
185 For all this paragraph: ACCUE, CM7 ASS1 261, CEE-TR 11/65.
186 ACCUE, CM7 ASS1 261, 27/09/1966, CEE-TR 17/66, Annex IV.
187 ACCUE, CM7 ASS1 262, CEE-TR 6/67, 2/05/1967.
188 ACCUE, CM7 ASS1 262, 2/05/1967, Doc. CEE-TR 7/67.
189 ACCUE, CM7 ASS1 262, 11/03/1969, Doc. CEE-TR 9/69.
190 AHCE, BAC 15 1993 34 1976, 26/10/1976.
191 ACCUE, CM7 ASS1 260, Rec. n° 2/71, 15–18/03/1971.
192 Douglas S. Massey et al., "Theories of International Migration: A Review and Appraisal," *Population and Development Review* (1993), p. 431.
193 ACCUE, CM7 ASS1 260, Rec. n° 2/71.
194 Böhning, *The Migration of Workers in the United Kingdom and the European Community*, pp. 90–1.
195 AHUE, CM2 1968 1006, T/216/68 (SOC), GSQ Meeting, 4–5/04/1968.
196 OJEC, 19/10/1968, L 257/1.
197 OJEC, 5/07/1971, L 149/1.
198 See Chapter 2.
199 ACCUE, CM6 EAMA2 736, T/395/65 (EAMA), 13–14/09/1965.
200 ACCUE, CM6 EAMA1 309, II, 10/11/1967, Doc. CEE/EAMA/15/68.
201 ACCUE, CM6 EAMA1 309, 8/03/1968, Doc. CEE-EAMA/22/68.
202 ACCUE, CM6 EAMA2 736, 28/01/1971.
203 ACCUE, Liste Rouge 70282, 22/06/1973, I/131/73.
204 Böhning, *The Migration of Workers in the United Kingdom and the European Community*, pp. 132–3.
205 AHCE, BAC 134 1987 170 (1970–1972), XIV/571/71-F.
206 AHCE, BAC 134 1987 170, Note of H. Henze, 5/10/1971.
207 AHCE, BAC 134 1987 170: (1) 19/11/1971, T/614/71; (2) 10/12/1971, Doc. n° 803.
208 JORF, 1972–1973, n° 113.
209 AHCE, BAC 134 1987 170, Doc. n° 803.
210 OJEC, L 73, 27/03/1972.

## 4 A PROTECTIONIST STATUS QUO, 1973–1984

1 Heinz Werner, "Migration and Free Movement of Workers in Western Europe," in *Les Travailleurs étrangers en Europe occidentale*, ed. P. J. Bernard (Paris: Mouton, 1976)p. 68.
2 Marcel Berlinghoff, "An den Grenzen der Aufnahmefähigkeit: Die Europäisierung des Anwerbestopps 1970–1974. Ein Vergleich der restriktiven Migrationspolitik in der Schweiz, der Bundesrepublik Deutschland und in Frankreich" (Heidelberg, 2011), p. 232.

## NOTES

3   ACCUE, Liste Rouge 31316, SEC (77) 3954.
4   Werner, "Migration and Free Movement of Workers in Western Europe," p. 71.
5   ACCUE, LR 32172, 23/03/1979, Annex.
6   Tapinos, *L'Immigration étrangère en France: 1946–1973*, Travaux et documents—Institut national d'études demographiques (Paris: Presses universitaires de France, 1975), p. 119, fn. 3.
7   Federico Romero, *Emigrazione e Integrazione europea, 1945–1973*, Studi di storia (Roma: Edizioni lavoro, 1991), p. 125.
8   Philip L. Martin and Marion F. Houstoun, "The Future of International Migration," *Journal of International Affairs* 33, no. 2 (1979), p. 316.
9   Source: ACCUE, CM5 ADH3 488, Annex. Note: Luxembourg excluded. No data for Greeks in France and the Netherlands. No data for Portuguese in the Netherlands.
10  ACCUE, CM5 ADH3 1630, CONF-P/9/81, Portuguese Declaration, 29/04/1981, Annexes 1 and 3.
11  ACCUE, CM5 ADH3 488, 15/10/1981.
12  ACCUE, CM5 ADH2 30-I, COM(78) 338 final, 12/07/1978.
13  ACCUE, CM5 ADH2 40-I, Greek Declaration, 11/12/1978. World Bank. http://data.worldbank.org/indicator/SP.POP.TOTL?end=2015&locations=GR&start=1960&view=chart. Access date: 15/03/2017.
14  Kostas Infantis, "State Interests, External Dependency Trajectories and 'Europe': Greece," in *European Union Enlargement: A Comparative History*, ed. Wolfram Kaiser and Jurgen Elvert (London: Routledge, 2004), pp. 86, 94; Eirini Karamouzi, *Greece, the EEC, and the Cold War, 1974–1979: The Second Enlargement* (London: Palgrave Macmillan, 2014), chap. 2.
15  ACCUE, CM5 ADH2 40-I, Greek Declaration, 11/12/1978.
16  ACCUE, CM5 ADH2 15.14, 06/12/1978 Meeting, German Proposal, 6/10/1978.
17  ACCUE, CM5 ADH2 40-I, Greek Declaration, 11/12/1978.
18  ACCUE, CM5 ADH2 22-IV, 2/04/1979, Doc. 44.
19  OJEC, 19/11/1979.
20  ACCUE, Liste Rouge 74150, S/250/74 (NT 11) (SOC 2), GSQ Meeting, 13–14/02/1974.
21  ACCUE, Liste Rouge 74138, 16/07/1976.
22  ACCUE, Liste Rouge 74138, S/1244/76 (NT 17), Addendum 2, 13/07/1976.
23  AHCE, BAC 15 1993 34, CEE-TR 6/76 1–2/03/1976.
24  ACCUE, Liste Rouge 74532, Decision 2/76, CEE-TR 43/76, Art. 2.
25  Ibid., Art. 6.
26  Ibid., Art. 5.
27  ACCUE, Liste Rouge 74532, 13/12/1976.
28  ACCUE, Liste Rouge 74534, Decision 1/80, Arts. 6 and 16.
29  ACCUE, Liste Rouge 74160, 8805/80 NT 13, 14/07/1980.
30  OJEC, 13.9.82, C 238/55–57, 8/07/1982 Resolution.
31  ACCUE, Liste Rouge 74141, 8510/82, ASSRE 218, 8/07/1982.
32  ACE, Doc. 5892, 05/05/1988, n° 164.
33  ACCUE, Liste Rouge 74141.
34  For this paragraph: ACCUE, Liste Rouge 74534, 1/06/1981.
35  ACCUE, Liste Rouge 74534, 30/09/1981.
36  ACCUE, Liste Rouge 74534, CEE-TR 110/84.
37  Jürgen Elvert, "A Fool's Game or a Comedy of Errors? EU Enlargements in Comparative Perspective," in *European Union Enlargement: A Comparative History*, ed. Wolfram Kaiser and Jürgen Elvert (London: Routledge, 2004), pp. 213–4.
38  Ricardo Martín De La Guardia, "In Search of Lost Europe: Spain," in *European Union Enlargement: A Comparative History*, ed. Wolfram Kaiser and Jurgen Elvert (London: Routledge, 2004), pp. 107–8.
39  ACCUE, CM5 ADH3 481, COM(78) 630 final, 29/11/1978.
40  ACCUE, CM5 ADH3 182, Document de travail du Président du groupe ad hoc adhésion Espagne.
41  ACCUE, CM5 ADH3 481, COM(78) 630 final.

## NOTES

42  ACCUE, CM5 ADH3 481, Doc. n° 38.
43  ACCUE, CM5 ADH3 483, Telex, 11/09/1984, Annex.
44  31 December 1995 for Luxemburg.
45  OJEC, L 302, 15/11/1985, Accession Treaty, Articles 56, 58, 60, 216, 218, 220.
46  Ibid., Arts. 57, 217.
47  Décret n° 82–1015, JORF, 2/12/1982, p. 3644; Insee. www.insee.fr/fr/themes/calcul-pouvoir-achat.asp. Access date: 15/03/2017; John M. Abowd, Francis Kramarz, Thomas Lemieux, and David N. Margolis, "Minimum Wages and Youth Employment in France and the United States," in *Youth Employment and Joblessness in Advanced Countries*, ed. David G. Blanchflower and Richard B. Freeman (Chicago: University of Chicago Press, National Bureau of Economic Research, January 2000), pp. 466–7.
48  ACCUE, Liste Rouge 31978, Assembly Resolution, 16/11/1976, pp. 49–54.
49  OJEC, C 293/12, 13/12/1976.
50  Between 1973 and 1984, the unemployment rate in the Community increased from an average of 1–3 percent to an average of 8–14 percent. In France, where wage standards were the most rigid as a consequence of the largest increase in the minimum wage, the general unemployment rate increased fivefold from 2.1 percent in the third quarter of 1969 to 10.1 percent in the third quarter of 1984. For those aged 15–24, who were largely unskilled, the increase was stronger: the unemployment rate increased sevenfold from 3.7 percent in the third quarter of 1969 to 24.6 percent in the third quarter of 1984. Sources: (1) OECD Labour Force Statistics. http://stats.oecd.org/Index.aspx?DatasetCode=LFS_SEXAGE_I_R#. Access date: 15/03/2017; (2) INSEE, ILO Unemployment. www.bdm.insee.fr/bdm2/choixCriteres?codeGroupe=1533. Access date: 15/03/2017.
51  Douglas S. Massey, Joaquin Arango, and Edward Taylor, *Worlds in Motion: Understanding International Migration at the End of the Millennium* (Oxford: Oxford University Press, 2005), p. 111.
52  For this paragraph: ACCUE, Liste Rouge 41301, 2222/74 (RP/CRS 42) Extr. 5, COREPER Meeting, 18–20/12/1974.
53  ACCUE, Liste Rouge 44725, 18/06/1976.
54  ACCUE, Liste Rouge 44725, Résolution finale.
55  ACCUE, Liste Rouge 40855, 1292/75 (ES 103), GEQ Meeting, 30–31/10/1975, Annex I.
56  ACCUE, Liste Rouge 40860, 1479/77 (RP/CRS 41) Extr. 2, COREPER Meeting, 7–9/12/1977.
57  For this paragraph: EEC Commission, COM (78) 468 final, 22/09/1978, Annex A.
58  COM (78) 468 final.
59  UNESCO, *Statistiques des étudiants à l'étranger* (Paris, 1982).
60  COM (78) 468 final.
61  AHCE, DG SJ BDT (32) 92 352, Mémoire déposé par la Commission, 16/03/1984.
62  UNESCO, *Statistiques des étudiants à l'étranger*.
63  AHCE, DG SJ BDT (32) 92 352, 16/03/1984.
64  For this paragraph: AHCE, DG SJ BDT 371 91 2794, JUR (81) D/4516, Annex.
65  AHCE, DG SJ BDT 371 91 2794, Note for the attention of Chefs de cabinet.
66  AHCE, DG SJ BDT 371 91 2794, JUR (81) D/4516.
67  Court Ruling, 26/05/1982, Case 149/79.
68  AHCE, DG SJ BDT 371 91 2794, Note for Chefs de cabinet.
69  European Commission, *First Annual Report to the European Parliament on Commission Monitoring of the Application of Community Law 1983*. COM (84) 181 final, 11 April 1984.
70  COM (86) 204 final.
71  European Commission, *Second Annual Report to the European Parliament on Commission Monitoring of the Application of Community Law 1984*. COM (85) 149 final, 23 April 1985.
72  European Commission, *Third Annual Report to the European Parliament on Commission Monitoring of the Application of Community Law 1985*. COM (86) 204 final, 1 September 1986.
73  European Commission, *Évaluation du fonctionnement du Marché intérieur*. COM (83) 80 final, 18 February 1983.

NOTES

74 Simone Alberdina Wilhelmina Goedings, *Labor Migration in an Integrating Europe: National Migration Policies and the Free Movement of Workers, 1950–1968* (The Hague: Sdu Uitgevers, 2005), p. 36; OJEC, L 169/1–28, 29/06/1987, Article 6 (3).
75 ACCUE, Liste Rouge 32164, 12/11/1975, Doc. 375/75, Avis Commission Affaires sociales, Enquête fédérale du travail.
76 Ibid., Annexe à l'avis de la Commission des Affaires culturelles, Tableau synoptique.
77 OJEC, 196/299, 13/11/1975 Session, Interventions of Guido Brunner.
78 ACCUE, Liste Rouge 32158, 1271/75 (SOC 239), GSQ Meeting, 22/10/1975.
79 ACCUE, Liste Rouge 32038, 1276/75 (SOC 243).
80 OJEC, L 199/32–33, 6/08/1977.
81 ACCUE, Liste Rouge 32161, T/781/76 (SOC), GSQ Meeting, 12/10/1976.
82 ACCUE, Liste Rouge 32159, R/1230/76 (SOC 131), Annex.
83 ACCUE, Liste Rouge 32160, R/1487/76 (SOC 157), GSQ Meeting, 15/06/1976.
84 ACCUE, Liste Rouge 32158, 377/76 (SOC 97), GSQ Meetings, 11/02 and 17/03/1976.
85 OJEC, L 199/32–33, 6/08/1977, Art. 2.
86 Ibid., Art. 3.
87 ACCUE, Liste Rouge 32162, R/1832/77 (SOC 173), Annex.
88 ACCUE, Liste Rouge 35112, 1976 ESF Activities Report, COM (77) 398 final.
89 Emmanuel Comte, "The Origins of French Support for European Monetary Integration, 1968–1984," in *Max Weber Programme Red Number Series* (San Domenico di Fiesole: European University Institute, 2016), p. 7.
90 ACCUE, Liste Rouge 31431, 5225/79 (SOC 38), GSQ Meeting, 27/02/1979.
91 ACCUE, Liste Rouge 31431, 5824/79 (SOC 50), GSQ Meeting, 20–21/03/1979, Annex.
92 ACCUE, Liste Rouge 31436, Decision 79/642, Art. 8.
93 Ibid., Art. 2.
94 ACCUE, Liste Rouge 31432, 6525/79 FIN 235 (SOC 73), 27/04/1979.
95 ACCUE, Liste Rouge 31436, Arts. 4 and 6.
96 ACCUE, Liste Rouge 31432, 6525/79 FIN 235 (SOC 73).
97 ACCUE, Liste Rouge 31434, Doc. 91/79, 10/04/1979.
98 ACCUE, Liste Rouge 32052, EP Debates, 24/09/1975, p. 190.
99 ACCUE, Liste Rouge 35112, V/686/77F.
100 ACCUE, Liste Rouge 32036, 1057/75 (SOC 188), GSQ Meeting, 16/09/1975.
101 ACCUE, Liste Rouge 32049, CES 1123/75.
102 Ibid.
103 ACCUE, Liste Rouge 32038, 1276/75 (SOC 243), Annex.
104 ACCUE, Liste Rouge 32095, CES 694/83. André Lebon, "L'Aide au retour des travailleurs étrangers," *Économie et statistique* 113, no. 1 (1979).
105 ACCUE, Liste Rouge 32049, CES 1123/75.
106 Ibid.
107 Ibid.
108 ACCUE, Liste Rouge 32526, 10190/80.
109 ACCUE, Liste Rouge 32526, 12403/80 (SOC 466), GSQ Meeting, 9/12/1980, Annex.
110 ACCUE, Liste Rouge 32527, 5880/81 (SOC 93).
111 ACCUE, Liste Rouge 32527, 6425/91 (SOC 110).
112 ACCUE, Liste Rouge 32036, 939 f/75 (SOC 159), GSQ Meeting, 23/07/1975; ACCUE, Liste Rouge 32038, 1276/75 (SOC 243), Annex; ACCUE Liste Rouge 32039, R/2991/75 (SOC 280), Annex.
113 ACCUE, Liste Rouge 32036, 1125/75 (SOC 198), GSQ Meeting, 24/09/1975.
114 ACCUE, Liste Rouge 32164, European Parliament, Doc. 375/75, 12/11/1975.
115 ACCUE, Liste Rouge 32589, COM(75) 132 final, 2/04/1975, Annex.
116 ACCUE, Liste Rouge 32593, 8014/80 (SOC 226), Annex II, GSQ Meetings, 20/02 and 7/03/1980.
117 Ibid.

## NOTES

118 ACCUE, Liste Rouge 32519, Note des services de la Commission.
119 ACCUE, Liste Rouge 32589, R/1997/75 (SOC 157), GSQ Meeting, 15/07/1975.
120 ACCUE, Liste Rouge 32589, R/2216/75 (SOC 179), GSQ Meeting.
121 ACCUE, Liste Rouge 32589, COM(75) 132 final, Annex.
122 ACCUE, Liste Rouge 32589, R/2216/75 (SOC 179).
123 ACCUE, Liste Rouge 32591, R/1104/76 (SOC 124), GSQ Meeting.
124 ACCUE, Liste Rouge 32592, 4275/80, GSQ Meeting, 15/01/1980.
125 ACCUE, Liste Rouge 32515, 6537/81 (SOC 121), Annex.
126 ACCUE, Liste Rouge 68448, 11013/80 (SOC 394), 5/11/1980.
127 ACCUE, Liste Rouge 68448, 10168/83 (SOC 273), GSQ Meeting, 25/10/1983.
128 ACCUE, CM2 1974 1416, 1048/74 (ES 99), GEQ Meeting, 28–29/03/1974, Annex I.
129 ACCUE, CM2 1974 1416, 1048/74 (ES 99), Annex I.
130 OJEC, 20/01/1975, L 14/10, Art. 8 (2).
131 ACCUE, Liste Rouge 32510, 6574/79 (SOC 76), 2/05/1979.
132 ACCUE, Liste Rouge 32512, 9839/79 (SOC 218), 16/10/1979.
133 ACCUE, Liste Rouge 32510, 6574/79 (SOC 76).
134 ACCUE, Liste Rouge 32514, 11814/1/80 (SOC 440).
135 ACCUE, Liste Rouge 2379, European Parliament, Doc. 1–506/80, 24/10/1980, Annex III.
136 ACCUE, Liste Rouge 2374, 7455/80 DS 5, Council's Ad Hoc Group on Special Rights.
137 AHCE, DG SJ BDT (32) 92 352, 16/03/1984, Mémoire Commission.
138 ACCUE, Liste Rouge 2375, 11102/81 DS 1, 23/11/1981.
139 Ferdinand Wollenschläger, *Grundfreiheit ohne Markt: Die Herausbildung der Unionsbürgerschaft im Unionsrechtlichen Freizügigkeitsregime*, Verfassungsentwicklung in Europa (Tübingen: Mohr Siebeck, 2007), p. 103.
140 ACCUE, Liste Rouge 2375, 6911/83 DS 4, 10/05/1983.
141 Catherine Wihtol de Wenden, *Citoyenneté, nationalité et immigration* (Paris: Arcantère, 1987), pp. 81–91.
142 ACCUE, Liste Rouge 2357, T/289/76 (DS), Special Rights Group Meeting, 16/03/1976.
143 ACCUE, Liste Rouge 2375, 8343/80 DS 6, Special Rights Group.
144 Arlette Heymann-Doat, "Les Institutions européennes et la citoyenneté," in *Les Étrangers dans la cité: expériences européennes*, ed. Olivier Le Cour Grandmaison and Catherine Wihtol de Wenden (Paris: La Découverte, 1993), p. 184.
145 Andrew Moravcsik, *The Choice for Europe: Social Purpose and State Power from Messina to Maastricht*, Cornell Studies in Political Economy (Ithaca, NY: Cornell University Press, 1998), p. 346.
146 Anthony M. Messina, *The Logics and Politics of Post-WWII Migration to Western Europe* (New York: Cambridge University Press, 2007), p. 141.
147 ACCUE, Liste Rouge 31316, SEC (77) 3954.
148 OJEC, Minutes of the EP meeting of 10 October 1978, Speech by German MEP Jahn.
149 ACCUE, Liste Rouge 32191, 97/77 (SOC 25), GSQ Meeting, 18/01/1977.
150 ACCUE, Liste Rouge 32037, R/3110/75 (SOC 299), 12/12/1975, Annex.
151 ACCUE, Liste Rouge 32041, R/231/76 (SOC 33), 28/01/1976, Resolution on the Action Programme for migrant workers and their families, Annex, Statements to be included in the minutes of the session of the Council.
152 *Bulletin des Communautés européennes*, December 1974, n° 12, pp. 7–13.
153 ACCUE, Liste Rouge 2574, R/2717/75 (UP 2), Council's group on passport union, 5/11/1975.
154 ACCUE, Liste Rouge 32172, 8003/79 (SOC 140).
155 ACCUE, Liste Rouge 2580, 7098/81, 29/06/1981.
156 ACCUE, Liste Rouge 25202, T/304/77 (SOC) (DEA), GSQ Meeting, 30/03/1977.
157 Groupe œcuménique, *La population algérienne en France* (Paris: Centre d'information et d'études sur les migrations méditerranéennes, 1981).
158 ACCUE, Liste Rouge 25202, T/304/77 (SOC) (DEA), GSQ Meeting, 30/03/1977.
159 ACCUE, Liste Rouge 25201, I/464/76 (SOC).

160 ACCUE, Liste Rouge 25202, T/304/77 (SOC) (DEA).
161 ACCUE, Liste Rouge 25202, T/166/77 (SOC) (DEA), GSQ Meeting, 15/02/1977.
162 ACCUE, Liste Rouge 25202, T/246/77 (SOC) (DEA), 15/03/1977, Communiqué of the General Commission of the Euro-Arab Dialogue.
163 ACCUE, Liste Rouge 25202, T/304/77 (SOC) (DEA).
164 ACCUE, Liste Rouge 25202, Cairo Meeting, 6–8/02/1979.
165 ACCUE, Liste Rouge 25202, T/304/77 (SOC) (DEA).
166 R. van Gendt, *Services pour le retour et la réinsertion des travailleurs émigrés: Rapport de synthèse* (Paris: OECD, 1977), p. 59, par. 44.
167 ACE, Doc. 6266, 12/07/1990.
168 ACCUE, Liste Rouge 25202, T/166/77 (SOC) (DEA), GSQ Meeting, 15/02/1977.
169 ACCUE, Liste Rouge 25201, I/464/76 (SOC), p. 3.
170 ACCUE, Liste Rouge 25201, I/465/76 (SOC), p. 10, GSQ Meeting, 15/12/1976.
171 ACCUE, Liste Rouge 25201, I/34/77 (SOC) (DEA 7), GSQ Meeting, 26/01/1977.
172 ACCUE, Liste Rouge 25201, I/36/77 (SOC) (DEA 8).
173 Annex XV.
174 ACCUE, Liste Rouge 83948, CES 352/82, 9/04/1982.
175 ACCUE, Liste Rouge 83948, CES 691/82.
176 ACCUE, Liste Rouge 68488, SEC (81) 466, 20/03/1981, Commission WP, UN Resolution 34/172.
177 ACCUE, Liste Rouge 32104, 7019/85 (SOC 160).
178 ACCUE, Liste Rouge 68488, SEC (81) 466.
179 ACCUE, Liste Rouge 68488, 6008/81 (SOC 101), GSQ Meeting, 24/03/1981.
180 ACCUE, Liste Rouge 68488, 9572/81 (SOC 277), 29/09/1981.
181 ACCUE, Liste Rouge 32104, 7019/85 (SOC 160).
182 ACCUE, Liste Rouge 32104, 6841/86 (SOC 147), GSQ Meeting, 14/04/1986.
183 ACCUE, Liste Rouge 32104, 4607/87 (SOC 17), Annex.
184 ACCUE, Liste Rouge 68488, SEC (81) 466.
185 ACCUE, Liste Rouge 68488, 6008/81 (SOC 101), GSQ Meeting.
186 ACCUE, Liste Rouge 68488, 9572/81 (SOC 277).
187 ACCUE, Liste Rouge 32104, 4607/87 (SOC 17), GSQ Meeting, 28/01/1987.
188 International Convention on the Protection of the Rights of All Migrant Workers and Members of Their Families, New York, 18/12/1990. https://treaties.un.org/Pages/ViewDetails.aspx?src=IND&mtdsg_no=IV-13&chapter=4&clang=_en. Access date: 15/03/2017.

## 5 A SELECTIVE AND REGIONALIST REGIME, 1984–1992

1 Andrew Moravcsik, *The Choice for Europe: Social Purpose and State Power from Messina to Maastricht*, Cornell Studies in Political Economy (Ithaca, NY: Cornell University Press, 1998), pp. 314–78; Éric Bussière, Michel Dumoulin, and Sylvain Schirmann, eds., *Milieux économiques et intégration européenne au XX$^e$ siècle: La relance des années Quatre-Vingts (1979–1992): Colloque des 1$^{er}$ et 2 décembre 2005* (Paris: Comité pour l'Histoire économique et financière, 2007); Simone Paoli, "The Migration Issue in France-Italy Relations from the Schengen Agreement (1985) to the Establishment of the Schengen Area (1995)" (paper presented at the conference *Peoples and Borders: Seventy Years of Movement of Persons in Europe, to Europe, from Europe (1945–2015)*, Padua, University of Padua, 6–8 November 2014); Simone Paoli, "The Schengen Agreements and Their Impact on Euro-Mediterranean Relations: The Case of Italy and the Maghreb," *Journal of European Integration History* 21, no. 1 (2015).
2 Russell King, "Migration and the Single Market for Labour: An Issue in Regional Development," in *The European Challenge: Geography and Development in the European Community*, ed. Mark Blacksell and Allan M. Williams (Oxford: Oxford University Press, 1994).
3 Moravcsik, *The Choice for Europe*, p. 359.
4 Ibid., pp. 364, 369, 374. Simone Paoli, "Migration in European Integration: Themes and Debates," *Journal of European Integration History* 22, no. 2 (2016), p. 289.

## NOTES

5 ACCUE, Liste Rouge 1603, COM (83) 80 final.
6 ACCUE, Liste Rouge 1444, CES 219/83.
7 ACCUE, Liste Rouge 1847.
8 ACCUE, Liste Rouge 1842.
9 ACCUE, Liste Rouge 1847.
10 ACCUE, Liste Rouge 1842, Telex n° 074.
11 ACCUE, Liste Rouge 1603, COM (83) 80 final.
12 Hans C. Taschner, *Schengen oder die Abschaffung der Personenkontrollen an den Binnengrenzen der EG* (Saarbrücken: Europainstitut der Universität des Saarlandes, 1990), p. 10.
13 ACCUE, Liste Rouge 2596, 5614/83 UP 3, Working group on a passport union, 10/03/1983.
14 ACCUE, Liste Rouge 2596, 10544/83 UP 15, 14/11/1983.
15 ACCUE, Liste Rouge 2596, 5614/83 UP 3.
16 ACCUE, Liste Rouge 2596, 6610/83 UP 5, 27/04/1983.
17 ACCUE, Liste Rouge 2596, 7734/84 (Presse 102), 7/06/1984.
18 Moravcsik, *The Choice for Europe*, p. 359.
19 AN, 5 AG 4 CM 41, dossier 4, sous-dossier 2, Conseil des Ministres du 20/06/1984, Communication du ministre des Affaires européennes.
20 Moravcsik, *The Choice for Europe*, p. 360.
21 AN, 5 AG 4EG 69, dossier 1, Note, 10/05/1989.
22 European Council on 25 and 26 June 1984 in Fontainebleau, DOC/84/2. http://europa.eu/rapid/press-release_DOC-84-2_fr.htm. Access date: 15/03/2017.
23 JORF, 3/08/1984, pp. 2565–6.
24 Moravcsik, *The Choice for Europe*, p. 360.
25 AN, 5 AG 4 EG 41, dossier 1, Réunion chez le Président sur Milan, 11/06/1985, 9:30.
26 AN, 5 AG 4 EG 41, dossier 1, Déjeuner 12/06/1985.
27 For this paragraph: ACCUE, Liste Rouge 1842, Accord.
28 Taschner, *Schengen oder die Abschaffung der Personenkontrollen an den Binnengrenzen der EG*, p. 15.
29 AN, 5 AG 4 EG 41, dossier 1, 'Marché intérieur – Transports.'
30 AN, 5 AG 4 4767, extr., Archives of Jacques Attali, European Council, Milan, 28–29/06/1985.
31 OJEC, L 169/1–28, 29/06/1987.
32 AN, 5 AG 4 EG 67, dossier 2, 28/11/1989, Fiche II.
33 AN, 5 AG 4 CM 41, dossier 4, sous-dossier 2: (1) Note Yannick Moreau, 19/06/1984; (2) Service de Presse.
34 ACCUE, Liste Rouge 1842, Accord, Art. 30.
35 AN, 5 AG 4 EG 68, dossier 1, Jean-Marc Sauvé to Cabinet du Premier Ministre, 6/02/1989.
36 OJEC, L 169/1–28, 29/06/1987.
37 OJEC, L 169/25, 29/06/1987.
38 Paoli, "The Schengen Agreements and Their Impact on Euro-Mediterranean Relations."
39 King, "Migration and the Single Market for Labour," p. 237.
40 AN, 5 AG 4 EG 68, dossier 1, Note Isabelle Renouard, 18/04/1989.
41 AN, 5 AG 4 EG 67, dossier 2, "Libre circulation des personnes en Europe. Les enceintes de négociation," 9/11/1989. This was the immigration group within the group of coordinators of the Twelve on the free movement of persons.
42 ACCUE, Liste Rouge 1575, 15/09/1989 Meeting.
43 AN, 5 AG 4 EG 68, dossier 1, Jean-Marc Sauvé to Premier Ministre, 6/02/1989.
44 AN, 5 AG 4 EG 69, dossier 1, Note 18/07/1989. Annexe I.
45 AN, 5 AG 4 EG 68, dossier 1, Group of Coordinators, 13/04/1989.
46 AN, 5 AG 4 EG 67, dossier 2, *The Economist*, 11/08/1989.
47 Ibid.
48 AN, 5 AG 4 EG 68, dossier 1, Note E. Cazimajou, 20/02/1989.
49 AN, 5 AG 4 EG 69, dossier 1, E. Guigou to Président, 13/12/1989.
50 Ibid., Recipient's handwritten note.
51 AN, 5 AG 4 EG 68, dossier 1, 6/02/1989.

## NOTES

52 AN, 5 AG 4 EG 68, dossier 2, Rapport Groupe de travail II, 1/12/1988; OJEC, 22/09/2000, Convention, Art. 22, par. 1.
53 AN, 5 AG 4 EG 68, dossier 1, 2 March.
54 AN, 5 AG 4 EG 68, dossier 1, Note Georges Chacornac, 9/12/1988.
55 AN, 5 AG 4 AH 18, dossier 1, Telex, 23/10/1989.
56 AN, 5 AG 4 EG 67, dossier 2, Note Jean-Paul Tran-Thiet, 14/11/1989.
57 AN, 5 AG 4 AH 18, dossier 1, Jean-Pierre Puissochet to Cabinet du ministre d'État, 22/01/1990.
58 AN, 5 AG 4 EG 69, dossier 1, Telex E. Cazimajou, 18/12/1989.
59 AN, 5 AG 4 EG 69, dossier 1, J.-P. Huchon to Jean-Louis Bianco, 14/12/1989; AN, 5 AG 4 EG 69, dossier 1, Telex Boidevaix, 14/12/1989; AN, 5 AG 4 AH 18, dossier 1, Bérengère Quincy, 29/01/1990.
60 AN, 5 AG 4 EG 68, dossier 1, Isabelle Renouard, 18/04/1989.
61 AN, 5 AG 4 EG 68, dossier 1, E. Guigou to Président, 18/04/1989.
62 AN, 5 AG 4 EG 69, dossier 1, Telex E. Cazimajou, 15/11/1989.
63 AN, 5 AG 4 AH 18, dossier 1, 29/01/1990, Cresson-Dankert Meeting Preparation.
64 AN, 5 AG 4 AH 18, dossier 1, É. Guigou to Président.
65 AN, 5 AG 4 AH 18, dossier 1, Note by the Chairman of the German delegation to the Schengen consultation, 13/03/1990.
66 AN, 5 AG 4 AH 18, dossier 1, SGCI, 11/05/1990.
67 OJEC, 22/09/2000, Schengen Convention, Declaration of the FRG.
68 AN, 5 AG 4 AH 18, dossier 1, 29/01/1990, Cresson-Dankert Meeting Preparation.
69 AN 5 AG 4 AH 18, dossier 1, Note, 1/06/1990.
70 OJEC, 22/09/2000, Schengen Convention, Art. 2, par. 2 and Art. 9, par. 2.
71 Ibid., Art. 26.
72 ACCUE, Liste Rouge 1574, CIRC 3608/89.
73 ACCUE, Liste Rouge 1575, Réunion du groupe des coordonnateurs, 15/09/1989.
74 ACCUE, Liste Rouge 1574, CIRC 3608/89, Declaration of E. Cazimajou, 17/03/1989.
75 OJEC, C 254, 19/08/1997, pp. 1–12.
76 Article 4 Dublin; Article 35 Schengen.
77 Article 5 Dublin; Article 30, par. 1, a) Schengen.
78 Article 6 Dublin; Article 30, par. 1, e) Schengen.
79 ACCUE, Liste Rouge 1575, Réunion du groupe des coordonnateurs, 15/09/1989.
80 Article 9 Dublin; Article 36 Schengen.
81 Maarten P. Vink, "Negative and Positive Integration in European Immigration Policies," *European Integration online Papers (EIoP)* 6, no. 13 (2002).
82 OJEC, C 224, 31/08/1992 Treaty on European Union, Title II: Treaty instituting the European Community, new Article 100C.
83 Serge de Waersegger, *Le Soir* (Belgian newspaper), 11/06/1991.
84 AN, 5 AG 4 AH 18, dossier 1, Minutes of the meeting of the Central Negotiating Group, on 31/05/1990.
85 ACCUE, Liste Rouge 43450, CIRC 3650/90.
86 OJEC, 22/09/2000, pp. 63–5, Accession Agreement of Italy to the Schengen Convention.
87 ACE, Doc. 6817, 26/04/1993.
88 King, "Migration and the Single Market for Labour," p. 236.
89 Index Mundi, Germany Unemployment Rate. www.indexmundi.com/germany/unemployment_rate.html. Access date: 15/03/2017.
90 Douglas S. Massey, Joaquin Arango, and Edward Taylor, *Worlds in Motion: Understanding International Migration at the End of the Millennium* (Oxford: Oxford University Press, 2005), pp. 111–2.
91 Conclusions of the Fontainebleau European Council, *Bulletin des Communautés européennes*, June 1984, n° 6.
92 ACCUE, Liste Rouge 40866, 4471/85 ETS 2, Annex, 28/01/1985.
93 ACCUE, Liste Rouge 44725, 6/06/1983, Annex, 15/09/1982.
94 ACCUE, Liste Rouge 44725, Søren Prahl to Président, 29/04/1985.

## NOTES

95  OJEC, 21/08/1985, L 223/15–25.
96  Article 1.
97  ACCUE, Liste Rouge 40866, 7296/85 (Presse 91).
98  ACCUE, Liste Rouge 1850.
99  ACCUE, Liste Rouge 35136.
100  ACCUE, Liste Rouge 35134, COM (86) 257 final.
101  AHCE, DG SJ BDT (32) 92 353, Rapport d'audience.
102  Ibid., Commission intervention.
103  ACCUE, Liste Rouge 34830, COM (85) 756 final, 20/12/1985.
104  ACCUE, Liste Rouge 34852, COM (89) 235 final, 29/05/1989.
105  ACCUE, Liste Rouge 34830, COM (85) 756 final.
106  ACCUE, Liste Rouge 34830, 5926/86 EDUC 16 (SOC 98), 20–21/03/1986.
107  ACCUE, Liste Rouge 34830, COM (85) 756 final.
108  ACCUE, Liste Rouge 34830, 5926/86 EDUC 16 (SOC 98).
109  ACCUE, Liste Rouge 34831, Decision 87/327.
110  ACCUE, Liste Rouge 34855, Anna Hermans, 14/11/1990.
111  ACCUE, Liste Rouge 34831, Decision 87/327, annex, action 3.
112  ACCUE, Liste Rouge 34830, 9858/86 EDUC 61 (SOC 322), 5/11/1986.
113  OJEC, 30/12/1989, L 395/23, Decision 89/663.
114  ACCUE, Liste Rouge 34852, COM (89) 235 final.
115  Source: European Commission, Erasmus Facts, Figures & Trends, 2012–2013, p. 30. http://ec.europa.eu/dgs/education_culture/repository/education/library/statistics/ay-12-13/facts-figures_en.pdf. Access date: 15/03/2017.
116  ACCUE, Liste Rouge 34855, Anna Hermans, 14/11/1990.
117  ACCUE, Liste Rouge 34852, 10195/89 EDUC 93 (SOC 426).
118  OJEC, L 1, 3/01/1994, pp. 3–522.
119  Ibid., Protocol 15.
120  ACCUE, Liste Rouge 35136, Directive 89/48: Considérants and Article 4.
121  ACCUE, Liste Rouge 35136, Declarations, Ad Article 2.1.
122  ACCUE, Liste Rouge 35138, Nicole Fontaine, 6/11/1985.
123  AN, 5 AG 4 TB 59, dossier 2, Brussels Meeting Minutes, 29/04/1992.
124  Robert A. Mundell, "A Theory of Optimum Currency Areas," *American Economic Review* (1961).
125  ACCUE, Liste Rouge 31497, COM (88) 382 final, 11/07/1988.
126  INSEE, ILO Unemployment Rate, 1968–2004. www.bdm.insee.fr/bdm2/choixCriteres?codeGroupe=1533. Access date: 15/03/2017.
127  AN, 5 AG 4 4767, Mémorandum pour un progrès de la construction de l'Europe.
128  ACCUE, Liste Rouge 31497, COM (88) 382 final.
129  King, "Migration and the Single Market for Labour," p. 236.
130  ACE, Doc. 6211, 24/04/1990.
131  ACCUE, Liste Rouge 68412, Report of the Committee on Social Affairs, 27/01/1993.
132  Marco Martiniello, "European Citizenship," in *Migration and European Integration: The Dynamics of Inclusion and Exclusion*, ed. Robert Miles and Dietrich Thränhardt (Madison, NJ: Fairleigh Dickinson University Press, 1995), pp. 43–6.
133  ACCUE, Liste Rouge 4385, Fontainebleau European Council Conclusions.
134  Speech by François Mitterrand in Front of the Bundestag, 20/01/1983. http://discours.vie-publique.fr/notices/847900500.html. Access date: 15/03/2017.
135  Arrêt de la Cour du 15 janvier 1986, Pietro Pinna contre Caisse d'allocations familiales de la Savoie, Affaire 41/84, *Recueil de jurisprudence 1986*.
136  Ettore Recchi, *Mobile Europe: The Theory and Practice of Free Movement in the EU* (London: Palgrave Macmillan, 2015), p. 51.
137  OJEC, L 331, 16/11/1989, Regulation 3427/89.
138  AN, 5 AG 4 AH 10, dossier 4, Note 4/04/1989.

139 In: Finn Laursen and Sophie Vanhoonacker, *The Intergovernmental Conference on Political Union: Institutional Reforms, New Policies and International Identity of the European Community* (Maastricht: European Institute of Public Administration, 1992), p. 277.
140 Ferdinand Wollenschläger, *Grundfreiheit ohne Markt: Die Herausbildung der Unionsbürgerschaft im Unionsrechtlichen Freizügigkeitsregime*, Verfassungsentwicklung in Europa (Tübingen: Mohr Siebeck, 2007), p. 111.
141 ACCUE, Liste Rouge 62273, 9233/90 ADD 1 REVTRAT 16, Annex VII, 18/10/1990.
142 In: Laursen and Vanhoonacker, *The Intergovernmental Conference on Political Union*, p. 304.
143 ACE, Doc. 6266, 12/07/1990.
144 For this paragraph: ACCUE, Liste Rouge 9524, Panayotis Lambrias, 12/12/1985.
145 Massey et al., *Worlds in Motion*, p. 117.
146 For this paragraph and the next: ACCUE, Liste Rouge 2393, COM (86) 487 final, 03/10/1986.
147 www.cvce.eu/obj/message_conjoint_de_francois_mitterrand_et_helmut_kohl_paris_18_avril_1990-fr-89369c53-5d93-4e56-8397-825ca92c86f5.html. Access date: 15/03/2017.
148 ACCUE, Liste Rouge 2381, 8429/89 DS 19, 5–6/09/1989.
149 ACCUE, Liste Rouge 2381, Students Directive, Article 1.
150 ACCUE Liste Rouge 2387, Directive 90/365, Article 1.
151 ACCUE, Liste Rouge 2385, Directive 90/364, Article 1.
152 AN, 5 AG 4 CDM 18, dossier 4.
153 ACCUE, Liste Rouge 62273, 8724/90 UP 1 REVTRAT 12, 21/09/1990.
154 ACCUE, Liste Rouge 62273, 8724/1/90 REVTRAT 12.
155 ACCUE, Liste Rouge 62273, 9233/90 ADD 1 REVTRAT 16, Annex VII.
156 ACCUE Liste Rouge 62273, 10356/90 REVTRAT 18, 30/11/1990.
157 www.cvce.eu/obj/message_conjoint_de_francois_mitterrand_et_helmut_kohl_paris_6_decembre_1990-fr-e0df114a-728b-4fd8-9b24-394878bc0b5d.html. Access date: 15/03/2017.
158 OJEC, C 224, 31/08/1992, EU Treaty, Article J.1, par. 4.
159 Ibid., Article J.4, par. 1.
160 ACCUE, Liste Rouge 68422, SEC (89) 924 final.
161 ACCUE, Liste Rouge 74814, José Mendes Bota, A3–0393/91, 20/12/1991.
162 ACCUE, Liste Rouge 68422, SEC (89) 924 final.
163 ACE, Doc. 6266.
164 King, "Migration and the Single Market for Labour," p. 240.
165 ACCUE, Liste Rouge 68830, SEC (90) 1813 final, 10/10/1990.
166 Massey et al., *Worlds in Motion*, p. 121.
167 Ibid., p. 117.
168 ACE, Doc. 6211, 24/04/1990.
169 King, "Migration and the Single Market for Labour," p. 235.
170 Massey et al., *Worlds in Motion*, p. 117.
171 OECD Results: ACE, Doc. 6211.
172 ACCUE, Liste Rouge 74814, A3–0393/91.
173 ACCUE, Liste Rouge 74814, Minutes of the Meeting of May 14, 1992.
174 ACCUE, Liste Rouge 74145, TR 15/86 REV. 1, 14/10/1986; ACCUE, Liste Rouge 74142, Note, 29/10/1986.
175 ACCUE, Liste Rouge 74147, Note, 11/11/1986.
176 ACCUE, Liste Rouge 74147, Note, 17/11/1986.
177 ACCUE, Liste Rouge 74148, 10791/86 NT 24, Art. 3.
178 ACCUE, Liste Rouge 74145, TR 15/86 REV. 1.
179 ACCUE, Liste Rouge 74148, 10791/86 NT 24, Articles 6 and 13 bis.
180 ACCUE, Liste Rouge 74142, TR 14/86 REV. 1, 14/10/1986.
181 ACCUE, Liste Rouge 74148, 10791/86 NT 24.
182 ACCUE, Liste Rouge 74142, Note, 29/10/1986.
183 ACCUE, Liste Rouge 74148, 10791/86 NT 24, Articles 5 and 8.
184 Ibid., Article 1 bis.

NOTES

185 Affaire 12/86, *Recueil de jurisprudence 1987*, p. 3719. http://eur-lex.europa.eu/smartapi/cgi/sga_doc?smartapi!celexplus!prod!CELEXnumdoc&lg=fr&numdoc=61986CJ0012. Access date: 15/03/2017.
186 ACCUE, Liste Rouge 68422, SEC (89) 924 final.
187 ACE, Doc. 5913, 16/06/1988.
188 IOM Constitution. www.iom.int/jahia/webdav/site/myjahiasite/shared/shared/mainsite/about_iom/iom_constitution_fr_booklet.pdf. Access date: 15/03/2017.
189 For this paragraph: (1) ACE, Doc. 5705, 27/02/1987; (2) ACE, Doc. 5913; (3) ACCUE, Liste Rouge 74148, A3–0393/91.
190 OJEC, L 229, 17/08/1991, p. 248. http://eur-lex.europa.eu/JOHtml.do?uri=OJ:L:1991:229:SOM:FR:HTML. Access date: 15/03/2017.
191 www.rfi.fr/actufr/articles/037/article_20103.asp. Access date: 15/03/2017.
192 ACCUE, Liste Rouge 74148, Report A3–0393/91.
193 *International Herald Tribune*, 25/09/1990.
194 ACCUE, Liste Rouge 74148, Report A3–0393/91.
195 ACCUE, Liste Rouge 74148, Resolution A3–0393/91.
196 ACE, CM/Del/Dec(92)469, 23/01/1992.
197 Richard Gillespie, "Northern European Perceptions of the Barcelona Process," *Revista CIDOB d'afers internacionals*, no. 37 (1997), pp. 67–8.
198 Marco Montanari, "The Barcelona Process and the Political Economy of Euro Mediterranean Trade Integration," *JCMS: Journal of Common Market Studies* 45, no. 5 (2007), p. 1020.
199 Gillespie, "Northern European Perceptions of the Barcelona Process," p. 73.

CONCLUSION

1 OJEU, L 329, 30/12/1993, pp. 34–8, Directive 93/109.
2 OJEU, L 368, 31/12/1994, pp. 38–47, Directive 94/80.
3 Marco Martiniello, "European Citizenship," in *Migration and European Integration: The Dynamics of Inclusion and Exclusion*, ed. Robert Miles and Dietrich Thränhardt (Madison, NJ: Fairleigh Dickinson University Press, 1995), p. 365; Sue Collard, "French Municipal Democracy: Cradle of European Citizenship?," *Journal of Contemporary European Studies* 18, no. 1 (2010), p. 95.
4 Official Journal of the EU (OJEU), L 18, 21/01/1997, Directive 96/71.
5 OJEU, L 229, 29/06/2004, Directive 2004/38.
6 OJEU, C 340, 10/11/1997, Amsterdam Treaty, Protocol integrating the Schengen acquis into the framework of the European Union. Protocol on the application of certain aspects of Article 7a of the Treaty establishing the European Community to the United Kingdom and Ireland.
7 OJEU, C 340, 10/11/1997, Amsterdam Treaty, Article 2.
8 For all following statistical results: (1) Ettore Recchi, *Mobile Europe: The Theory and Practice of Free Movement in the EU* (London: Palgrave Macmillan, 2015), pp. 52–76. (2) Dieter Bräuninger, "The Dynamics of Migration in the Euro Area," *Deutsche Bank AG*, 14/07/2014. www.dbresearch.com/PROD/DBR_INTERNET_EN-PROD/PROD0000000000338137/The+dynamics+of+migration+in+the+euro+area.pdf. Access date: 15/03/2017.
9 Robert O. Keohane and Joseph S. Nye, *Power and Interdependence*, 4th ed. (Boston: Longman, 2012), p. 37.
10 Alan S. Milward, *The Frontier of National Sovereignty: History and Theory, 1945–1992* (London; New York: Routledge, 1993), p. 29; Andrew Moravcsik, *The Choice for Europe: Social Purpose and State Power from Messina to Maastricht*, Cornell Studies in Political Economy (Ithaca, NY: Cornell University Press, 1998), p. 491. Fernando Guirao, Frances M. B. Lynch, and Sigfrido M. Ramírez Pérez, *Alan S. Milward and a Century of European Change*, Routledge Studies in Modern European History (New York: Routledge, 2012), p. 93.
11 Moravcsik, *The Choice for Europe*, p. 346.

# SOURCES

## Archives

### OECD Archives, Paris (AOECD)

Committee for European Economic Cooperation (CEEC). Box 366:
- Bundle 1.
- Bundle 2. 11/07/1947–21/09/1947. Proposals and Delegations.
- Bundle 3. 11/07/1947–22/09/1947. Statements by Delegates.
- Bundle 4. 21/07/1947–15/09/1947. Executive Committee Minutes.
- Bundle 5. 16/03/1948–14/04/1948. Working Party, Committee II (Draft Convention on Privilege and Immunities).
- Bundle 9. 15/03/1948–10/04/1948. Proposals for a Draft Multilateral Agreement and Constitution.
- Bundle 10. 16/03/1948–15/04/1948. CEEC–Working Party C.R. of 18/03/1948–15/04/1948.
- Bundle 15. 19/03/1948–10/04/1948. Committee III, Multilateral Agreement (March 1948–April 1948)

Organisation for European Economic Cooperation (OEEC).
- Box 9, Bundle 6. Manpower Division.
- Films 48, 124, 125, 126, 129, 192. Manpower Committee.
- Film 301. Tourism Committee.
- Films 52, 85. Executive Committee.
- Films 46, 49, 71, 84, 107, 110, 159, 160, 177, 178. Council.
- Film 548. Conference on reorganisation of the OEEC.

### Archives centrales du Conseil de l'Europe, Strasbourg (ACE)

Congress of Europe, The Hague. Verbatim Reports.
Documents online: www.coe.int/en/web/documents-records-archives-information/home. Access date: 15/03/2017.

## SOURCES

Archives historiques de l'Union européenne, Florence (AHUE)

MAEF, 501. DE-CE, 1944–1960, CECA A.30.5, Elaboration du traité, 07/1950–07/1952.

MAEI, PS20. Affari economici – 1950, Uff. II, Versamento D b.28, Delegazione italiana, Piano Schuman, 1950, Salari e questoni sociali.

AH 9, 116, 124. Assemblée ad hoc. Sous-commission des attributions.

CM1 1954 194, 196, 197, 200. Libre circulation de la main-d'œuvre.

CM1 1955 282. Libre circulation de la main-d'œuvre.

Règlement concernant la sécurité sociale des travailleurs migrants.
- CM2 1958 931. 19/06/1958–30/06/1958.
- CM2 1958 932. 01/07/1958–17/07/1958.

CM2 1958 946. Fonds de réétablissement du Conseil de l'Europe. Exercice 1956–1957. Rapport du Gouverneur au Conseil d'Administration. 1$^{er}$ février 1958.

CM2 1961 220. 11/08/1961–02/01/1962. Entraves à la libre circulation de personnes.

Programme général pour la suppression des restrictions à la liberté d'établissement.
- CM2 1961 318. 22/12/1959–22/03/1960.
- CM2 1961 321. 19/05/1961–12/06/1961.
- CM2 1961 332. 08/09/1960–14/10/1960.
- CM2 1961 338. 10/02/1961.
- CM2 1961 339. 02/02/1961–06/03/1961.

Règlement n° 15 relatif aux premières mesures pour la réalisation de la libre circulation des travailleurs, et directive du Conseil du 16 août 1961.
- CM2 1961 379. 25/01/1961–28/02/1961.
- CM2 1961 383. 06/06/1961–12/06/1961.

CM2 1961 390. 31/10/1961–05/06/1962. Règlement n° 16 portant modification du règlement n° 3 concernant la sécurité sociale des travailleurs migrants.

CM2 1963 626. 29/06/1962–11/12/1962. Directive 63/261/CEE du Conseil du 02.04.1963.

Règlement n° 36/63/CEE du Conseil du 02.04.1963 concernant la sécurité sociale des travailleurs frontaliers.
- CM2 1963 716. 16/07/1962–28/08/1962.
- CM2 1963 719. 13/02/1963–07/03/1963.

CM2 1963 727. 22/03/1963–29/05/1963. Règlement n° 73/63/CEE du Conseil du 11.07.1963.

CM2 1964 998. 18/10/1963–25/10/1963. Directive 64/220/CEE du Conseil du 25.02.1964.

CM2 1964 1140. Premier programme commun 64/307/CEE pour favoriser l'échange de jeunes travailleurs au sein de la Communauté.

Règlement n° 38/64/CEE du Conseil du 25.03.1964 et directive 64/240/CEE du Conseil du 25.03.1964.

SOURCES

- CM2 1964 1168. 05/06/1963–10/07/1963.
- CM2 1964 1169. 03/07/1963–10/09/1963.
- CM2 1964 1184. 04/02/1964–06/02/1964.
- CM2 1964 1189. 25/03/1964–09/01/1967.
- CM2 1964 1196. 06/09/1962–28/11/1962.

CM2 1967 994. 03/02/1965–18/01/1966. Directives 67/530/CEE, 67/531/CEE et 67/532/CEE du Conseil du 25/07/1967.

CM2 1967 1112. 03/04/1967–30/05/1967. Mise en œuvre des articles 47–49 de l'Accord d'Athènes.

CM2 1967 1113. 06/06/1966–30/05/1967. Assistance au développement du potentiel ouvrier grec.

CM2 1968 875. 19/02/1968–17/04/1968. Directive 68/192/CEE du Conseil du 05/04/1968.

Directive 68/363/CEE du Conseil du 15/10/1968.
- CM2 1968 878. 09/04/1965–24/03/1966.
- CM2 1968 882. 16/11/1966–08/09/1967.
- CM2 1968 884. 09/01/1968–15/10/1968.

CM2 1968 925. 09.02.1967–15.06.1968. Directive 68/415/CEE du Conseil du 23/12/1968.

CM2 1968 927. 22/03/1967–04/04/1968. Avis du gouvernement allemand pour l'activité des avocats.

CM2 1968 982. 19/09/1967–15/12/1967. Problèmes de main-d'œuvre dans la Communauté en 1966/1967.

Règlement (CEE) n° 1612/68 du Conseil du 15/10/1968.
- CM2 1968 1005. 20/01/1968–07/03/1968.
- CM2 1968 1006. 25/03/1968–06/05/1968.
- CM2 1968 1008. 29/05/1968–04/07/1968.
- CM2 1968 1009. 25/06/1968–15/07/1968.
- CM2 1968 1011. 16/07/1968–30/07/1968.
- CM2 1968 1013. 12/09/1968–15/10/1968.
- CM2 1968 1018. 29/04/1969–04/06/1969.

Directive 68/360/CEE du Conseil du 15/10/1968.
- CM2 1968 1019. 19/12/1966–05/03/1968.
- CM2 1968 1020. 14/03/1968–13/06/1968.
- CM2 1968 1021. 20/06/1968–30/07/1968.

CM2 1969 1058. 16/01/1969–10/04/1969. Evolution du marché de l'emploi dans la Communauté).

Directive 71/18/CEE du Conseil.
- CM2 1970 1021. 10/02/1969–11/01/1971.
- CM2 1970 1023. 06/11/1969–24/06/1970.

CM2 1971 1227. 18/11/1970–26/11/1970. Travailleurs de pays tiers occupés dans les États membres.
Règlement (CEE) n° 1408/71 du Conseil du 14/06/1971.
- CM2 1971 1257. 10/07/1968–29/10/1968.
- CM2 1971 1259. 20/11/1968–30/01/1969.
- CM2 1971 1262. 13/03/1969–23/05/1969.
- CM2 1971 1264. 18/06/1969–18/07/1969.
- CM2 1971 1265. 15/07/1969–13/10/1969.
- CM2 1971 1269. 28/10/1969–14/11/1969.
- CM2 1971 1270. 04/11/1969–13/11/1969.

CM3 NEGO1 44, Comité intergouvernemental: sous-commission des problèmes sociaux. Rapport de la commission pour la C.P.E.
CM3 NEGO 229. Conférence intergouvernementale: Historique des articles 48, 49, 50 et 51 du traité.
CM3 NEGO 230. Conférence intergouvernementale: Historique des articles 52, 53, 54, 55, 56, 57 et 58 du traité.

## Archives centrales du Conseil de l'Union européenne, Brussels (ACCUE)

*The files 'Liste rouge' were declassified.
CM1 1953 61. Visas pour l'Allemagne et l'Italie.
CM1 1955 282. Libre circulation de la main-d'œuvre. 1954/1955.
CM1 1956 336. Obstacles à la mobilité des travailleurs et problèmes sociaux de réadaptation.
CM1 1956 343, 346. Élaboration de la convention européenne de sécurité sociale des travailleurs migrants.
Convention européenne de sécurité sociale des travailleurs migrants.
- CM1 1957 360. Réunion des ministres les 24 et 25 janvier 1957. 11/01/1957–07/02/1957.
- CM1 1957 362. Réunion des ministres les 26 et 27 juillet 1957. 18/06/1957–13/06/1958.
- CM1 1957 365. 11/03/1957–25/05/1957.
- CM1 1957 368. 15/01/1957–28/02/1957.

CM1 1959 359. Rapports de la commission des affaires sociales de l'A.P.E.
CM1 1961 321. Application de l'article 69 du Traité C.E.C.A. 01/09/1960–10/11/1960.
CM2 1959 856, 857, 858. Directives sur le droit d'établissement dans les P.T.O.M. et D.O.M. 1958–1959.

CM2 1961 375. Problèmes conjoncturels de main-d'œuvre dans la Communauté en 1961. 27/07/1961–23/10/1961.

Convention concernant l'égalité de traitement des nationaux et des non-nationaux en matière de sécurité sociale, Conférence internationale du travail, Genève, 1962.

- CM2 1962 908. 25/08/1960–02/06/1961.
- CM2 1962 909. 19/10/1961–26/03/1962.
- CM2 1962 910. 07/06/1962–27/06/1962.

CM2 1964 1131. Problèmes de main-d'œuvre dans la Communauté en 1963. 29/07/1963–27/08/1963.

CM2 1966 1044. Recommandations du Conseil d'association CEE-Turquie. 29/10/1965–28/11/1966.

Règlement (CEE) n° 1408/71 du Conseil du 14/06/1971.

- CM2 1971 1274. 21/11/1969–28/01/1970.
- CM2 1971 1291. 17/05/1971–14/06/1971.
- CM2 1971 1295. 01/03/1966–14/12/1968.
- CM2 1971 1298. 18/04/1966–30/07/1969.

Règlement (CEE) n° 574/72 du Conseil du 21/03/1972.

- CM2 1972 1411. 21/07/1971–26/11/1971.
- CM2 1972 1417. 23/02/1972–11/11/1974.

CM2 1973 1670. Déclarations des États membres prévues à l'article 5 du règlement 1408/71. 26/11/1971–20/11/1972.

CM2 1974 1416. 29/06/1972–11/07/1974. Directive 75/34/CEE du Conseil du 17/12/1974.

CM2 1974 1440. Propositions de directives du Conseil pour les activités du médecin et du praticien de l'art dentaire. Retirées par la Commission, 04/11/1974. 18/03/1969–10/07/1970.

Propositions de directives du Conseil pour les activités de l'architecte. Retirées par la Commission, 04/11/1974.

- CM2 1974 1476. 14/08/1969–27/01/1970.
- CM2 1974 1477. 02/03/1970–28/07/1970.
- CM2 1974 1480. 18/08/1971–06/11/1974.
- CM2 1974 1481. 22/05/1967–11/03/1969.
- CM2 1974 1482. 10/07/1972–11/06/1974.

CM2 1974 1487. Propositions de directives du Conseil pour les activités exercées d'une façon ambulante. Retirées par la Commission, 04/11/1974. 16/06/1972–16/10/1972.

Proposition de directive du Conseil fixant la liberté d'établissement dans l'agriculture. Retirée par la Commission, 04/11/1974.

- CM2 1974 1543. 03/02/1969–06/08/1970.
- CM2 1974 1544. 24/06/1970–06/11/1974.

CM2 1975 2174. 4ᵉ rapport sur le logement des travailleurs migrants et de leur famille, 1971–1972. 12/02/1975–18/02/1975.

CM3 NEGO 6. Réunion des ministres des Affaires étrangères, Messine, 01–03/06/1955.

CM3 NEGO 44, 45. Comité intergouvernemental: sous-commission des problèmes sociaux.

CM3 NEGO 253. 1956–1957. Conférence intergouvernementale: historique de l'article 132 du traité C.E.E.: Association des P.T.O.M.

CM3 NEGO 254. 1956–1957. Conférence intergouvernementale: historique des articles 133, 134, 135 et 136: Association des P.T.O.M. Application à l'Algérie.

CM3 NEGO 255. 1956–1957. Convention relative à l'Association des P.T.O.M.

CM5 ADH1 115. Entretiens entre la délégation britannique et la délégation de la Commission. 25/01/1962–05/06/1962.

CM5 ADH1 197. Nationalité et citoyenneté britannique. 29/03/1962–11/05/1962.

CM5 ADH2 15. 9ᵉ session CEE-Grèce le 06/12/1978. Farde 14. 29/09/1978–06/12/1978.

CM5 ADH2 22-IV. Prises de position du Conseil. Mesures transitoires et/ou de sauvegarde. Politique sociale.

CM5 ADH2 30-I. Prises de position du Conseil. Application du droit dérivé par la Grèce. Politique sociale.

CM5 ADH2 40-I. Prises de position du Conseil. Politique sociale.

CM5 ADH3 182. Mesures transitoires avec l'Espagne dans le secteur social. 20/03/1979–12/12/1983.

CM5 ADH3 481. Libre circulation des travailleurs. 29/11/1978–10/10/1983.

CM5 ADH3 483. Sécurité sociale des travailleurs migrants avec l'Espagne. 19/05/1980–15/01/1985.

CM5 ADH3 488. Situation sociale des travailleurs espagnols. 15/10/1981.

CM5 ADH3 1630. Libre circulation des travailleurs avec le Portugal. 13/12/1979–16/07/1985.

CM6 EAMA1 309. Droit d'établissement et prestation de services. Dossier II. 12/04/1966–01/02/1971.

CM6 EAMA2 736. Droit d'établissement, article 29 de la Convention de Yaoundé. 06/10/1965–28/01/1971.

CM7 ASS1 260. Recommandation n° 2/71 de la Commission parlementaire mixte CEE-Turquie. 18/03/1971–24/03/1971.

CM7 ASS1 261. Main-d'œuvre en Turquie. 20/07/1965–17/11/1966.

CM7 ASS1 262. Main-d'œuvre en Turquie. Farde 1. 17/11/1966–12/06/1967.

Liste Rouge 1444. Traitement par le C.E.S. du renforcement du marché intérieur. 27/07/1982–17/05/1983.

Travaux du Groupe des coordonnateurs (libre circulation des personnes).
- Liste Rouge 1574. 3/1. 17/02/1989–19/05/1989.
- Liste Rouge 1575. 3/2. 26/06/1989–30/10/1989.

Liste Rouge 1603. Evaluation du fonctionnement du marché intérieur. 21/02/1983–25/10/1983.

Liste Rouge 1842. Suppression des obstacles frontaliers. 28/06/1982–20/10/1987.

Prises de position à l'égard du Marché Intérieur.
- Liste Rouge 1847. 24/02/1983–05/07/1983.
- Liste Rouge 1850. 01/07/1988–19/01/1989.

Liste Rouge 2357. Droits spéciaux. 3/13. 27/10/1975–26/11/1976.

Proposition du 31/07/1979 de directive relative au droit de séjour des ressortissants des États membres sur le territoire d'un autre État membre.
- Liste Rouge 2374. 1/7. 12/09/1979–03/06/1980.
- Liste Rouge 2375. 2/7. 11/07/1980–03/10/1983.
- Liste Rouge 2379. 6/7. 21/09/1979–15/12/1980.

Liste Rouge 2381. Directive 90/366/CEE du 28/06/1990. 1/4. 26/06/1989–24/07/1992.

Liste Rouge 2385. Directive 90/364/CEE du 28/06/1990. 1/2. 26/06/1989–13/07/1990.

Liste Rouge 2387. Directive 90/365/CEE du 28/06/1990. 1/2. 26/06/1989–13/07/1990.

Liste Rouge 2393. Droit de vote aux élections municipales des citoyens de la Communauté (03/10/1986). 03/10/1986–01/07/1987.

Mise en œuvre du point 10 du communiqué final du Sommet de Paris des 09–10/12/1974.
- Liste Rouge 2574. 9/3. 24/10/1975–11/11/1975.
- Liste Rouge 2580. 9/9. 12/06/1980–18/01/1984.

Liste Rouge 2596. Résolution du Conseil du 07/06/1984 relative au franchissement des frontières intracommunautaires. 3/1. 09/07/1982–09/06/1984.

Liste Rouge 4385. Europe des citoyens. 25/06/1984–06/12/1989.

Liste Rouge 9524. Développement des régions défavorisées par l'attraction de nouveaux résidents. Traitement par l'Assemblée. 12/12/ 1985–22/01/1986.

Liste Rouge 25201. Déclaration relative aux conditions de vie et de travail des travailleurs étrangers (Projet de). 30/11/1976–27/04/1979.

Liste Rouge 25202. Formation professionnelle des travailleurs migrants en vue de leur réintégration dans leur pays d'origine. 08/12/1976–27/04/1979.

Liste Rouge 31316. Logement des travailleurs migrants. 01/12/1977–08/12.1977.

Décision 79/642/CEE du 16/07/1979.
- Liste Rouge 31431. 05/03/1979–27/03/1979.
- Liste Rouge 31432. 06/04/1979–08/05/1979.

- Liste Rouge 31434. Traitement par l'Assemblée. 21/03/1979–09/05/1979.
- Liste Rouge 31436. 16/07/1979–16/12/1979.

Liste Rouge 31497. 1$^{er}$ rapport sur le 3$^e$ programme d'échange de jeunes travailleurs (1985–1987). 08/07/1988–18/07/1988.

Liste Rouge 31978. Résolution de l'Assemblée du 16/11/1976 sur l'abus du principe de la libre circulation des travailleurs. 15/11/1976–09/12/1976.

Résolution du Conseil du 09/02/1976, programme d'action en faveur des travailleurs migrants.

- Liste Rouge 32036. 4/20. 04/08/1975–09/10/1975.
- Liste Rouge 32037. 5/20. 06/10/1975–18/12/1975.
- Liste Rouge 32038. 6/20 07/11/1975–27/11/1975.
- Liste Rouge 32039. 7/20. 25/11/1975–08/12/1975.
- Liste Rouge 32041. 9/20. 02/12/1975–05/04/1976.
- Liste Rouge 32049. 17/20. 30/10/1975–17/01/1976.
- Liste Rouge 32052. 20/20. 31/07/1975–20/10/1975.

Liste Rouge 32095. Avis du 25/10/1984 de la section des affaires sociales du C.E.S. sur les travailleurs migrants. 1/2. 03/07/1984–02/10/1984.

Liste Rouge 32104. Proposition de décision du Conseil du 20/07/1983, Convention internationale sur la protection des droits de tous les travailleurs migrants et de leur famille. 08/07/1983–21/07/1988.

Proposition de directive du Conseil visant à la scolarisation des enfants migrants.

- Liste Rouge 32158. 18/09/1975–12/04/1976.
- Liste Rouge 32159. 21/04/1976–12/05/1976.
- Liste Rouge 32160. 08/06/1976–25/06/1976.
- Liste Rouge 32161. 18/10/1976–26/11/1976.
- Liste Rouge 32162. 29/11/1976–18/07/1977.

Liste Rouge 32164. Traitement par l'Assemblée de la proposition de directive visant à la scolarisation des enfants migrants. 08/08/1975–20/11/1975.

Liste Rouge 32172. Consultation sur les politiques migratoires vis-à-vis des États tiers. 1/6. 23/03/1979–02/08/1979.

Liste Rouge 32191. 5/13. 14/12/1976–29/04/1988. Proposition du 04/11/1976 de directive concernant la lutte contre la migration illégale et l'emploi illégal.

Règlement (CEE) 1390/81 du 12/05/1981.

- Liste Rouge 32510. 22/30. 05/05/1979–17/05/1979.
- Liste Rouge 32512. 24/30. 19/10/1979–16/11/1979.
- Liste Rouge 32514. 26/30. 29/10/1980–02/03/1981.
- Liste Rouge 32515. 27/30. 20/12/1978–09/04/1981.

Liste Rouge 32519. Résolution de l'Assemblée du 17/06/1980 sur la modification des règlements 1408/71 et 574/72. 30/04/1980–14/07/1980.

Proposition d'un règlement du Conseil du 18/06/1980 modifiant le règlement 1408/71.

- Liste Rouge 32526. 1/5. 18/06/1980–15/12/1980.
- Liste Rouge 32527. 2/5. 22/01/1981–30/05/1991.

Proposition de règlement du Conseil du 10/04/1975 modifiant les règlements 1408/71 et 574/72.
- Liste Rouge 32589. 1/10. 10/04/1975–14/10/1975.
- Liste Rouge 32591. 3/10. 17/12/1975–09/12/1976.
- Liste Rouge 32592. 4/10. 07/04/1980–19/06/1980
- Liste Rouge 32593. 5/10. 27/06/1980–29/10/1980.

Décision 87/327/CEE du Conseil du 15/06/1987 (Erasmus).
- Liste Rouge 34830. 1/4. 20/12/1985–18/06/1987.
- Liste Rouge 34831. 2/4. 15/06/1987–30/12/1989.

Liste Rouge 34852. Décision 89/663/CEE du Conseil du 14/12/1989 (Erasmus). 1/3. 12/05/1989–30/12/1989.

Liste Rouge 34855. Résolution du P.E. du 25/02/1991 sur la dimension européenne au niveau universitaire. 14/11/1990–25/02/1991.

Liste Rouge 35112. Activités communautaires en faveur de l'éducation des migrants. 29/03/1978–16/10/1978.

Directive 89/48/CEE du Conseil du 21/12/1988 relative à un système général de reconnaissance des diplômes.
- Liste Rouge 35134. 22/07/1985–30/05/1988.
- Liste Rouge 35136. 22/07/1985–30/05/1988.
- Liste Rouge 35138. 22/07/1985–30/05/1988.

Directive 85/384/CEE du Conseil du 10/06/1985. Proposition de directive du 16/05/1967.
- Liste Rouge 40844. 3/3. 22/05/1967–29/03/1968.
- Liste Rouge 40855. 11/26. 22/07/1975–20/01/1977.
- Liste Rouge 40860. 16/26. 30/11/1977–03/01/1978.
- Liste Rouge 40866. 17/07/1980–10/06/1985.

Liste Rouge 41301. Directive 75/363/CEE du Conseil du 16/06/1975. 1/2. Remaniement suite à l'arrêt de la Cour de Justice dans l'affaire 2/74. 18/11/1974–11/06/1975.

Liste Rouge 43450. Groupe coordonnateurs 'Libre circulation des personnes.' 16/07/1990–09/01/1991.

Liste Rouge 44725. Prises de position concernant la réalisation de la liberté d'établissement et de la libre prestation de services pour les activités non salariées de l'architecte. 18/06/1976–06/01/1988.

Liste Rouge 62273. Conférence intergouvernementale sur l'Union politique. 1/8. 18/06/1990–10/12/1990.

Liste Rouge 68412. Conditions de vie et de travail des citoyens de la Communauté dans les régions frontalières. 27/11/1990–27/01/1993.

SOURCES

Liste Rouge 68422. Intégration sociale des migrants des pays tiers. 22/06/1989–29/06/1989.

Liste Rouge 68448. Proposition de règlement du Conseil du 10/04/1975 modifiant les règlements 1408/71 et 574/72 relatif à l'uniformisation du système de paiement des prestations familiales. 06/11/1980–05/02/1988.

Liste Rouge 68488. Convention sur la protection des droits de tous les travailleurs migrants et de leurs familles (ONU). 20/03/1981–10/05/1982.

Liste Rouge 68830. Politiques d'immigration et intégration sociale des immigrés dans la Communauté. 16/03/1990–13/04/1992.

Liste Rouge 70282. Approche globale pour les relations de la Communauté avec les pays du bassin méditerranéen. Volet main-d'œuvre. 22/06/1973.

Liste Rouge 74141. Régime de visa établi par deux pays membres pour les ressortissants turcs. 13/10/1980–13/09/1982.

Article 12 de l'accord d'Ankara.
- Liste Rouge 74138. 28/04/1976–21/09/1976.
- Liste Rouge 74142. 06/03/1986–17/11/1986.
- Liste Rouge 74145. 3/6. 14/10/1986–21/10/1986.
- Liste Rouge 74147. 5/6. 11/11/1986–17/11/1986.
- Liste Rouge 74148. 6/6. 06/10/1988–28/01/1992.

Liste Rouge 74150. Article 39 du Protocole additionnel à l'Accord d'Ankara. 2/9. 08/02/1974–27/02/1974.

Liste Rouge 74160. Décision n° 3/80 du Conseil d'Association CE-Turquie, du 19/09/1980. 2/2. 15/07/1980–07/06/1991.

Liste Rouge 74532. Décision du Conseil d'Association CEE-Turquie n° 2/76 relative à la mise en œuvre de l'article 12 de l'accord d'Ankara. 23/09/1976–10/01/1977.

Liste Rouge 74534. Problèmes d'application de la décision n° 1/80 du Conseil d'Association CEE-Turquie. 07/03/1980–06/02/1987.

Liste Rouge 74814. Traitement par l'Assemblée sur les répercussions de la création du Marché unique sur les travailleurs migrants des PVD. 20/12/1991–15/06/1992.

Liste Rouge 83948. Travailleurs migrants A.C.P. dans la C.E.E. 16/06/1982–08/10/1982.

Archives historiques de la Commission européenne, Brussels (AHCE)

Recommandation concernant l'activité des services sociaux à l'égard des travailleurs se déplaçant dans la Communauté.
- BAC 6 1977 465.
- BAC 6 1977 470 (1967).

BAC 7 1986 1626 (1963–1964). Rapport sur l'application du règlement n° 15 et de la directive du 16/08/1961.

BAC 26 1969 208 (1962). Sécurité sociale des travailleurs frontaliers et des travailleurs saisonniers.

BAC 38 1984 344 (1969). Libre prestation des services des avocats, médecins, dentistes, architectes, pharmaciens.

BAC 42 1991 323 (1961–1964). Application du régime des baux ruraux aux agriculteurs ressortissant des autres États membres et reconnaissance de leur droit de muter d'une exploitation à une autre.

BAC 134 1987 170 (1970–1972). Adhésion du Royaume-Uni.

BAC 144 1992 250 (1964–1965). Règlement 38/64: activité des services sociaux à l'égard des travailleurs se déplaçant dans la Communauté.

BAC 201 1989 309 (1939–1973). Libre circulation des travailleurs. Suite à donner au cas d'infraction présumée.

Affaire 2/74: Arrêt de la Cour de Justice du 21 juin 1974 – Jean Reyners contre État belge.
- BAC 371 1991 1728. 1971–1974. Vol. 1.
- BAC 371 1991 1729. 1974. Vol. 2.

Arrêt de la Cour du 13 février 1985. Françoise Gravier contre Ville de Liège. Affaire 293/83.
- DG SJ BDT (32) 92 352.
- DG SJ BDT (32) 92 353.

DG SJ BDT 371 91 2794. Arrêt de la Cour du 26 mai 1982. Commission des Communautés européennes contre Royaume de Belgique. Affaire 149/79.

## Archives nationales, Paris (AN)

F7: Ministry of the Interior.
- F7 16046. Sûreté nationale. Service de la carte d'identité et des passeports. Artisans.
- F7 16066. Relations avec la Sarre, étrangers refoulés de Sarre, 1948–1955.
- F7 16100. Etrangers dans les départements du Haut-Rhin, du Bas-Rhin, de la Moselle et des Alpes-Maritimes, 1946–1961.
- F7 16115. Allemagne et Autriche, 1947–1952.

5 AG 4: Archives of the Presidency of François Mitterrand.
- 5 AG 4 4767. Archives de Jacques Attali. Conseil européen, Milan, 28–29/06/1985.
- 5 AG 4 AH 10, dossier 4. Archives d'Alain Holleville. Droit d'éligibilité et droit de vote des ressortissants européens. 1988–1990.
- 5 AG 4 AH 18, dossier 1. Archives d'Alain Holleville. Accords de Schengen. 1989–1990.

- 5 AG 4 CDM 18, dossier 4. Archives de Caroline de Margerie (1990–1992).
- 5 AG 4 CM 41, dossier 4, sous-dossier 2. Archives du conseil des ministres. Conseil des Ministres du 20 juin 1984. Accord international relatif à la circulation des citoyens au sein de la communauté européenne. 1984.
- Archives d'Élisabeth Guigou.
  5 AG 4 EG 41, dossier 1. Conseil européen de Milan, 28–29/05/1985.
  5 AG 4 EG 67, dossier 2. Accords de Schengen. 1989.
  5 AG 4 EG 68, dossier 1. Accords de Schengen, conseil restreint du 19/04/1989. 1988–1989.
  5 AG 4 EG 68, dossier 2. Accords de Schengen. 1989.
  5 AG 4 EG 69, dossier 1. Accords de Schengen. 1988–1989.
- 5 AG 4 TB 59, dossier 2. Archives de Thierry Bert. Application des accords de Schengen. 1989–1995.

Auswärtiges Amt, Politisches Archiv, Berlin (AAPA)

B2: 221-09, Montan-Union, Europäische Gemeinschaft für Kohle und Stahl, Schumanplan. 104, 1953–1958.

B10:
- 022-48, Grundsatzfragen der Europäischen (West-)Integration. 140, 1954–1955. Europarat.
- 221-35-12. 703.
- 221-35-21. 704, Europarat.
- 224-23-00. 871, Sachverständigenkonferenz über die Gründung einer Europäischen Politischen Gemeinschaft in Paris, Band 5, Jan.–Mai 1954.
- 224-23-41. 884, Sachverständigenkonferenz über die Gründung einer Europäischen Politischen Gemeinschaft in Paris – Dokumente des Wirtschaftsausschusses, Band 2, Feb. 1954.
- 224-44-30, Wirtschaftliche Zuständigkeiten. 890, Art. 82 bis 87 des Entwurfs der Satzung einer EG, Mai–Okt. 1953.
- 225-10-01. 900, Außenministerkonferenzen – Messina, 1–2/6/1955, Band 1, Feb.–Jun 1955.
- 412-00. 1877: Ein-und Auswanderung – Allgemeines, Band 1, Dez. 1949–Sep. 1950.
- 412-00: 2365.
  *Tätigkeitsbericht des Ständigen Sekretariats für das Auswanderungswesen im Vereinigten Wirtschaftsgebiet*, Bremen, Jan. 1949.
  Office of administration. *Unemployment in Western Germany. A Graphic Study.* Jan. 1950.

B15: Sekretariat für Fragen des Schuman-Plans (1950–1954).

## Official publications

Bulletin des Communautés européennes. Luxembourg: Office des publications officielles des Communautés européennes.

Commission administrative pour la sécurité sociale des travailleurs migrants. *Premier rapport annuel sur la mise en œuvre des règlements concernant la sécurité sociale des travailleurs migrants. Année 1959.* Luxembourg: Office des publications officielles des Communautés européennes, March 1961.

Commission administrative pour la sécurité sociale des travailleurs migrants. *Quatrième rapport annuel sur la mise en œuvre des règlements concernant la sécurité sociale des travailleurs migrants. Année 1962.* Luxembourg: Office des publications officielles des Communautés européennes.

Communauté économique européenne. *Textes. Sécurité sociale des travailleurs migrants. État au 1$^{er}$ janvier 1965. Liste des instruments intervenus entre les États membres en matière de sécurité sociale et mentionnés à l'annexe D du règlement n° 3, à l'annexe 6 du règlement n° 4, ainsi qu'à l'annexe 1 du règlement n° 36/63/CEE du Conseil du 2 avril 1963.* Luxembourg: Office des publications officielles des Communautés européennes, 1965.

European Commission. *First annual report to the European Parliament on Commission monitoring of the application of Community law 1983.* COM (84) 181 final, 11 April 1984.

European Commission. *Second annual report to the European Parliament on Commission monitoring of the application of Community law 1984.* COM (85) 149 final, 23 April 1985.

European Commission. *Third annual report to the European Parliament on Commission monitoring of the application of Community law 1985.* COM (86) 204 final, 1 September 1986.

European Commission. *Proposal for a Directive of the European Parliament and of the Council on services in the internal market.* COM (2004) 2 final, 13 January 2004.

*Journal officiel de la République française* (JORF).

- Year 1972–1973, n° 113, 14 December 1972, pp. 6105–8. Compte rendu intégral de la séance du 13/12/1972.
- Year 1973–1974, n° 75, 20 December 1973, pp. 6105–8. Compte rendu intégral de la séance du 19/12/1973.

## Printed sources, collections of documents, memoirs

Adenauer, Konrad. *Memoirs, 1945–1953.* London: Weidenfeld, 1966.

Auriol, Vincent, and Pierre Nora. *Journal du Septennat, 1947–1954.* Vol. 1. 1947, Paris: A. Colin, 1970.

Ballini, Pier Luigi, and Antonio Varsori. *L'Italia e l'Europa: 1947–1979* [in Italian, English, and French.]. 2 vols. Soveria Mannelli: Rubbettino, 2004.

Gaulle, Charles de. *Discours et Messages.* 5 vols. Vol. 1. Pendant la guerre, juin 1940–janvier 1946, Paris: Plon, 1970.

Millot, Roger. "Le Secteur des Professions Libérales." In *Les Aspects économiques de la liberté d'établissement et de prestation de services dans la Communauté économique européenne*, edited by Commission des Communautés européennes, 114–29. Pont-à-Mousson, France: Services des publications des communautés européennes, 1967.

Monnet, Jean. *Mémoires.* Le Livre de Poche. New ed. Paris: Librairie générale française, 2007.

# BIBLIOGRAPHY

Asselain, Jean Charles. *Histoire économique du XX<sup>e</sup> siècle. La réouverture des économies nationales (1939 aux années 1980)*. Collection "Amphithéâtre." Paris: Presses la Fondation nationale des sciences politiques, Dalloz, 1995.

Bade, Klaus J. " 'Preussenganger' und 'Abwehrpolitik': Ausländerbeschäftigung, Ausländerpolitik und Ausländerkontrolle auf dem Arbeitsmarkt in Preussen vor dem ersten Weltkrieg." *Archiv für Sozialgeschichte* 24 (1984): 91–162.

———. *L'Europe en mouvement. La migration de la fin du XVIII<sup>e</sup> siècle à nos jours*. Translated by Olivier Mannoni. Faire L'europe. Paris: Éd. du Seuil, 2002.

———. *Migration in European History*. Oxford: Blackwell, 2003.

Baudelot, Christian, and Anne Lebeaupin. "Les salaires de 1950 à 1975." *Economie et statistique* 113, no. 1 (July–August 1979): 15–22.

Berlinghoff, Marcel. "An den Grenzen der Aufnahmefähigkeit: Die Europäisierung des Anwerbestopps 1970–1974. Ein Vergleich der restriktiven Migrationspolitik in der Schweiz, der Bundesrepublik Deutschland und in Frankreich." Heidelberg, 2011.

Berstein, Serge, Jean-Claude Casanova, and Jean-François Sirinelli. *Les années Giscard: La politique économique 1974–1981*. Paris: Armand Colin, 2009.

Bertola, Giuseppe, and Pietro Garibaldi. *The Structure and History of Italian Unemployment*. CESIFO Working Paper, 2003.

Blanc-Chaléard, Marie-Claude. *Les immigrés et la France: XIX<sup>e</sup>-XX<sup>e</sup> siècles*. Paris: La Documentation française, 2003.

Böhning, Wolf Rüdiger. *The Migration of Workers in the United Kingdom and the European Community*. London: Oxford University Press, 1972.

Boswell, Christina, and Andrew Geddes. *Migration and Mobility in the European Union*. Basingstoke: Palgrave Macmillan, 2011.

Bussière, Éric, Michel Dumoulin, and Sylvain Schirmann, eds. *Milieux économiques et intégration européenne au XX<sup>e</sup> siècle: La relance des années Quatre-Vingts (1979–1992): Colloque des 1<sup>er</sup> et 2 décembre 2005*. Paris: Comité pour l'Histoire économique et financière, 2007.

Cahn, Jean-Paul, and Ulrich Pfeil. *L'Allemagne, 1945–1961: De la catastrophe à la construction du Mur*. Villeneuve-d'Ascq: Presses universitaires du Septentrion, 2008.

Clayton, Marina Maccari. "'Communists of the Stomach': Italian Migration and International Relations in the Cold War Era." *Studi Emigrazione* no. 155 (2004): 575–98.

Collard, Sue. "French Municipal Democracy: Cradle of European Citizenship?" *Journal of Contemporary European Studies* 18, no. 1 (2010): 91–116.

Comte, Emmanuel. "Les origines de la citoyenneté européenne, de 1974 à 1992." In *L'Europe des citoyens et la citoyenneté européenne. Évolutions, limites et perspectives*, edited by Michel Catala, Stanislas Jeannesson, and Anne-Sophie Lamblin-Gourdin, 69–87. Bern: Peter Lang, 2016.

———. "The Origins of French Support for European Monetary Integration, 1968–1984." In *Max Weber Programme Red Number Series*, 23 pages. San Domenico di Fiesole: European University Institute, 2016.

Cross, Gary S. *Immigrant Workers in Industrial France: The Making of a New Laboring Class*. Philadelphia: Temple University Press, 1983.

Dahlberg, Kenneth A. "The EEC Commission and the Politics of the Free Movement of Labour." *JCMS: Journal of Common Market Studies* 6, no. 4 (1967): 310–33.

Dancygier, Rafaela M. *Immigration and Conflict in Europe*. Cambridge: Cambridge University Press, 2010.

Destradi, Sandra. "Regional Powers and Their Strategies: Empire, Hegemony, and Leadership." *Review of International Studies* 36, no. 4 (2010): 903–30.

Ducci, Roberto, and Bino Olivi. *L'Europa incompiuta*. Vol. 22. Padova: Cedam, 1970.

Dumoulin, Michel. *Mouvements et politiques migratoires en Europe depuis 1945: Le cas italien*. Bruxelles: Éditions Ciaco, 1989.

Elvert, Jürgen. "A Fool's Game or a Comedy of Errors? EU Enlargements in Comparative Perspective." In *European Union Enlargement: A Comparative History*, edited by Wolfram Kaiser and Jürgen Elvert, 189–208. London: Routledge, 2004.

Fauri, Francesca. "Free but Protected? Italy and Liberalization of Foreign Trade in the 1950s." In *Explorations in OEEC History*, edited by Richard Griffiths, 139–48. Paris: OECD, 1997.

Feldstein, Helen S. "A Study of Transaction and Political Integration Transnational Labour Flow within the European Economic Community." *JCMS: Journal of Common Market Studies* 6, no. 1 (1967): 24–55.

Gaddis, John Lewis. *We Now Know: Rethinking Cold War History*. Oxford; New York: Clarendon Press; Oxford University Press, 1997.

———. *The Cold War: A New History*. New York: Penguin Press, 2005.

Gillespie, Richard. "Northern European Perceptions of the Barcelona Process." *Revista CIDOB d'afers internacionals* no. 37 (1997): 65–75.

Gilpin, Robert. *War and Change in World Politics*. Cambridge; New York: Cambridge University Press, 1981.

Goedings, Simone Alberdina Wilhelmina. *Labor Migration in an Integrating Europe: National Migration Policies and the Free Movement of Workers, 1950–1968*. The Hague: Sdu Uitgevers, 2005.

Guirao, Fernando, Frances M. B. Lynch, and Sigfrido M. Ramírez Pérez. *Alan S. Milward and a Century of European Change*. Routledge Studies in Modern European History. New York: Routledge, 2012.

Haas, Ernst B. "Words Can Hurt You; or, Who Said What to Whom about Regimes." *International Organization* 36, no. 2 (1982): 207–43.

Haddad, Emma. *The Refugee in International Society: Between Sovereigns*. Cambridge: Cambridge University Press, 2008.

Henry, Louis. "Evolution démographique de L'Europe, 1938–1947, d'après un article de Grzegorz Frumkin dans le Bulletin économique pour L'Europe." *Population* 4, no. 4 (1949): 743–8.

Herbert, Ulrich. *Geschichte der Ausländerpolitik in Deutschland: Saisonarbeiter, Zwangsarbeiter, Gastarbeiter, Flüchtlinge*. Munich: CH Beck, 2001.

Heymann-Doat, Arlette. "Les institutions européennes et la citoyenneté." In *Les Étrangers dans la cité: Expériences européennes*, edited by Olivier Le Cour Grandmaison and Catherine Wihtol de Wenden, 176–91. Paris: La Découverte, 1993.

Infantis, Kostas. "State Interests, External Dependency Trajectories and 'Europe': Greece." In *European Union Enlargement: A Comparative History*, edited by Wolfram Kaiser and Jurgen Elvert, 75–98. London: Routledge, 2004.

Kaitila, Ville. "Convergence of Real GDP Per Capita in the EU 15: How Do the Accession Countries Fit In?" In *European Network of Economic Policy Research Institute Working Papers*. Brussels, 2004.

Karamouzi, Eirini. *Greece, the EEC, and the Cold War, 1974–1979: The Second Enlargement*. London: Palgrave Macmillan, 2014.

Keeler, John T. S. "De Gaulle et la Politique agricole commune de L'Europe: Logique et héritages de l'intégration nationaliste." In *De Gaulle en son siècle, Tome V, L'Europe*, edited by Institut Charles de Gaulle, 155–66. Paris: Plon, 1992.

Keohane, Robert O. *After Hegemony: Cooperation and Discord in the World Political Economy*. A Princeton Classic Edition. 1st Princeton classic ed. Princeton, NJ: Princeton University Press, 2005.

Keohane, Robert O., and Joseph S. Nye. *Power and Interdependence*. 4th ed. Boston: Longman, 2012.

Kindleberger, Charles Poor. *The World in Depression, 1929–1939*. History of the World Economy in the Twentieth Century. Berkeley: University of California Press, 1973.

King, Russell. "Migration and the Single Market for Labour: An Issue in Regional Development." In *The European Challenge: Geography and Development in the European Community*, edited by Mark Blacksell and Allan M. Williams, 218–41. Oxford: Oxford University Press, 1994.

Klein, Ronald Stanley. *The Free Movement of Workers: A Study of Transnational Politics and Policy-Making in the European Community*. Ph.D. Dissertation, George Washington University: 1981. University Microfilms, 1983.

Laursen, Finn, and Sophie Vanhoonacker. *The Intergovernmental Conference on Political Union: Institutional Reforms, New Policies and International Identity of the European Community*. Maastricht: European institute of public administration, 1992.

Lebon, André. "L'aide au Retour des Travailleurs Étrangers." *Économie et statistique* 113, no. 1 (1979): 37–46.

Ludlow, N. Piers. *The European Community and the Crises of the 1960s: Negotiating the Gaullist Challenge*. Cass Series-Cold War History. London; New York: Routledge, 2006.

Maestripieri, Cesare. *La libre circulation des personnes et des services dans la CEE*. Heule, Belgium: Uga, 1971.

Maihofer, Werner, ed. *Noi Si Mura*, Selected Working Papers of the European University Institute, 1986.

Martens, Albert. *Les immigrés: Flux et reflux d'une main-d'œuvre d'appoint. La politique belge de l'immigration de 1945 à 1970*. Sociologische Verkenningen. Leuven, Krakenstr, 3: Universitaire Pers, 1976.

Martin, Philip L., and Marion F. Houstoun. "The Future of International Migration." *Journal of International Affairs* 33, no. 2 (1979): 311–33.

Martín De La Guardia, Ricardo. "In Search of Lost Europe: Spain." In *European Union Enlargement: A Comparative History*, edited by Wolfram Kaiser and Jürgen Elvert, 99–118. London: Routledge, 2004.

Martiniello, Marco. "European Citizenship." In *Migration and European Integration: The Dynamics of Inclusion and Exclusion*, edited by Robert Miles and Dietrich Thränhardt, 43–6. Madison, NJ: Fairleigh Dickinson University Press, 1995.

Massey, Douglas S., Joaquin Arango, Graeme Hugo, Ali Kouaouci, Adela Pellegrino, and J. Edward Taylor. "Theories of International Migration: A Review and Appraisal." *Population and Development Review* (1993): 431–66.

Massey, Douglas S., Joaquin Arango, and Edward Taylor. *Worlds in Motion: Understanding International Migration at the End of the Millennium*. Oxford: Oxford University Press, 2005.

Meade, J. E. *Negotiations for Benelux: An Annotated Chronicle, 1943–1956*. Princeton Studies in International Finance. Princeton, NJ: International Finance Section, Dept. of Economics and Sociology, Princeton University, 1957.

Mechi, Lorenzo. *L' Organizzazione internazionale del lavoro e la ricostruzione europea: Le basi sociali dell'integrazione economica (1931–1957)*. Storia E Memoria. Roma: Ediesse, 2012.

Messina, Anthony M. *The Logics and Politics of Post-WWII Migration to Western Europe*. New York: Cambridge University Press, 2007.

Meyers, Eytan. *Multilateral Cooperation, Integration, and Regimes: The Case of International Labor Mobility*. Center for Comparative Immigration Studies, University of California, San Diego, Working Paper 61, 2002.

Milward, Alan S. *The Reconstruction of Western Europe, 1945–51*. Berkeley: University of California Press, 1984.

———. *The Frontier of National Sovereignty: History and Theory, 1945–1992*. London; New York: Routledge, 1993.

Milward, Alan S., George Brennan, and Federico Romero. *The European Rescue of the Nation-State*. Berkeley: University of California Press, 1992.

Molle, Willem, and Aad Mourik. "International Movements of Labour under Conditions of Economic Integration: The Case of Western Europe." *JCMS: Journal of Common Market Studies* 26, no. 3 (1988): 317–40.

Montanari, Marco. "The Barcelona Process and the Political Economy of Euro-Mediterranean Trade Integration." *JCMS: Journal of Common Market Studies* 45, no. 5 (2007): 1011–40.

Moravcsik, Andrew. *The Choice for Europe: Social Purpose and State Power from Messina to Maastricht*. Cornell Studies in Political Economy. Ithaca, NY: Cornell University Press, 1998.

Morawska, Ewa. "Labor Migrations of Poles in the Atlantic World Economy, 1880–1914." *Comparative Studies in Society and History* 31, no. 2 (1989): 237–72.

Mundell, Robert A. "A Theory of Optimum Currency Areas." *American Economic Review* (1961): 657–65.

Paoli, Simone. "The Migration Issue in France-Italy Relations from the Schengen Agreement (1985) to the Establishment of the Schengen Area (1995)." Paper presented at the Conference *Peoples and Borders: Seventy Years of Movement of Persons in Europe, to Europe, from Europe (1945–2015)*, Padua, University of Padua, 6–8 November 2014.

———. "The Schengen Agreements and Their Impact on Euro-Mediterranean Relations: The Case of Italy and the Maghreb." *Journal of European Integration History* 21, no. 1 (2015): 125–46.

———. "Migration in European Integration: Themes and Debates." *Journal of European Integration History* 22, no. 2 (2016): 279–96.

Petrini, Francesco. "Il '68 e la crisi dell'età dell'oro." *Annali dell'Istituto Ugo La Malfa* 22 (2007): 47–71.

Poidevin, Raymond, and European Community Liaison Committee of Historians. *Histoire des débuts de la Construction européenne, mars 1948-mai 1950: Actes du colloque de Strasbourg, 28–30 novembre 1984*. Bruxelles: Bruylant, 1986.

Puchala, Donald J., and Raymond F. Hopkins. "International Regimes: Lessons from Inductive Analysis." *International Organization* 36, no. 2 (1982): 245–75.

Rass, Christoph. *Institutionalisierunsprozesse auf einem internationalen Arbeitsmarkt: Bilaterale Wanderungsverträge in Europa zwischen 1919 und 1974*. Studien zur historischen Migrationsforschung (Shm). Paderborn: Schöningh, 2010. doi:9783506770684.

Recchi, Ettore. *Mobile Europe: The Theory and Practice of Free Movement in the EU*. London: Palgrave Macmillan, 2015.

Rieben, H. "Intra-European Migration of Labour and Migration of High-Level Manpower from Europe to North America." In *North American and Western*

*Economic Policies*, edited by C. P. Kindleberger and A. Shonfield, 452–87. London: Macmillan, 1971.

Romero, Federico. *Emigrazione e Integrazione europea, 1945–1973*. Studi di storia. Roma: Edizioni lavoro, 1991.

———. "Migration as an Issue in European Interdependence and Integration: The Case of Italy." In *The Frontier of National Sovereignty: History and Theory, 1945–1992*, edited by Alan Steele Milward, 33–58. London: Routledge, 1993.

Rosental, Paul-André. "Migrations, souveraineté, droits sociaux. Protéger et expulser les étrangers en Europe du XIXe siècle à nos jours." *Annales. Histoire, sciences sociales* 2, no. 6 (2011): 335–73.

Sala, Roberto. "Il controllo statale sull'immigrazione di manodopera italiana nella Germania federale." *Annali dell'Istituto storico italo-germanico in Trento / Jahrbuch des italienisch-deutschen historischen Instituts in Trient* (2004): 119–52.

Soysal, Yasemin Nuhoglu. *Limits of Citizenship: Migrants and Postnational Membership in Europe*. Chicago: University of Chicago Press, 1994.

Tapinos, Georges Photios. *L'Immigration étrangère en France: 1946–1973*. Travaux et documents—Institut national d'études démographiques. Paris: Presses universitaires de France, 1975.

Taschner, Hans C. *Schengen oder die Abschaffung der Personenkontrollen an den Binnengrenzen der EG*. Saarbrücken: Europainstitut der Universität des Saarlandes, 1990.

Torpey, John. *L'Invention du passeport: États, citoyenneté et surveillance*. Translated by Elisabeth Lamothe. Paris: Belin, 2005.

Tosi, Luciano. "Un obiettivo italiano a lungo perseguito: La libera circolazione della manodopera." In *L'Italia e la dimensione sociale nell'Integrazione europea*, edited by Luciano Tosi, 183–98. Padova: Cedam, 2008.

Trachtenberg, Marc. *A Constructed Peace: The Making of the European Settlement, 1945–1963*. Princeton Studies in International History and Politics. Princeton, NJ: Princeton University Press, 1999.

Vink, Maarten P. "Negative and Positive Integration in European Immigration Policies." *European Integration online Papers (EIoP)* 6, no. 13 (2002).

Warlouzet, Laurent. "The Deadlock: The Choice of the CAP by De Gaulle and Its Impact on French EEC Policy (1958–69)." In *Fertile Ground for Europe? The History of European Integration and the Common Agricultural Policy since 1945*, edited by Kiran Klaus Patel, 98–117. Baden-Baden: Nomos, 2009.

Werner, Heinz. "Migration and Free Movement of Workers in Western Europe." In *Les Travailleurs étrangers en Europe occidentale*, edited by P. J. Bernard, 65–85. Paris: Mouton, 1976.

Wihtol de Wenden, Catherine. *Citoyenneté, nationalité et immigration*. Paris: Arcantère, 1987.

Winand, Pascaline. "The U.S. and European Integration from the Second World War to the Mid-1950s. Opportunities, Challenges, and Control." In *America, Europe, Africa, 1945–1973*, edited by Éric Remacle and Pascaline Winand,

83–104. Bruxelles, Bern, Berlin, Frankfurt am Main, New York, Oxford, Wien: Peter Lang, 2009.

Wollenschläger, Ferdinand. *Grundfreiheit ohne Markt: Die Herausbildung der Unionsbürgerschaft im Unionsrechtlichen Freizügigkeitsregime*. Verfassungsentwicklung in Europa. Tübingen: Mohr Siebeck, 2007.

Young, Oran R. "Regime Dynamics: The Rise and Fall of International Regimes." *International Organization* 36, no. 2 (1982): 277–97.

# INDEX

Adenauer, Konrad 45–8, 57, 61, 183
Africa 9, 50, 53, 76–7, 82, 88, 108, 112, 138, 142; African, Caribbean, and Pacific States 140, 174–5; Associated African and Malagasy States 54–5, 107
agriculture 5, 7, 38, 40, 47, 53, 61–2, 67, 75–6, 91, 96–7, 180; Common Agricultural Policy (CAP) 5, 7, 62, 67–8, 75, 91, 97, 180
Algeria *see* Maghreb
Alphand, Hervé 18
Ankara agreement 71, 104–6, 114, 116, 173
Australia 26–7, 74
Austria 7, 11–13, 21, 27, 29, 72, 146, 160

Benelux 7, 18–21, 34, 48, 56, 73, 93, 107, 112, 145–50
Berlin 21, 45, 137, 166
Bidault, Georges 12, 18, 20
Brussels Pact 43
Brussels Treaty 19, 28, 31

Canada 27, 70, 72
Cold War 3–5, 7, 9–10, 12, 26–7, 40, 45, 71, 75, 166, 177, 180, 183
Commission of the Communities 6, 51, 60, 85, 87, 91–4, 114–15, 123–5, 128, 132, 144, 158, 173, 175
Common Agricultural Policy (CAP) *see* agriculture
Common Foreign and Security Policy (CFSP) 167–9
*Confédération générale du travail* (CGT) *see* trade unions
Conference on security and cooperation in Europe (CSCE) 94, 169
Council of Europe 6, 24–5, 30–2, 34, 46–8, 72–3, 104, 115; Congress of Europe 13–14
Council of the European Economic Community: Committee of Permanent Representatives (COREPER) 6, 120–1, 133–4, 156; Group on Social Questions 57
Czechoslovakia 12, 74, 153

Denmark 28–9, 92, 115, 119, 134–6, 139, 141, 146, 155, 160, 165, 170
*Deutscher Gewerkschaftsbund* (DGB) *see* trade unions

Economic and Social Committee (ESC) 6, 53, 58, 60–2, 97, 100, 103, 129–30, 144
Erhard, Ludwig 32–3, 43, 61
Euro-Arab Dialog 138–40
European Coal and Steel Community (ECSC) 5–7, 34–8, 41–8, 63, 180
European Court of Justice 6, 81, 101–2, 123, 163, 173, 178
European Defence Community 40, 43
European Free Trade Association (EFTA) 160
European Political Community 38–41, 48

Finebel 20
frontier workers 28, 30, 65–9, 162

Gaulle, Charles de 16
German Democratic Republic 21, 38, 43–50, 152–3, 179
Greece 2, 7, 8, 25–9, 70–2, 75, 77, 104, 106, 110, 113–14, 117–18, 131–2, 141, 150, 162, 164–5, 171–3, 180–1, 183

Hallstein, Walter 43–9, 57, 183
Hungary 11–12, 72, 153

International Labour Organisation 17, 73–4; International Labour Office 17, 78
International Organisation for Migration 27, 71–2, 173–6
Ireland 28–31, 92, 133, 150, 156, 165

233

# INDEX

Kohl, Helmut 146–7, 151, 167–9, 183

Latin America 26, 144, 171, 174
Lemaignen, Robert 51

Maghreb 33, 55, 77, 108, 151, 165; Algeria 25, 36, 50–2, 62, 107, 138, 171; Morocco 164, 170–1; Tunisia 138–9, 171
Marshall Plan 3, 17, 20, 23; Economic Cooperation Administration 20, 25–6, 32
Mitterrand, François 6, 146–8, 151, 167–9, 174
Mollet, Guy 51
Morocco *see* Maghreb

North Africa *see* Maghreb
North Atlantic Treaty Organisation (NATO) 26, 32, 43, 45
Norway 27, 29, 92, 136

Organisation for Economic Cooperation and Development (OECD) 70, 139, 187, 189; Committee for European Economic Cooperation (CEEC) 17–20; Manpower Committee 19, 25, 32; Organisation for European Economic Cooperation (OEEC) 6, 18–19, 23–6, 30–4, 48, 69, 70, 73
Overseas: *Départements d'outre-mer* 50–4, 106, 107; Overseas Countries and Territories (OCT) 52–4; *Territoires d'outre-mer* (French overseas territories) 50–3

recognition of diplomas and qualifications 1, 8, 9, 35–7, 59, 87, 98–102, 118, 120–9, 142, 145, 152, 156–62, 182
Russia *see* Soviet Union

Schengen 1, 3, 6, 9, 143, 147–56, 170, 177
Schuman, Robert 34–5
Schumann, Maurice 83, 86, 88, 93
social security benefits 1, 2, 5, 27, 31–2, 84–5, 88–9, 95, 104–5, 114–15, 125, 129–35, 140–2, 180–3; childbirth allowances 92; family allowances 4, 8, 44, 62–8, 73–4, 90–2, 132–4, 137, 163; healthcare 65, 67
Soviet Union, Russia 4, 7, 9, 13, 23–4, 39, 45–8, 74, 94, 166, 168, 179, 180, 183
Storch, Anton 36–7, 46–7, 64
strikes 13, 33, 80–1, 85, 119
students 100, 120–2, 135, 140, 158–61, 167, 182; Erasmus 158–62, 182
Sweden 27–33, 136, 160
Switzerland 7, 15, 17–18, 20, 27–9, 33, 69–72, 79, 112, 160

trade unions 6, 17–18, 25, 36–7, 44, 57, 60, 69, 78, 81, 86, 97, 102, 119, 129–30, 140, 170, 181; *Confédération générale du travail* (CGT) 37, 78, 81, 86; *Deutscher Gewerkschaftsbund* (DGB) 36, 43, 60, 100
Truman, Harry 13, 25–6
Tunisia *see* Maghreb

United Nations 27, 140–1, 154

Western (European) Union 19, 47, 163

young people 24–5, 49–50, 53, 59, 94, 96, 100, 127–8, 161, 181
Yugoslavia 12, 149–53, 170–1